Bellièvre
and Villeroy

Bellièvre

POWER IN FRANCE UNDER

EDMUND H. DICKERMAN

and Villeroy

HENRY III AND HENRY IV

BROWN UNIVERSITY PRESS • PROVIDENCE

International Standard Book Number: 0–87057–131–1
Library of Congress Catalog Card Number: 70–127365
Brown University Press, Providence, Rhode Island 02912
© *1971 by Brown University. All rights reserved*
Published 1971
Printed in the United States of America
By Connecticut Printers, Inc.
On Warren's Olde Style
Bound by Stanhope Bindery
Designed by Richard Hendel

TO MY SON SAMUEL

Contents

Preface   ix

Acknowledgments   xi

1. The Men and Their Times   3

2. The State and Government   27

   GOVERNMENT   27
   FRANCE   35
   ROYAL AUTHORITY   41
   HENRY III   51
   CATHERINE DE MEDICI   66
   HENRY IV   70
   THE MINISTERS   77

3. War and Foreign Policy   85

   WAR   85
   FOREIGN POLICY   89
      Spain   95
      England   103
      The Dutch Republic   107
      The German Protestant Principalities   109
      Savoy, Tuscany, and the Venetian Republic   111
      The Papacy   114

4. Society and the Economy   119

   THE NOBILITY   119
   THE BUREAUCRACY   122
   THE CLERGY   126

THE PEASANTS 131
THE HUGUENOTS 133
THE ECONOMY 139

5. Conclusion 147

Appendix. Chronological List of Events 153

Notes 157

Bibliography 189

Index 197

 Preface

ONE OF a historian's most exciting tasks is to discover how men of the past viewed their world. If they were informed, intelligent, and sensitive, and their times were of great import for the future, it may be possible to recreate a significant segment of the Weltanschauung of the past.

Two men—Nicholas de Neufville, sieur de Villeroy (1543–1617), and Pomponne de Bellièvre, sieur de Grignon (1529–1607)—because they were influential ministers of the kings of France for over forty years and because a large body of their correspondence has survived, offer a historian such an opportunity. Theirs was a crucial era in France's history, that of the Wars of Religion, the beginnings of France's ascent to European hegemony, the Renaissance, and the Catholic Reformation.

This study seeks to discover and recreate the Weltanschauung of Villeroy and Bellièvre in an era when Frenchmen were called on to confront the problems raised by rapid social, economic, political, and intellectual change. Since they were busy statesmen rather than scholars, Villeroy and Bellièvre did not ordinarily express their thoughts in systematic treatises; however, by their actions and in numerous letters they did comment on issues that they considered relevant to their age. It seems reasonable to assume that they also spoke for an important segment of what we today call the enlightened public.

To organize into coherent form what the ministers lived and felt as chaotic reality, this study has been divided into five chapters. Chapter 1 treats Villeroy and Bellièvre primarily as human beings. Their characters, revealed by word and deed, are compared with those of persons with whom the ministers were in frequent contact. From this comparison emerges the gulf between the ethics of the court and those of the ministers. The long friendship between Villeroy and Bellièvre is traced, both to shed further light on their characters and to display the tensions that royal service produced. The ministers' cultural outlook is then surveyed to determine to what degree they were *au courant* with the glories of the French Renaissance.

Chapter 2 focuses on Villeroy's and Bellièvre's views of politics. In chapter 2 are considered the nature of the monarchy they served, their philosophy of rule, their definition of royal sovereignty, their concept of and feelings toward France, their opinions of their royal masters, and their sense of professional identity as royal ministers. It is clear that they knew the basic weaknesses of the monarchy they served and that they accommodated their philosophy of government to those weaknesses. They also perceived the importance of absolute royal sovereignty, had a deep feeling for and a clear conception of France, knew their kings' strengths and weaknesses, and felt a deep pride in their ministerial status.

Chapter 3 presents the ministers' outlook on war and foreigners. Their views of France's friends and foes, as well as their policy recommendations toward them, show the extent to which the future Europe of the nations was embedded in the Europe of the kings. The ministers' attitude toward war, which they abhorred but condoned, helps to explain why peace was such a rare phenomenon under the *ancien régime*.

Chapter 4 turns to the ministers' views of society and the economy. Their concept of each group's function, from the nobility to the peasantry, reveals how Villeroy and Bellièvre stood astride the medieval and modern worlds. They were at once committed to the tested and traditional by temperament and drawn to the new and untested by necessity.

Chapter 5 is an assessment of Bellièvre's and Villeroy's perspicacity as commentators on, and molders of, late sixteenth- and early seventeenth-century France. With few exceptions they discerned the needs of the present and the trends of the future and, as royal ministers, were in an advantageous position to translate their perceptions into reality.

 Acknowledgments

THIS BOOK is a greatly metamorphosed version of a doctoral dissertation presented to the Department of History of Brown University. Many debts of gratitude have been incurred in its long gestation. A Brown University traveling fellowship enabled me to spend an exciting year in Paris and to utilize the magnificent manuscript collection of the Bibliothèque Nationale. A grant from the University of Connecticut Research Foundation allowed me to gather microfilm, some of which enriched the present study, and the same foundation provided typing services for the manuscript. Professor Orest A. Ranum of Johns Hopkins University recommended the study for publication and offered several helpful suggestions for its improvement. To Margaret Ellickson Dickerman I wish to offer thanks for her moral support at a crucial stage of the manuscript's composition. My friends and colleagues at the University of Connecticut, Professor James L. McKelvey and Professor Marvin R. Cox, have generously offered their suggestions and encouragement, for which I am very grateful. Most of all, I wish to express my deep appreciation to Professor William F. Church of Brown University, a splendid scholar and kind friend, who offered me far more of his time and encouragement during this study's genesis than anyone could reasonably ask.

Bellièvre
and Villeroy

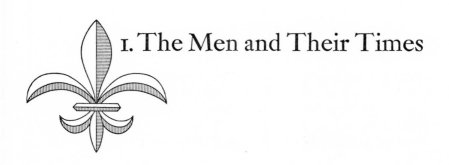

1. The Men and Their Times

FOLLOWING ONE of two modes of ascent open to ambitious bourgeois families in early modern France, the Bellièvre family spent
a century establishing itself as part of the municipal elite of Lyons
before moving into royal service. Beginning in the 1430s, when
two Bellièvre brothers settled in Lyons, the family, by entering
the corporation of notaries, the church benefices, and the municipal council of Lyons, established itself in the city's ruling oli-
garchy. By carefully amassing offices, passing them on to their
progeny, and marrying into similarly ambitious and upwardly
mobile families, the Bellièvres became part of the lower nobility,
the *noblesse de cloche*. The next upward step, entrance into royal
service, was taken by Claude Bellièvre, father of Pomponne. In
1531 he received the post of *avocat du roi* in the *sénéchaussée* of
Lyons and the *bailliage* of Maçon. Soon afterwards he added the
posts of *procureur général* of the parlement of Grenoble and
président of the parlement of Grenoble, offices which he held until his retirement from public life in 1544 or 1545. By the time of
his retirement, Claude Bellièvre had, through his offices in the
parlement, raised his family to the status of the *noblesse de robe*.
It remained for Pomponne to solidify and expand the family's
place as royal servants into membership in that narrow group
known as *grands officiers*. Like other ambitious men, among them
Villeroy, Pomponne de Bellièvre turned the royal administrative
system into a vast family enterprise.[1]

The other path into the upper reaches of the bureaucracy, ascent through the hierarchy of royal offices, was the one traveled
by the Villeroys. The great-great-grandfather of Nicholas de
Neufville, sieur de Villeroy, may have begun his career as a fish-
monger; he later served Philip, duke of Burgundy, as a maître
d'hôtel. During the fifteenth century the family played a promi-

nent part in the municipal government of Paris and, by the time
of Villeroy's grandfather, had begun a rapid climb through offices in the royal household. The latter, Nicholas I (d. 1549), obtained the posts of *secrétaire du roi* (1507), *secrétaire des finances, trésorier de France,* and *secrétaire de la chambre,* and
finished his career as a member of the *conseil des affaires* of
Henry II. His son Nicholas II (d. 1594) was an equally distin-
guished royal servant. He acquired the posts of *secrétaire des
finances* (1539), *trésorier de France,* lieutenant general of the
Ile-de-France, *gouverneur* of Pontoise, Mantes, and Meulan, *pré-
vôt des marchands* of Paris (1568), and *trésorier de l'Ordre de
Saint-Michel.* Nicholas III, the subject of this study, thus began
life blessed by the fact that the Villeroys had served the kings of
France for two generations.[2]

While Villeroy's youth was probably spent at court, Bellièvre's
was spent in Lyons. After his education in the law, he entered
royal service in 1554 by obtaining the office of councillor in the
parlement of Chambéry. Because of his family's influence, he also
enjoyed the incomes of several benefices in the collegiate churches
of Lyons. In 1559 Bellièvre's prospects rose when he was summoned to court. In 1560 and again in 1562, he was sent to Switzerland to settle minor disputes between France and the cantons.
His dexterity at diplomacy brought him advancement to the post
of ambassador to the Gray League in 1564. There he managed to
tighten France's ties with her traditional source of fighting men
and to offset growing Spanish influence. His success led to pro-
motion to ambassador to the Swiss Confederation, a post that he
filled successfully from 1566 to 1571. During the decade of the
1560s, Bellièvre was accumulating offices. He was lieutenant general of the *bailliage* of Vermandois (1562–64) and lieutenant
general of the *sénéchaussée* of Lyons (1564–70); and in 1566
was made a *conseiller* of the Parlement of Paris. His astute service
to the crown in Switzerland, along with the favor of Jean Morvilliers, bishop of Orléans, led to Bellièvre's being made in 1570 a
conseiller d'état. Secure in the favor of the queen mother, Catherine de Medici, Bellièvre—after brief missions to the Swiss to
calm fears aroused by the Saint Bartholomew's Day massacre and
to Poland as Catherine's personal agent to her son Henry, re-

cently elected king of Poland—began a career at court that lasted until his death thirty-three years later.[3]

Villeroy had barely emerged from adolescence when he entered royal service. At only sixteen he was made a *secrétaire des finances* (1559). Thus, during the same year the fortunes of both Villeroy and Bellièvre were tied to the court. Villeroy, favored by his family connection, soon caught the eye of Catherine de Medici, who sent him on several minor missions: in 1559 he went to Spain to implement a small point of the Treaty of Cateau-Cambrésis, and in the same year he traveled to Rome to iron out a dispute over precedence between France and Spain.

After this, Villeroy remained at court, where in 1563 he helped to prepare the Edict of Pacification, except, perhaps, for 1567, when he may have gone to England to try to arrange a marriage between Elizabeth and the king's brother, the duke of Anjou. In any case, Villeroy's travels outside of France ended in November 1567, when, at the age of twenty-four, he was made a secretary of state. Thus young Villeroy, a favorite of Charles IX, and trusted by Catherine de Medici, embarked on a fifty-year career as a secretary of state and minister to four kings of France. In 1561 he married the beautiful Magdalene de Laubespine, of an old secretarial family.[4]

With the accession of Henry III to the throne, Bellièvre and Villeroy began a joint service to Henry III and Henry IV that would last more than thirty years. Villeroy served almost without interruption as the minister of three kings. Under Henry III (1574–88), Villeroy was not only the king's favorite secretary but also his close friend until 1588, when Henry, made desperate by the coercion of the Catholic League, suspected Villeroy's loyalty and dismissed him. Denied royal employment and drawn by family loyalty, Villeroy joined the league, in which his son had already taken office. As one of the leading advisers to the league chieftain, the duke of Mayenne, and as his principal negotiator with the royalists, Villeroy spent the years from 1589 to 1593 trying to negotiate a compromise solution to France's divisions. On Henry IV's conversion, Villeroy expressed an interest in returning to royal employ and accepted a post as secretary of state in September 1594. Thus began his service to Henry IV, who so esteemed Villeroy that he is alleged to have said: "I have handled more business today with M. de Villeroy than I have with the others in six months."[5] Henry's assassination ended their fruitful relationship, but the old minister remained to serve Henry's wife, the regent, Marie de Medici. From 1610 until 1616, when he was forced out of office by the queen's favorite, Concini, Villeroy was one of Marie's principal advisers. His death in December 1617 brought a long and successful career to a close.

Villeroy held only one important office, that of secretary of state; but in his hands the office gradually evolved from a horizontal to a vertical administrative jurisdiction. At first, like the other two or three secretaries, Villeroy was responsible for administering several provinces of France and for communicating with several foreign powers. When he returned to office in 1594, Villeroy ceased to concern himself with matters of internal administration and took over exclusive control of communication with France's ambassadors abroad. Although his staff consisted of only a few clerks until his son-in-law Brulart de Puysieux became his assistant in 1606, Villeroy was in effect secretary of state for foreign affairs. His role thus reflected in practice the clear division of internal and diplomatic administration that was to be rationalized fully by Louis XIV.

With some significant deviations, Bellièvre's career followed a path similar to Villeroy's. During the reign of Henry III he was principal negotiator for the king and Catherine with the monarchy's foes. The crown's important dealings with the factious duke of Anjou, the Huguenot rebels, and the Catholic League were all directed by Bellièvre. He also played a major role in administering the realm's finances. When Henry III dismissed Villeroy, Bellièvre too was sent into retirement; unlike Villeroy, however, he refused to join the league but sat out the conflict at his estate until March 1593, when he accepted Henry IV's offer of a place in the *conseil d'état*. For the next six years (1593–98) Bellièvre performed such important diplomatic and administrative tasks as helping to reconcile the duke of Mayenne, spending fifteen months as the king's proconsul in his native Lyons (1594–95), helping to amass funds for Henry's war with Spain (1595–97), and directing the negotiations that culminated in the Peace of Vervins. At the death of Chancellor Cheverny in August 1599 Bellièvre was elevated to the chancellorship, an office he filled to the king's satisfaction until 1601. Then he came into open conflict with Henry by resisting the king's violation of the independence of the *noblesse de robe* and with both Henry and Sully by opposing their plan to make royal offices hereditary (the *paulette*). Bellièvre fought for his position for four years, before losing the seals to Nicholas Brulart de Sillery in January 1604. From then until his death on 5 September 1607, Bellièvre languished in semidisgrace, stripped of all but the empty title of chancellor.

Unlike Villeroy, Bellièvre held many offices during his career. In addition to the chancellorship, he was a *président* of the Parlement of Paris (1576–80) and held a variety of high fiscal posts. From 1571 to 1574 he served as a member of Charles IX's *conseil des finances*. When Henry III suppressed the council, he named Bellièvre his superintendent of finance, a post that he held until the body was restored in 1582 and he was made one of eleven councillors collectively charged with control of finances. Appointed by Henry IV to his reorganized *conseil des finances* in 1595, Bellièvre served on it for the rest of his life. His experience at first gave him a decisive voice in fiscal matters, but his dispute with Henry and Sully ultimately resulted in his complete muzzling.

Although the two ministers were close friends and generally agreed in their policy views, they had entirely different personalities and styles of operation. A strong impression of what Villeroy and Bellièvre were like as men emerges from their extensive correspondence.

Villeroy's salient trait was serenity, a fusion of calm self-confidence, stoic resignation to life's vicissitudes, and optimism. No matter how overwhelming France's problems seemed, Villeroy never lost faith that reasoned and calm discourse could solve them. He might bewail his native land's miseries and men's inconstancy, but he never abandoned the quest to alleviate the former and to avert the consequences of the latter. Disappointment, because it was expected, did not for long discourage him, and through each cry of despair there sounded a note of hope.

A tranquil exterior did not mean that Villeroy lacked passion. However, passion restrained by reason directed his actions. His fervent attachment to the French monarchy and to Catholicism buoyed up his spirits when the former seemed near perishing and the latter seemed about to wilt before the evangelical fervor of the Huguenots.

Accompanying Villeroy's calm was a certain coolness. He projected an image of competence, orderliness, diligence, and even charm, but not of warmth and sympathy. Villeroy was less tolerant of human foibles, less willing to concede integrity to opposing positions, and possibly less moved by human misery than was Bellièvre.

If he was somewhat cool and diffident, Villeroy was not furtive or hypocritical. He was usually frank and honest in the expression of his opinions. His *Mémoires d'estat*, for example, contain no great discrepancies when compared with his correspondence. His advice to his masters Henry III, Henry IV, and the duke of Mayenne was candid and bold. When dealing with foreign emissaries, Villeroy was evasive only when reasons of state demanded deceit. His frankness was itself a sign of a sense of security that only the threat of loss of royal favor could shake.

Villeroy, for all his power and prestige, never displayed a sense of self-importance. In his dealings with his subordinates, France's resident ambassadors abroad, Villeroy showed respect for their opinions and confidence in their capacities. He was careful to phrase his directions so as to avoid an imperious tone and often acknowledged the ambassadors' greater knowledge of a given problem.

The last facet of Villeroy's mode of operation was his ordered, methodical style. His instructions to France's diplomats were models of clarity and precision; his policy recommendations, clearheaded and practical; and his attention to his duties, unwavering. Year after year he operated in his efficient, if colorless, manner, so impressing his contemporaries with his abilities and energy that one of them observed that Villeroy displayed "order in his speeches, judgment in his writings, sincerity in his opinions [and] constancy and secrecy . . . in his resolve."[6]

Bellièvre's demeanor, although dignified, does not convey the studied calm of Villeroy's. Bellièvre was a more emotional man who was less successful in veiling his passions. Lacking the restrained tone of Villeroy's, his letters often ring with anguish, joy, and even humor. Bellièvre complained more than Villeroy, whether of the malevolence of France's foes, her friends' inconstancy, her servants' ineptitude, or fate's harsh judgments. Whereas Villeroy's prose is lean and precise, Bellièvre's is verbose and expansive, for he wrote as he talked—with enthusiasm and at length. Beneath his occasional cries of despair lay the same resilience that sustained Villeroy. Bellièvre's optimism, so necessary during years of ceaseless, often hopeless negotiations, seems to have been dissipated only during his last years, when he was out of favor and politically impotent. Then he may have grown world-weary but never cynical.

Although Bellièvre deemed public order fundamental to society's well-being, he did not show in his thoughts and deeds the same fastidious concern for order as did Villeroy. His bold, sprawling handwriting, so different from Villeroy's neat minuscule script, reflects the meandering pattern of his thoughts. Bellièvre could sum up a problem or propose a solution in a catch phrase or metaphor, but he was less effective in presenting a reasoned analysis than his colleague.

Bellièvre's passions were not those of Villeroy, but they were deeply felt. Bellièvre was a good Catholic, but he placed loyalty to France at least on a par with loyalty to his faith. His patriotism was no deeper than Villeroy's, but because his defense of his faith was less exalted, his patriotism appears more striking. His deepest passions were directed to the defense of the *noblesse de robe* in whose behalf he sacrificed both royal favor and power. Like many of his contemporaries, Villeroy refused to compromise his faith by recognizing the heretic Henry of Navarre as king. Bellièvre chose to defend a principle, the integrity of the *noblesse de robe*, when few others were willing to take the risk, and none had as much to lose as he.

Bellièvre was apparently less self-confident than Villeroy. He courageously defended his convictions but was timid when dealing with those to whom he felt socially inferior, like the king and the great nobles.

Bellièvre's warmth and kindness formed a striking contrast to Villeroy's coolness. Bellièvre was more tolerant of others, more forgiving, and more sympathetic with the frailties of human nature. He always had a kind word for those overwhelmed by their responsibilities, gave fatherly advice to those men engaging in duties with which he had long been familiar, and suffered with those whom he considered unjustly pilloried by men or fate. Like Villeroy, Bellièvre did not elevate his dignity to self-importance, and he showed the same respect for subordinates as Villeroy. Human suffering, common in his era, touched Bellièvre deeply. Whether it was France's suffering masses, alien refugees, the wife of a colleague, an informer scorned by those who had benefited from his informing, or a pamphleteer who chose to write for a losing cause, Bellièvre felt sympathy for their plight and did what he could to alleviate it. Passion for the just cause, compassion for the victims of misfortune, and humility before his inferiors—such were the feelings of a man endowed with, but not corrupted by, power.

THE period from 1560 to 1610 was probably not the worst epoch in France's history in terms of public disorders and private excesses, but it was little better than the worst. According to Bellièvre, "There have never been . . . worse times," and Villeroy complained of an age in which "neither reason nor honesty have great credit."[7] Even if it is conceded that public sins are always more visible than private virtues, the ministers' times were of the sort that try men's souls.

Bellièvre and Villeroy both preached and practiced the virtues that their times called Christian and that nineteenth-century men called bourgeois. This is not to say that the ministers had an identity as bourgeoisie: they simply rejected their noble contemporaries' chivalric ethic, along with their many vices, and considered themselves members of a segment of society standing between the masses and the hereditarily privileged. Both ministers had a clear sense of identity as royal ministers, and Bellièvre identified with the *noblesse de robe*. From this vantage point they adhered to certain values, and these values are reflected in their actions.

Courage on the battlefield, even when it became heroic folly, was to the nobles a cardinal virtue. Villeroy and Bellièvre, although they stood in awe of this sort of physical courage, did not aspire to emulate it and did not deem the glory it earned worth the risks it entailed. They had, however, their own less ostentatious brand of courage.

Bellièvre's physical courage, for all his fears that Henry IV would consider him timid, seldom failed him. He frequently underwent dangers and privations, especially in his younger days. When delivering funds in 1576 to John Casimir, the captain of German troops whose army was encamped south of Paris and who demanded a huge payment for leaving, Bellièvre saw soldiers brutally beat an assistant whom they mistook for him. The minister was understandably shaken but continued his negotiations until taken to Heidelberg as a hostage to guarantee payment of funds that he had been unable to deliver. Bellièvre's return to the mercenaries' camp emptyhanded, which led to his being abducted, was itself an act of courage. Two years later, in 1578, Bellièvre went to Antwerp to try to prevent the duke of Anjou from assuming leadership of the Dutch revolt. On the return trip two members of his party died of typhoid, the same disease that soon afterwards took the life of Don John of Austria, with whom Bellièvre had dealt shortly before. From 1580 to 1584 Bellièvre was almost constantly on the move, negotiating with the Huguenots. His travels took him across the frozen wastes of Guyenne in winter and through the malarial humidity of southern Languedoc in summer. Only once, during the summer of 1584, did he protest against the dangers that disease and brigands posed.[8] Even late in life, when afflictions of old age imposed their discomforts, Bellièvre did not willingly abandon the arduous life of moving from chateau to chateau with the court.

Bellièvre's intellectual courage matched his willingness to endure physical danger. When Elizabeth reprimanded him for his too forceful protest against Mary Stuart's execution, Bellièvre drafted a bold reply. Nor did he cower before Elizabeth's attempt to browbeat him into abandoning his mission to save Mary Stuart. While he was Henry IV's proconsul in Lyons (1594–95), Bellièvre did not hesitate to tell the king what the region needed.

He nagged Henry to send men and money, warning him that otherwise the region might be lost, and urging him to postpone his coronation and come south, even though he knew that his appeals had begun to irritate the king.[9] In his long struggle against the *paulette*, which led to his loss of royal favor, he showed courage of the first magnitude.

Villeroy, too, had to undergo privations and dangers in the monarchy's service. He found the return to court from Fleix, where he had just negotiated a peace with the Huguenots in 1580, arduous, for his coach had mired down, forcing him to abandon his baggage. His years in the service of the Catholic League, when the extremists in Paris were hostile to his attempts to effect a reconciliation with the king, were dangerous ones. Although the duke of Epernon swore to take Villeroy's life, the minister courageously refused to do anything that would compromise his loyalty to Mayenne. Villeroy endured life in the trenches before Amiens (1597), just as he did the winter campaign against Savoy in 1600 (the country, he wrote, was "so covered with snow that we will have trouble getting out of here, and still more living here") and the slow, uncomfortable trip from Lyons to Paris after the war. When he had to go to Metz in the winter of 1603 to meet some German princes, he voiced his resentment against "those who have compelled us to make this trip in this season";[10] but if Villeroy frequently complained, he did not evade dangers that had to be faced.

Villeroy's intellectual courage cannot be faulted. His Catholic League service, during which his integrity was maligned by both league extremists and some royalists, was his finest hour. He could have retired from the fray, but he preferred to act on his conviction that France could be saved only by the king's conversion. Even though he sometimes despaired that unless he was "better supported, assisted and believed," he would "labor in vain,"[11] Villeroy clung to his conviction until he succeeded. His abandonment of Bellièvre when the latter incurred the king's wrath was not a case of cowardice, but rather an agonizing choice between the ties of friendship and the duty owed to kings.

Both ministers were pacific men who lived in violent times. Even regicide was condoned by political thinkers and practicing statesmen. The Spanish ambassador in France, Bernadino de Mendoza, praised Jacques Clément's assassination of Henry III for "the signal favor that he just granted the Catholic religion."[12] To both ministers, however, violence against God's anointed was a mortal sin. Duels among the nobility were endemic, even though Henry IV made an effort to stamp them out; but Bellièvre and Villeroy had no sympathy with this form of private violence. Once when Sully and the duke of Epernon almost came to swords' points, Bellièvre stepped between them and negotiated a reconciliation. Villeroy sympathized with Mornay when he was set upon by an arrogant young noble with whom the old Huguenot refused to duel. At a court where Henry IV deemed war a school that tested honor and dispensed glory and where Sully gloried in his prowess in the use of artillery, the ministers were unmoved by such enthusiasm. When Sully looked forward to using his artillery against Savoy, Bellièvre firmly declared: "I detest this war." Villeroy resented the fact that his lack of enthusiasm led "our warriors to make fun of us."[13] By repudiating the private violence and national mayhem of their times, the ministers affirmed their peaceful natures.

Corruption in office was an accepted part of the sixteenth-century milieu, and only blatant corruption raised men's eyebrows. In the context of their times, Bellièvre and Villeroy were deemed honest men; had they been known to profit unduly from their offices, they would certainly have been labeled corrupt—their compatriot and Bellièvre's predecessor as chancellor, Cheverny, was repeatedly charged with corruption and forced to defend himself against his critics. Villeroy's personal income of 80,000 livres a year from his offices and estates must have reduced considerably the temptation to indulge in peculation.[14]

Men of the times were not only violent but vindictive. When Biron refused to confess or to beg the king's pardon for his treason and went to the scaffold without implicating his coconspirators, Henry IV ordered Bellièvre to publish an account of his last hours to show "the wretchedness of his courage." This was ignoble defamation, since Biron had died bravely. Bellièvre, who prepared the charges against Biron, urged a private execution to avoid shaming Biron's family, whose intervention in his behalf

Bellièvre deemed admirable. Villeroy also felt compassion for Biron, who, he said, showed "more concern for his relatives and his domestic affairs than for easing his conscience."[15]

Bellièvre's compassion and Henry IV's vindictiveness again clashed over the case of the former Catholic League pamphleteer Louis d'Orléans, who had fled Paris in 1594 and remained in exile in Flanders until 1602, when he asked permission to return to France. Although he had been sent passports and a promise of the king's pardon, on his arrival in Paris he was imprisoned in the Conciergerie. When he appealed to Bellièvre for release because the other leaguers had been pardoned, Bellièvre, who at Vervins had opposed the return of league émigrés ("If they have scorned the king's benevolence, they now suffer the harm they have brought upon themselves"), nevertheless urged his release. This charitable impulse was but an extension of his efforts to help unfortunate leaguers during the civil wars.[16]

The contrast between the ministers' loyalties to their families and the nobility's betrayal of relatives was sharp. The duke of Anjou incessantly intrigued against his brother, Henry III; Margaret of Valois joined the league against both her husband and her brother; and the count of Auvergne tried to place the blame for a plot against Henry IV on his sister Henriette, the king's mistress. To betray their own relatives would have been beyond the ministers' comprehension. Villeroy not only made every effort to secure his son Alincourt offices and favor but in 1588, after the king refused to give Alincourt the lieutenant-generalship of Lyons, and Alincourt accepted a post in the league, cast his lot with his son and the league. Villeroy also secured for his son the post of ambassador to Rome (1605–8). Even though Alincourt lacked his father's abilities (the Florentine ambassador called him "un da poco un inetto e un ignorante"),[17] Villeroy continued his efforts to promote his son's career.

Bellièvre was just as avidly protective of his family's interests. He worked diligently to secure his son Albert a succession of benefices, the most important of which was the archbishopric of Lyons. When Albert was forced to resign (probably because of mental aberration), Bellièvre tried desperately but unsuccessfully to secure him admission to the *cour des aides*. Another son, Nicholas, became a councillor in the Parlement of Paris. During the league years Bellièvre also tried to protect friends and relatives from the destruction of war. When his cousin Jacques Faye d'Espesses died in 1590, Bellièvre went to great lengths to see that his offices passed to his heirs.[18]

Villeroy consoled Sully on the death of his son, and Bellièvre reminded Constable Montmorency after his wife's death that he still had a beautiful granddaughter. Although there may have been political motives in commiserating with the misfortunes of such powerful men, there was also, from the tone of the letters, genuine sympathy. There can be no doubt of Villeroy's concern for his family, and Bellièvre's affection for his was revealed by his fear, when he was dismissed by Henry III without the royal pensions he had been promised, that he would be unable to provide for his relatives.[19]

At a time when betrayal of causes was frequent, the ministers stood steadfast in their integrity. The duke of Mayenne's undercover dealings with the Spanish while Villeroy was trying to reach a compromise peace with Henry IV offended Villeroy's sense of honor. Bellièvre, too, was shocked when pledges were broken. The duke of Nemours, whom the citizens of Lyons had imprisoned when they rejoined Henry IV in 1594, promised Bellièvre that he would, if given certain guarantees, return to loyalty to Henry IV. But when Bellièvre asked him to honor his pledge after he had escaped from prison, Nemours replied: "I had consented to turn over the places only to have my liberty, which God having had the grace to give me, I do not see that I have a great deal with which to concern myself."[20]

In an age when disease was common, Bellièvre and Villeroy enjoyed robust health. Catherine de Medici was increasingly discomfited by gout, toothache, headache, and myriad other afflictions as she doggedly sought to protect her sons' thrones. Henry III was troubled by constant ill-health, for which he was forever seeking remedies, and his brother Anjou contracted tuberculosis, from which he died. Even Henry IV, of sturdier stock, found that his long campaigns took their toll on his system, for by the last decade of his life he was suffering from gout, bladder trouble, and frequent "fevers."[21]

Only twice was Villeroy disabled by a long illness. In the fall of 1583 he contracted a fever that kept him away from court for six months, and in 1606 bladder stones sent him to bed for an equal period. Both times he was impatient to get back to his post at court.[22]

Bellièvre also had two serious illnesses that kept him away from his duties. The first was in 1592, when he was incapacitated for two months with a "maligne humeur bileuse," his recovery doubtless hastened because he preferred taking bluebarbe and chicory in syrup to a purge. Five years later he was prevented from arranging the peace conference with Spain by a fever that lasted about two months. Other than these two bouts with illness, Bellièvre seems to have had good health until near the end of his life. The only chronic affliction he suffered from was insomnia, which had troubled him since his youth.[23]

Good fortune and hereditary robustness doubtless accounted for the ministers' good health, but so, too, did their lack of interest in the hunt and other strenuous pleasures. While Henry IV hunted, Villeroy and Bellièvre performed the less arduous—and less dangerous—chores of royal ministers, and there is no evidence that either Bellièvre or Villeroy kept mistresses or forsook sobriety.[24]

No doubt Villeroy and Bellièvre had human foibles, but in their public lives, which is all we can know, they were men of exemplary virtue. If their sins died with them, the surviving evidence suggests that their virtues were sufficient to excuse many peccadillos.

AMONG the high bureaucrats serving the kings of France between 1550 and 1650, deep and lasting friendships were the exception, not the rule.[25] Even the collaboration of Villeroy and Brulart de Sillery was founded less on affection than on common goals and a shared resentment of the personality and some of the policies of the duke of Sully. Also, their relationship was not, initially at least, one of equals, for Sillery's advancement depended in part on Villeroy's favor. Although co-operation between royal ministers was common even when personal antipathies existed (Villeroy and Sully, for example, collaborated fruit-fully even though they had little affection for one another), this was not always the case.[26] The tensions between the *bon Français* led by Richelieu and the *dévots* headed by Marillac from 1624 to 1630, for example, grew severe enough to precipitate a dissolution of the ministry and its recomposition with Richelieu and his *créatures* after the Day of Dupes.

The most intimate ties between the crown's great bureaucrats were those of blood and patronage. All the ministers served the interest of their relatives, and powerful ministers like Richelieu retained the loyalty of their *créatures* as much by the favors they granted as by the affection they inspired.[27] Close friendship between unrelated equals seems to have been a rare phenomenon.

The long friendship and collaboration of Bellièvre and Villeroy, a relationship of equals, was apparently unique in its time. Like most long friendships it was built on shared values, congenial temperaments, prolonged proximity, and a mutual need for friendship's consolations. Only near the end did political differences blight their intimacy.

The reign of Henry III, with all its uncertainties and tragedies, was the period when the ministers were closest. As the two principal advisers of a weak and vacillating king faced with multisided rebellion among his subjects, Villeroy and Bellièvre needed each other's support when all else seemed to be falling apart. Even foreign observers knew of their friendship. Edward Stafford, the English ambassador, deemed Bellièvre Villeroy's "especial and private friend," and Bernadino de Mendoza, the Spanish emissary, was also aware of their intimacy.[28]

Villeroy, looking back on their service to Henry III, remarked to Bellièvre that in serving their master their constant goal had been to preserve his authority above all else.[29] No differences over policy marred their relationship, and a tireless, if futile, quest for peace and order bound them together.

During Bellièvre's many diplomatic missions, Villeroy tried to lighten his colleague's burdens. In 1576, when Bellièvre faced invading German mercenaries demanding ransom for their departure, Villeroy tried to prod Henry III into advancing funds more rapidly. Bellièvre's frequent dealings with the Huguenots

between 1580 and 1584, which finally drove him to complain of
having endangered his health "too much," evoked Villeroy's
sympathy and aid. He cheered his colleague with assurances of
the king's trust, reminded him that no one could accomplish what
he could not carry out, and looked after Bellièvre's family in his
absence. Especially during Bellièvre's arduous negotiations with
the Catholic League between 1585 and 1588, when he faced outraged magnates with little but rhetoric to veil royal impotence,
Bellièvre appreciated a friend to whom he could confide his anger
at the leaguers and his exasperation with the king.[30]

Bellièvre returned Villeroy's aid and comfort. It was he who
recommended Villeroy to Henry III. And when the secretary
was insulted and humiliated by the duke of Epernon in 1587,
Bellièvre promoted a reconciliation because of "the friendship
between [Villeroy] and me." Earlier, in 1582, when a follower
of the duke of Anjou, Nicholas Salcède, charged Villeroy and
others with treasonous dealings with Spain, Bellièvre helped
Villeroy by listening to his complaints of injustice, investigating
the charges to prove their falsity, and urging Anjou to repress
rumors of them, so that Villeroy's reputation would not be
harmed. After Villeroy's dismissal by Henry III, Bellièvre helped
to ease his friend's anguish. During the six months between Villeroy's dismissal by the king and his taking service with the Catholic League, he poured out his grief and bitterness to Bellièvre:
"We have never been Huguenots or leaguers. We have done
what the king commanded us to do and have served him where
and as he wished. . . . We have had as a guide our consciences
fortified by several reasons that we have presented to the censure
and good judgment of His Majesty." And when Villeroy decided to join Mayenne, because "the court has not wanted either
to speak of me or to seek to protect me in my estates and properties," Bellièvre did not reproach him as Villeroy had feared he
might.[31]

Most important of all, during Henry III's sad reign the two
ministers were united by outrage and frustration against those
who by neglect or intent harmed France. Bellièvre, after vainly
pleading with Henry III to release him from a fruitless mission,
felt free to confide to Villeroy, "I am so tired of these horns that

if you do not help me get out of here I will die tomorrow. . . . To discuss in vain, I can no longer do it." Later, when trying to persuade Elizabeth to spare Mary Stuart's life, Bellièvre could grumble to Villeroy that "it is a great misfortune for servants when they [kings] propose to them [servants] things which are not in their power." Villeroy could confide his anger against Epernon and feel confident that Bellièvre would burn his letter. There were doubtless innumerable times when the two men shared their grievances and satisfactions, for Villeroy frequently mentioned his preference for dealing by word of mouth rather than by letter.[32]

The years from 1589 to 1593, when Villeroy served the league and Bellièvre remained neutral in retirement, were a milestone in the ministers' relationship. On the one hand, danger to their native land and themselves appeared to draw them even closer together; but, on the other hand, different allegiances and prolonged separation seem to have impaired their former intimacy. Bellièvre sensed this and early in their separation offered to maintain a frank exchange of ideas by sending a porter for any letter that Villeroy might wish to write him in code.[33]

Before the two ministers joined Henry IV, their goals—the conversion of the king and the salvation of France—were identical. Bellièvre could easily have echoed Villeroy, who claimed, "I am fond of my religion and the welfare of the state. . . . There is nothing in the world that I hold so dear." Bellièvre supported Villeroy's efforts to find a compromise settlement. If Villeroy grew discouraged at his repeated failures, Bellièvre cheered him; "On you has fallen the burden of speaking for peace," he reminded him. If royalists questioned Villeroy's integrity, Bellièvre assured them that they were mistaken. Even while Villeroy served the league, Bellièvre considered him the model for those who wished to save France. Villeroy was grateful for Bellièvre's trust, for, as he put it, "Who does not lose his friends . . . in times like these?"[34]

The physical separation of the two ministers was almost total for five years. On several occasions they planned to visit one another, but the insecurity of the roads, the pressure of Villeroy's duties, and Bellièvre's reluctance to leave Grignon thwarted their plans. They seem to have met only once during those years, in the spring of 1592, when Bellièvre entertained a gathering of league and royalist delegates seeking a negotiated peace.[35]

Separation did not prevent Villeroy and Bellièvre from doing each other numerous favors. Safeguarding each others' properties from the ravages of war had a high priority. Bellièvre, when he withdrew to Grignon, left his house in Paris in Villeroy's care. He also wrote to prominent royalists asking for protection for Villeroy's estates as well as his own. Villeroy reciprocated by persuading Mayenne to spare Bellièvre's estates and even managed to obtain compensation for Bellièvre for losses caused by foraging troops. In early 1591, when Villeroy at his estate at Pontoise was surrounded by plundering league troops, Bellièvre took the trouble to send his friend artichokes and bottled water, although he himself, threatened by a league garrison commanded by Villeroy's son, was scarcely more secure. Not long afterwards, Villeroy assured his old colleague, "I love my friends to the end, as I know you do."[36]

The strains of war and conflicting loyalties created momentary tensions between the ministers. Villeroy felt that Bellièvre's retirement from public life was too cautious, and Bellièvre resented Villeroy's attempt to draw him back into it. Bellièvre had already refused several overtures from Mayenne but was tentatively ready, by mid-1590, to consider entering Henry IV's employ. Villeroy, who was trying to reopen negotiations for a truce with Henry IV, suggested that Bellièvre be nominated as the king's delegate to a conference; but Bellièvre, who believed that if he negotiated with the league he would be blamed as he had been two years before, feared that Villeroy's nomination would bring "disfavor rather than favor." He also disliked the idea of returning to royal service on a leaguer's initiative: "Am I in such an evil predicament that they think I want to return to court by means of M. de Villeroy . . . ? It is for the master to choose." Bellièvre was most deeply hurt because his chances for a return to royal service were blighted in this way and felt compelled to write a draft of a letter and a memoir to prove his past and present loyalty to Henry IV. Villeroy was probably hurt by his friend's actions, for a few months later he wrote: "We have been unalike in but one thing. It is that you have certainly conducted yourself with a great deal more prudence than I have." Although the two men's relations quickly returned to their former trust, Bellièvre must have felt Villeroy's reproach: a year later he still insisted that Villeroy should have dealt with Mornay and not suggested him.[37]

The two old friends were reunited in royal service in September 1594, when Villeroy was appointed a secretary of state. Bellièvre, who had joined Henry in April 1593 after requesting a position as councillor of state, worked for Villeroy's return to power. Villeroy, after vainly trying to persuade Mayenne that revolt was unjustified after Henry's conversion, swore an oath of loyalty to the king in March. Bellièvre's good words for him, combined with the secretary Revol's death, brought Villeroy back to power. When Villeroy tried to thank Bellièvre, the latter explained (quite rightly) that Henry had chosen Villeroy because "he wanted to favor his affairs."[38]

During the next five years (1594–98), as they strove to win the war and secure the peace, the two ministers resumed their pattern of assistance and mutual reinforcement. During Bellièvre's year in Lyons as Henry IV's proconsul (1594–95), Villeroy repeatedly assured him that his handling of overwhelming problems in "the purgatory where you are" was exemplary. They shared common worries because of shortages of funds, the king's tendency to risk his life on the battlefield, and the pope's delay in granting Henry an absolution for apostacy. Both ministers were eager for peace and collaborated in urging their master to seek it. When peace talks finally began, Bellièvre conducted the negotiations, which Villeroy directed from court. Their mutual trust was reflected in their congratulations after successfully completing the peace treaty: Villeroy assured Bellièvre that "if your negotiations had been handled by others, things would not have succeeded as happily as they have," while Bellièvre replied that he could not have surmounted the many difficulties he faced "without your having spent some restless nights."[39] With peace finally secured, all seemed auspicious for the ministers' harmonious collaboration in behalf of France's reconstruction.

At first all went well. Bellièvre, who became chancellor in

August 1599, remained in Paris, while Villeroy constantly moved about with the peripatetic court; but the two ministers agreed on all aspects of policy. On the horizon, however, appeared the rising star of the duke of Sully, whose struggle with Bellièvre for control of the *conseil des finances* indirectly broke the ties between the two old friends.[40]

The conflict between Bellièvre and Sully, which flared up in late 1602 over the issue of making certain royal fiscal offices hereditary, put Villeroy's friendship to the test. If he sided with the chancellor against Sully and Henry IV, his own career would be threatened. Villeroy at first promised Bellièvre "to help as much as I can" in his friend's effort to block the establishment of hereditary officeholding. Soon, however, Villeroy was warning Bellièvre that Henry's sympathies lay with Sully and that "His Majesty . . . finds such disputes very disagreeable, and very often wrongs those who are wisest and most moderate." The secretary admitted to Bellièvre that he had not dared to raise the issue with the king and hinted strongly that Bellièvre should relax his opposition. Bellièvre continued, however, to withhold the seals from edicts that he deemed harmful to the state or *noblesse de robe*, and Villeroy gradually lost patience with his friend. At first he urged Bellièvre to seal the king's edicts to demonstrate his loyalty, but when Bellièvre remained adamant, Villeroy finally spoke harshly, warning his friend that royal servants who could not be "obedient to the will of the king and receive all his commands . . . must leave his service."[41] This was Villeroy's last warning: when Bellièvre refused to heed it, Villeroy could not have continued to support his friend without jeopardizing his own career.

During the last years of Bellièvre's life (1603–7), he was gradually stripped of power and his former friends fell away. Villeroy, probably regretfully, abandoned his alliance with the eclipsed chancellor for one with Brulart de Sillery. Late in 1603 the secretary even urged, with Sully's approval, that Bellièvre be stripped of the seals and that Sillery be made keeper of the seals in Bellièvre's place, a maneuver that is said to have angered and deeply hurt Bellièvre. And when Bellièvre did lose the seals two years later, appeals to Villeroy were ignored. Nevertheless, when

Villeroy's cipher clerk betrayed his code to the Spanish, Bellièvre, who handled the investigation, sympathized with Villeroy's having "raised an evil and unfaithful servant" and assured him of "good men's" support. The chancellor also supported Villeroy's efforts to persuade the king, against Sully's opposition, to intervene on the side of the Gray League against the Spanish in the Valtellina pass. Although Villeroy sympathized with Bellièvre's being "out of contention," telling him, "We have followed your good counsel, and believe that it was best of all," the secretary knew that his eclipse was permanent. When Bellièvre died in September 1607, Villeroy may have had fond memories of their former intimacy, but he mentioned his colleague's death only in passing.[42] Still, although the two men's concepts of the powers of kings and the duties of ministers differed, Villeroy had supported Bellièvre as long as he could without opposing the king's will and hazarding his own career.

VILLEROY and Bellièvre, like most men of power, showed little interest in knowledge for its own sake. They were not lacking in intelligence, but their cultural attainments were limited to those that were useful in performing their tasks as royal ministers—mastery of foreign languages, a clear, precise prose style, and a knowledge of history.

The formal education of both ministers in part dictated their future interests. After a brief period at the Collège de Navarre, Villeroy entered royal service at the age of sixteen. Although he was a friend of Ronsard, seems to have enjoyed poetry as a youth, and grew up at court, his long immersion in political life precluded his ever acquiring a humanist education. The son of a lawyer who was a humanist, Bellièvre had far more schooling, for after preliminary studies at Lyons, he studied law at Toulouse and Padua.[43] Bellièvre's background and training thus gave him a far greater acquaintance with the new learning than Villeroy had.

Villeroy and Bellièvre both had some facility in foreign languages. Villeroy spoke Italian, but apparently not well, for he excused himself from an unwanted interview with the legate on the ground of lack of fluency. Bellièvre, on the other hand, served as interpreter for Italian-speaking visitors to the king and felt completely at home with the language. He apparently learned some Greek as a youth, but the only evidence that he continued to use it are a few translations from Greek works among his papers. Bellièvre knew Latin, in which he occasionally composed formal treatises, but Villeroy seems not to have kept up whatever training he may have received in the language. Neither man knew German, and Bellièvre was forced to use an interpreter in dealing with the Dutch. Neither seems to have known English or more than the rudiments of Spanish. However, the ministers' linguistic skills proved sufficient for the conduct of the day-to-day business of government, for Italian was the language of diplomacy, neither minister was engaged as a diplomat for any appreciable time outside of France, and resident foreign ambassadors spoke either French or Italian.[44]

As a working statesman's guide, history was a part of the frame of reference of both ministers. In this discipline Villeroy again was less erudite than his colleague. Although the secretary referred to events in the immediate past—for example, the assistance given the Schmalkaldic League by Henry II and the traditional animosity between England and France since the Hundred Years War—he never invoked classical antiquity in his correspondence. Bellièvre, however, displayed a considerable knowledge of classical history. When arguing in defense of the Salic Law, he showed the ill effects of constitutional innovation on the Roman Empire, and by comparing the times of Horace and Cato with his own day concluded that the latter was worse. When he wanted to appeal to the duke of Epernon's patriotism, Bellièvre urged him to emulate the Roman republicans. Bellièvre also frequently invoked the proximate past. In a memoir praising the advantages of religious toleration, he reviewed the religious struggles of the sixteenth century to prove that history taught the futility of persecution. He criticized papal policy during his own lifetime for alienating France from Rome. To persuade the king to a particular course of action, Bellièvre often invoked historical precedents. During the civil wars, for instance, he feared that "this kingdom will fall into the same calamities as after the war with England." And he warned Henry III that if Henry of Navarre and his wife Margaret remained estranged, Elizabeth might show an interest in marrying Navarre in order to revive England's age-old claim to the Angevin inheritance. From his study of the past, Bellièvre assured Henry IV that according to "the wisest historians," those who lost the battles frequently won the wars.[45]

The ministers' literary and artistic interests were apparently slight. While Villeroy never mentioned any reading he had done, Bellièvre claimed to enjoy reading but did not specify what he read. In one of his last letters he expressed concern for the disposition of a deceased cleric's library and promised to take care of it. Bellièvre claimed to know the Scriptures; at least he felt qualified, while serving as a judge at the Mornay–Du Perron debate, to point out errors in Mornay's scriptural citations. Where art was concerned, both men seem to have enjoyed its decorative aspects without having any deep aesthetic appreciation. Although Villeroy called Conflans his "poor hermitage," his chateau and Bellièvre's Grignon were Renaissance buildings furnished as befitted the dwellings of *grands officiers* of France with Italian marble, gold-embossed wall hangings of Spanish leather, tapestries and pictures from Holland, and tapestries from Italy. Villeroy was also devoted to his gardens, in which he planted orange trees and melon seeds imported from Italy, and he once spoke facetiously of going home "to plant some cabbage."[46] Bellièvre's letters contain little information about his home, but his concern for its safety during the civil wars indicates his fondness for the house and its contents.

If Villeroy and Bellièvre had little time to absorb the humanist learning of their day, they were at least acquainted with some of France's leading thinkers and scholars. Both ministers knew Mornay, a man of considerable scholarly prowess. Bellièvre, who seems to have known Montaigne while the essayist was mayor of Bordeaux, also admired Du Haillan, the court historiographer, and wished to know him better. Learned clerics like Cardinal d'Ossat and Cardinal Du Perron were among the ministers' acquaintances, and Villeroy had known the cardinal of Lorraine, one of the leading voices at the final session of the Council of

Trent. Miss Sutherland's estimate of Villeroy as "the friend and patron of the poets and a 'perfect humanist' "[47] perhaps goes too far, but there is good evidence that Villeroy respected, even if he was not deeply involved in, classical culture.

The French nobility of the sixteenth century, in spite of the urging of men like Montaigne and La Noue that it prepare itself for rule by obtaining a good education, remained more committed to achieving dexterity with the sword than with the pen. The ministers were thus far better educated than their contemporaries among the nobility. But Villeroy and Bellièvre were not so well trained as were some aristocrats of Elizabethan England, where an interest in education flourished among the ruling classes. And compared with the masters of requests of Richelieu's day, as described by Mousnier,[48] the ministers seem but half-learned men.

Bellièvre's and Villeroy's educational limitations did not, however, detract from their intellectual achievements. They were life-long statesmen whose intellectual energies went into solving the enormous problems posed by their age. They reflected on important matters and arrived at intelligent, if not always novel, conclusions. If they could not compete with their more learned contemporaries in matters of formal erudition, they magnificently lived up to the humanist ideal of *la vita attiva*.

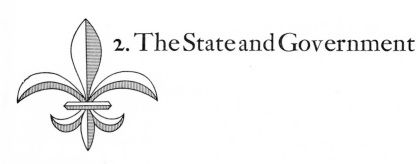

2. The State and Government

Government

The monarchy that Villeroy and Bellièvre served has been called a Renaissance monarchy,[1] a stage of royal government antecedent to the *ancien régime*'s final phase of monarchy—bureaucratic absolutism. Renaissance monarchs were strong only under certain conditions. When the loyalty of their politically potent subjects was assured by the judicious granting of pensions, benefices, and offices and when there were no great ideological issues to divide Frenchmen, kings like Francis I and Henry II ruled France, if not well, at least without major opposition.[2] But religious differences polarized opinion, and weak kings followed Francis and Henry. The period of the Wars of Religion, which saw France divided into two warring faiths, unleashed private passions and ambitions that kings like Henry III could not contain. Royal finances were inadequate for raising and maintaining the armies necessary to crush Huguenot and Catholic League rebels; the royal officials' traditions of discipline and honesty were too primitive and their numbers too few to maintain order; and dynastic patriotism's hold on Frenchmen was not deeply enough inculcated to overcome religious, regional, and corporate loyalties.[3] Without either their subjects' loyalties or an army and a bureaucracy adequate to impose their will, Renaissance monarchs had to rule as much by persuasion as by coercion.

Villeroy and Bellièvre, who served Renaissance kings, knew well the weaknesses of the monarchy, even if they probably could not have articulated them fully. The polarization of opinion that left the monarchy stranded between Huguenot and league rebels was to Villeroy the essence of his age's tragedy: "The king," he observed, "will have to guard himself from both sides now, in which consists our greatest misfortune." The dissolution of the bonds of loyalty to the crown was indicated, in

Villeroy's view, by the fact that "everyone has abandoned the tiller of the vessel to hurry to his own affairs." A constant lack of funds forced the monarch to parley when foreign invaders joined domestic rebels. As Bellièvre, who usually did the talking, put it, "They are armed, and we speak with empty hands. This means that our words, even when they come from the master's mouth, will have little effect." "We cannot make either war or peace," Villeroy said. "We are in such a state that we must fear all." When Henry III managed to field an army, he could not long maintain it. Villeroy complained, for example, that the duke of Mayenne's campaign against Navarre (1585–86) "consumes a great deal of money and ruins much of the country." Even victories were hollow if they could not be consolidated. The duke of Guise's destruction of the invading German mercenaries in 1587 only bettered the league's position, for Henry III, Bellièvre warned, lacked the funds to prevent league domination of his own forces. "We know our illness and cannot cure it," Villeroy lamented.[4]

The product of the weakness of Renaissance monarchy was government by diplomacy. Henry III and, until 1598, Henry IV had to deal with their powerful subjects much as if they were foreign powers possessing their own sovereignty.

Henry III's reign, the nadir of royal power in the sixteenth century, was the classic case of government by diplomacy. Henry was never able to impose a military solution on the Huguenot and league rebels: stalemate was followed by negotiations that ended in concessions; these in turn proved insufficient, and once again the cycle of conflict, negotiation, and concession began. Finally, in order to preserve his throne toward the end of his reign, Henry III was forced to ally himself with his heir and former foe, Henry of Navarre.[5]

Navarre, who became Henry IV in 1589, experienced the same dilemma for the first decade of his reign. Although he tried to win back his kingdom by force of arms, the task exceeded his resources. In order to secure his throne, he, too, had to bargain with, and make concessions to, his rebel Catholic subjects. From the time of his accession until his conversion four years later, Henry IV kept up intermittent diplomatic contacts with the league through its spokesman Villeroy.⁶ Ultimately the king granted the rebels the fundamental concession, his conversion. When even this proved insufficient, Henry did not hesitate to buy back the rebel magnates' loyalty with generous pensions and offices. Such league chieftains as Mayenne, Nemours, Villars, Joyeuse, Epernon, and Mercoeur were bought off when concession proved cheaper than war in regaining their loyalty.⁷ Henry's concessions diminished as victory approached, but, as penance for his decade of revolt, even Mercoeur, the last league holdout, was required only to marry his daughter to the king's bastard son.

Government by diplomacy ended with Henry IV's consolidation of his hold on France after 1598, but a certain deference to opposition did not. The king preferred to gain his powerful subjects' consent rather than coerce their obedience. His addresses to the Parlement of Paris when it opposed the Edict of Nantes and the admission of the Jesuits revealed a determination to gain his ends but were phrased as reasoned appeals as much as threats. Opposition from powerful magnates was endured with more tolerance and greeted with more alarm than one would expect from a monarch who claimed to be absolute. Biron's conspiracy was deemed such a danger that the duke was lured to court under false pretenses and then offered a pardon if he would confess and reveal his fellow conspirators. Only when he refused was he executed. Such followers as the baron of Lux and the prince of Joinville were pardoned when they confessed. For his knowledge of the plot the duke of Bouillon, a powerful Huguenot, was required only to request the king's pardon, an offer that Henry kept open for four years before deciding to humble the duke by force. When Bouillon finally capitulated, the only price he paid for his blatant contempt of royal authority was the loss of control of Sedan.⁸ These few examples show clearly that Henry IV, although he succeeded in imposing his will on his most restless subjects, did so very discreetly and was willing to give as well as take. His treatment of Bouillon contrasted sharply with Richelieu's handling of the dukes of Montmorency and Cinq-Mars.

Bellièvre and Villeroy were frequently the instruments of

government by diplomacy, and as the emissaries negotiating with the monarchy's foes they developed a philosophy of government that was an outgrowth of their diplomatic experience. Their faith in reasoned compromise and their caution, which would seem to be at odds with the ministers' commitment to royal absolutism, reflected the realities of monarchical power in their day. Kings might claim to possess absolute power, and the ministers might support their claim, but the hard fact remained that compromise was often necessary to govern the realm.

Compromise was necessary, Bellièvre saw, to maintain order. As he awaited the outcome of negotiations between emissaries from Henry IV and the league in 1592, Bellièvre knew that both sides would have to moderate their passions if an agreement were to be reached. His dictum was "If princes never come to agreements but when they love each other, there will be few agreements between princes." Villeroy's faith in the appeal of reasonable compromise sometimes weakened but never gave way. As he was about to begin the 1592 negotiations between Henry IV and the league, he wrote to Bellièvre: "In truth I do not think that these princes [the leaguers] want in their souls all the harm that their actions would seem to indicate. Each one defends himself as much and more from stubbornness and necessity than from hatred. . . . Now we must surmount and vanquish this stubbornness and necessity, for it seems that we will now be enlightened enough to see that war will serve neither one of us, and still less religion and the state." The primary obstacle, in Villeroy's view, was "the passion [that] blinds us on all sides."[9]

Caution, inculcated in the course of avoiding a hundred pitfalls, was the ministers' other guiding principle. As Bellièvre put it, there was "nothing more harmful of counsel than precipitateness." Time, he and Villeroy believed, was the great healer. Villeroy, while awaiting the outcome of Bellièvre's negotiations at Vervins, felt certain that "all matters can be agreed upon in time, directing them by degrees without hurrying them." When all else failed, he had long known, "one must learn to go on and gain time." Bellièvre agreed, for he had assured Henry III that "time and a moderate government of Your Majesty will assuage, if God pleases, the bitterness that suspicion has implanted in these men's [the Huguenots'] hearts." Villeroy and Bellièvre both knew that intemperate language was a luxury that caution did not permit. Bellièvre disapproved of royalists and leaguers attacking each other in print. "The wise man," he insisted, "knows how to gain the friendship of his enemy. If that does not work he resolves to harm with effects rather than offend with words." Villeroy, who had to maintain diplomatic amenities with Europe's princes, was careful to see that words did not needlessly offend. When Henry IV was displeased that Clement VIII did not condemn Spain's part in the Biron conspiracy, and told the pontiff so, Villeroy ordered France's ambassador in Rome "to tone down the language that His Majesty uses." A few years later, when another French ambassador in Rome wrote more forcefully than Villeroy deemed necessary, the secretary told him, "All that you have told His Holiness of Spanish infidelity and English malignity is true. . . . But when it is a question of putting in writing things that concern such princes one must be more circumspect and use more discretion than when one treats verbally." A cautious survey of the situation before making policy recommendations was, Bellièvre believed, crucial, for there was "no difference but in timing between advising well or badly." Finally, caution could mitigate disappointment as well as contribute to success. A strain of pessimism in the ministers was hardly surprising, given the woes that they had seen France endure. On the eve of a war with Savoy that he did not desire, Villeroy stoically said: "When we dispose ourselves for the worst, we will not be fooled when the best happens."[10]

A good deal of confusion once existed—and some still persists —concerning the nature of the king's councils. A *conseil d'en haut* was not created formally until 1615, but long before then the French kings and their intimate advisers had met to deal with matters of high policy. As Georges Pagès pointed out many years ago and as recent students of the period have confirmed, power rested in men, not councils. The confusion arose because contemporaries often referred to meetings of *conseils* when in fact no such formal bodies existed. They also failed to differentiate between four kinds of meetings, all of which were referred to indiscriminately as councils. First, there were the meetings of councils like the *conseil d'état et des finances*, which were more formal than the others. Second, there were meetings of the kings and their intimate advisers, which contemporaries referred to as *conseils d'état* or *conseils secrets*.[11] These were in fact, but not in law, meetings of a council. Third, kings often called *ad hoc* meetings of their ministers and important personages to solicit the opinions of the politically potent on major questions of policy—another of the monarchy's means of keeping its hand on the public pulse. Fourth, kings sometimes appointed commissions to discuss and advise on a given problem. These too were referred to as councils.

The *conseil d'état et des finances* was a permanent body that administered the realm's fiscal affairs. Real policy-making power did not rest in the council, whose members numbered fourteen in 1604, but rather in the individual or clique within the council whose views Henry IV shared. The struggle between Bellièvre and Sully for the control of the council was really a struggle for the king's support. Had the council been a place where policy was actually made by majority vote, Bellièvre would not have complained that the king and Sully ignored the advice of its majority.[12]

The outlines of royal policy were hammered out in meetings and through correspondence between the king and his ministers. This *conseil*, which contemporaries called the *conseil des affaires*, the king's "secretest cabinet," or the *consiglio private*, was what became under Louis XIV the *Conseil d'en haut*. Henry III called meetings of Villeroy, Bellièvre, his mother Catherine, and, by the 1580s, his favorite the duke of Epernon to discuss the recurring crises of his reign. Contemporaries frequently remarked on this sort of gathering: in 1577, when the question of war or peace with the Huguenots had to be resolved; in 1584, when the threat of Spanish intervention in Languedoc arose; several times during 1585 when the Catholic League began its campaign of coercion against the monarchy; in the spring of 1587, and again a year later, when league aggressions became blatant and could not be overlooked.[13]

Henry IV employed *ad hoc* gatherings of his ministers and the realm's magnates to sound out opinion on pressing issues. What contemporaries insisted on calling councils were in fact consultative assemblies on a small scale. Whenever war was imminent, for example, Henry convened a meeting of his ministers and nobles like Constable Montmorency, Marshal Lesdiguières, and the duke of Epernon to plan the campaign. Meetings of this sort were held before the war with Savoy (1600) and before the campaign in Juliers-Cleves (1610). To forestall the Biron conspiracy, Bellièvre, Sully, Sillery, Constable Montmorency, and the duke of Guise met frequently. If issues of great import arose, like those of permitting the return of the Jesuits and settling the dispute with Savoy over Saluzzo, magnates were invited to offer their opinions.[14] Such an expanded *conseil secret* proved useful to kings whose rule depended on their more powerful subjects' assent to the major outlines of royal policy.

Commissions to treat a given problem also were usually referred to by contemporaries as councils. For example, when Henry III was asked by the pope to introduce the decrees of Trent, he appointed a study group composed of Chancellor Cheverny, the cardinal of Bourbon, two archbishops, and a bishop to study the matter; this the nuncio considered a council.[15] And Henry IV asked Bellièvre to call a *conseil* of "Rosny, Chateauneuf, de Maisse, Villeroy, Sillery, Calignon and others that you judge appropriate" to arrange the disposition of his sister Catherine's estate.[16]

The variety of councils that contemporaries failed to distinguish among led earlier historians to focus on identifying the powers of councils rather than the influence of men. To speak of conciliar government is somewhat deceiving, for much of the decision making was done by letter and by informal gatherings of the kings' ministers with each other and with the king. During Henry III's reign, for example, Bellièvre was absent from the king about half of the time—sometimes for periods of a year—yet he was the king's principal minister except for Villeroy. The secretary, on the other hand, was seldom absent from the king's side for prolonged periods. A similar dispersion of personnel characterized Henry IV's reign. Sully and Bellièvre usually stayed in Paris to oversee their fiscal and judicial administrations, and met with the king only occasionally. Villeroy, however, because he drafted much of Henry's correspondence, remained with the king most of the time. Under neither monarch were frequent meetings of a "council" possible.[17] Rather than speaking of the king's councils as the focus of power, it would seem more appropriate to speak of the king's ministries, even if the term has anachronistic overtones. Relating to their master as individuals, the king's ministers together composed a ministry that under the king's direction shaped the policies and oversaw the administration of the monarchy.

If the term *ministry* is used to describe the group of individuals who were the kings' intimate advisers, it is possible to categorize the different types of relationships between kings and their ministers as the monarchy grew from a Renaissance into a bureaucratic monarchy. During the 1560s, when Catherine de Medici was regent for Francis II and Charles IX, she used as her intimate advisers her secretaries of state; the most influential of them, like Claude Laubespine and Villeroy, were in fact, if not in name, ministers. The organization was thus one of Catherine as prime minister and her relatively humble officers as her principal advisers. The ministries of Henry III and Henry IV had in common some of their personnel, the fact that neither king permitted the ascendancy of one minister to de facto prime minister status, and a broad distribution of power among several persons. Under Henry III, Villeroy and Bellièvre operated as equals, the only distinction between them being that Villeroy was concerned more with foreign relations, while Bellièvre was concerned more with finances. Henry IV's ministry saw a similar distribution of power and specialization, with Villeroy functioning essentially as secretary of state for foreign affairs. Bellièvre recognized the secretary's primacy in this area, as did even Sully, to whose decisions in all matters of finance the other ministers had to defer. This sort of plural ministry lasted into the regency of Marie de Medici, during which the *vieillards* Villeroy, Sillery, and Jeannin clung to power and tried to prevent the shipwreck of the monarchy. Louis XIII, when he assumed his majority, overthrew the brief reign of the queen's favorite, Concino Concini, only to place at the head of his ministry another favorite, the former royal falconer, the duke of Luynes. Luynes's death in 1621 was followed by a confused decade during which the ministry was torn between the *bons Français* headed by Richelieu and the *dévots* led by the keeper of the seals, Marillac. Richelieu's triumph with the Day of Dupes inaugurated a new kind of ministry, one headed by a prime minister. Richelieu built up a clientele of his *créatures,* the secretaries of state and the superintendents of finance, who were subservient to him. Richelieu stood between Louis XIII, whose prime minister he was in fact, and these *créatures,* who were the cardinal's allies and underlings. After Richelieu's death the same type of ministerial organization persisted under Mazarin, who, as the favorite of the queen mother, Anne, was the prime minister, assisted by such subordinate ministers as Chancellor Séguier, Superintendent Fouquet, and the secretaries of state Brienne and Le Tellier. Only when Louis XIV assumed his majority in 1661 did the pattern of a ministry headed by a prime minister end. Under Louis XIV the pattern of his grandfather Henry IV was restored, for Louis became his own prime minister and distributed power among men like Colbert, Le Tellier, Louvois, and Pomponne without permitting any one minister to dominate the ministry.[18]

It was within the context of Renaissance monarchy and a pluralistic allocation of ministerial powers that Bellièvre and Villeroy served the kings of France. Henry IV's supreme talent was, as one of his biographers has astutely concluded, "the art of making use of men well."[19] His good fortune was that there were available to serve him men like Bellièvre and Villeroy, whose talents were worth using.

France

An increasingly potent loyalty that held together the dynastic states emerging from the great upheavals of the sixteenth century was the ancestor of modern nationalism, dynastic patriotism. Devotion to their native land was displayed by statesmen as well as literary men in the France whose direction Richelieu was about to assume. Indeed, the emergence of patriotism was one of the features that made the sixteenth century the first modern century. Provincial particularism was a dying concept revived only momentarily by the divisions of the Wars of Religion. Even in Burgundy, where separatist traditions lingered into the late sixteenth century, the Wars of Religion did not lessen the Burgundians' awareness of being Frenchmen or patriots, however much the conflict may have shaken their loyalty to Henry III and Henry IV as individuals. The combined pressures of Henry IV's conversion and the threat of Spanish domination led to the repudiation of Mayenne and the Catholic League. The power struggles of the period, which had "a dynastic, not a national orientation," further solidified dynastic patriotism and necessitated the creation of new modes of international diplomacy. By the last years of Henry IV's reign André Duchesne could write unblushingly that France was "the radiance of the world, the light of Christianity."[20]

The existence of patriotic sentiment did not assure, however, that their native land would receive the prime loyalty of Frenchmen. For many, corporate loyalties to groups, regions, and patrons coexisted with patriotism, and sometimes the subordinate loyalty was to France. Examples abound in the years between 1560 and 1660. The league chieftain, Mayenne, for example, submitted to Henry IV only when his options had evaporated and he was guaranteed a modicum of personal power as *gouverneur* of the Ile-de-France and the payment of his enormous debts by the crown. The duke of Biron, for all the rewards heaped on him by Henry IV, sold his master out to Spain and Savoy for personal aggrandizement. Marseilles, during the wars of the league, abandoned its effort to exist as an urban republic only when the realities of military power and the demands of commerce obliged it to submit to Henry IV. The popular revolts so common during the Richelieu period were not cases of class warfare, as the Soviet historian Porshnev claims, but proof that large numbers of Frenchmen, usually organized around local *seigneurs* or officials, placed their group's interests above loyalty to their native land even while France was engaged in a desperate struggle with the Hapsburgs. The Fronde was not so much a defense of mythical constitutionalism against the encroachments of the new absolutism as a blind flailing out against the abuses of absolutism embodied in Mazarin's policies. It shows that in early seventeenth-century France the centrifugal forces of corporate loyalty still tugged against the centripetal forces of dynastic patriotism and that the monarch had yet to bind men's prime loyalty to the dynastic state.[21]

In spite of the studies that have delineated the growth and limitations of dynastic patriotism, little attention has been paid to the actual content of the patriotism of men in early modern France. To be loyal to one's native land demanded a consciousness of what the native land was. What, to proven patriots like Bellièvre and Villeroy, was France?

Their contemporaries knew that to the two ministers patriotism was a cardinal virtue. The English ambassador Edward Stafford believed Bellièvre to be "marvellously affected to this State and to his country" and to be "the best patriot in France." Years later the Dutch ambassador reported that Bellièvre was "deemed a good Frenchman by all." Henry of Navarre, even as the foe of Bellièvre's master, believed that Bellièvre always sought "the good of the state." Without false modesty, Bellièvre himself claimed that his goal was "always to love the king and desire his and the kingdom's prosperity." Villeroy demonstrated by his entire career that his promise to be "a good Christian and a true Frenchman" was not mere rhetoric.[22]

Villeroy and Bellièvre understood the importance of dynastic patriotism in keeping France intact. Bellièvre clearly foresaw that the league's Spanish support would discredit it once Henry IV had converted and that patriotism would rally the majority of Frenchmen behind France's legitimate and Catholic king. Villeroy, although he wished that Henry IV were "as powerful as he is loved," agreed.[23]

Had Villeroy and Bellièvre been asked how they felt about France, they would not have hesitated to explain their sentiments. They loved their native land, and had, as Villeroy rightfully claimed, spent their lives working toward "the same goal, which was to preserve [the king's] authority and the kingdom in their entirety in preference to everything else."[24] If they had been asked to explain what it was they loved, however, the ministers would probably have had to grope for an answer. France was many things to Bellièvre and Villeroy. Besides *La France*, they referred to their country as *la patrie, l'état*, and *le royaume*.[25] Although *fatherland, state*, and *kingdom* do not today have precisely the same meaning that they had in the ministers' day, these words seem to have carried approximately the same connotation: France was a state that was also a kingdom and the fatherland of those who were French.

Villeroy and Bellièvre might, if pressed, have defined *France* as a historic entity whose destiny they believed was to occupy the center of the European stage. France was also a territorial expanse, whose area might be increased (with extreme caution) but whose extent could not rightfully be diminished. France was also a linguistic unit. Not all who spoke French were Frenchmen, but those who lived in France and spoke other tongues were regarded with suspicion. Last and most important, France was to the ministers a Catholic kingdom, whose kings and religion were equally necessary to define her existence. The ministers never bothered to spell out their concept of France for posterity; but by reconstructing their scattered thoughts what they knew instinctively can be partially understood.

To the ministers France should have been the arbiter of Europe, not a battlefield for the ambitions of domestic magnates and foreign foes. To see "France, queen of the provinces . . . now exposed to the opprobrium and injury of some petty princes who would once have deemed themselves too honored to serve her" was to Bellièvre intolerable. Civil wars, he knew, were what undermined "the grandeur that this crown should possess." France resembled, Bellièvre said, "a man who has a small wound on his hand. Even though he has a robust and powerful body, it is no longer possible for him to make any exertion until his wound has healed. As long as these unfortunate civil wars last, we are wounded on the hand." Villeroy agreed on France's destiny but despaired that he could not "hope to see her risen and restored, as she should be, during our lifetime."[26] Only when peace was restored did Villeroy and Bellièvre, who always believed France to be in the right, see her assume her proper place in the European state system.

France was not only a nation with a proud history but also a territorial unit that could not legitimately be diminished. If part of the realm were lost, or seemed about to be, the ministers sprang to its defense. Bellièvre, for example, protested against Henry III's ceding Pignerol to the duke of Savoy to buy his amity. The duke's later usurpation of the marquisate of Saluzzo the ministers considered outrageous. During the last years of the war with Spain, when it looked as if England had designs on Calais, Villeroy and Bellièvre were alarmed. Villeroy warned the French ambassador in England that Elizabeth's promise of more military assistance might be used as a pretext for assailing the city of Calais. Spain's designs on French territory, which so angered the ministers during the league episode, did not cease even when the Spanish were forced to enter peace talks. Philip II at first asked for the revenues of Brittany and Auvergne for his daughter as the price of peace, which Bellièvre regarded as "unjust and beyond all reason." Then the Spanish demanded the right to keep some Picard cities that they had held for most of the war. Henry IV demanded their return and promised, "I will risk the rest of my kingdom and my life rather than slacken in this demand." When the Spanish archduke asked France to cede the county of Charolais at the peace conference, Bellièvre recommended refusal, because France should not "dismember her crown."[27]

On the other hand, Bellièvre and Villeroy recommended that France annex neighboring regions if circumstances permitted, but they insisted that the sensibilities of those annexed be respected. When Henry IV conquered Chambéry from Savoy in 1600, Bellièvre, who supervised the city's incorporation into France, urged Henry to give "these newly conquered people the most contentment we can" by creating a parlement at Chambéry. Although Henry IV hoped to receive ports in Flanders from the Dutch in return for increased subsidies (1605/6), Villeroy did not consider the ports worth the price of alienating the Dutch. Bellièvre weighed the military and political implications of Henry IV's campaign against Spanish Franche-Comté in 1595 and found the campaign frivolous; there was little hope of annexing it, and the minister would have preferred annexation of nearby Bresse, an area more easily assimilable and of greater strategic importance, which was annexed in 1600. Once a piece of territory had been conquered, however, the ministers were loath to lose it. Cambrai, the sole fruit of the duke of Anjou's Low Countries adventure, was threatened by the duke of Parma's forces in 1583, and Villeroy, in spite of the danger of increasing Spanish enmity, urged retention of the city.[28]

The French language, Bellièvre realized, was both a force for, and a sign of, patriotism. There had been deep resentment against Catherine de Medici's Italian favorites, even though they were among her (and France's) most devoted servants. When Marie de Medici was planning her journey to France to marry Henry IV, Bellièvre, remembering the hostility that Catherine's Italian-speaking followers had provoked, urged that Marie's servants be "all French."[29] Had his advice been followed, the unfortunate ascendancy of the Florentine adventurer, Concino Concini, over Marie when she was regent might have been avoided.

France was above all to Bellièvre and Villeroy a Catholic kingdom. Religion, king, and state were distinct but inseparable—all stood or fell together. Meeting the league threat to Henry III, Villeroy realized, was "a question of saving the king and the state." The king, as Bellièvre put it, was "the person on whose health the conservation of this state depends." The ministers were therefore appalled by Henry IV's bravado on the battlefield and the threats to his life by assassins, and Villeroy urged Henry to take every precaution to assure his survival. The ministers were also anxious about the succession, and in an age of high infant mortality even the birth of a dauphin only partially alleviated Villeroy's fears. Moreover, since France was not just a monarchy but a Catholic monarchy, whose ruler, the Most Christian King, had to be Catholic, Villeroy and Bellièvre worked tirelessly to secure Henry IV's conversion. Without it, Villeroy feared "the loss of our religion and of the kingdom." Since Villeroy believed religion "the principal foundation of all republics," Henry IV's conversion was "the only remedy to our misfortunes that remained." So eager were the ministers for it that they themselves refused to entertain any doubts as to its sincerity, and those who did were accused of hiding behind "a pretext to cover their own ambition." Having a Catholic king, however, was not in itself sufficient. As Bellièvre argued when the king was requesting a papal dissolution of his sterile marriage to Margaret of Valois, France needed an heir; otherwise there would be, "if not the total ruin of the state, at least a dangerous alteration and alienation of [men's] wills," on the king's death.[30] To Bellièvre, the essence of France was that it was a Catholic kingdom ruled by hereditary kings.

The ministers' consciousness of France, as well as their loyalty to their native land, was more highly developed than that of most of their contemporaries. For factious nobles France was more an object whose wealth they coveted than a focus of loyalty. By the masses France was probably best perceived as the patrimony of her kings, monarchs whom they seldom saw. To Bellièvre and Villeroy, however, France was a nexus of traditions, territories, persons, and ideals; although probably only half-consciously understood, this complex entity was no less efficacious in inspiring their heartfelt devotion.

Royal Authority

Royal authority was threatened during the Wars of Religion in two ways, for the Huguenots and Catholic Leaguers not only revolted; they also elaborated theoretical defenses for doing so. After the Saint Bartholomew's Day massacre of 1572, the Huguenots abandoned their protestations of loyalty to a king allegedly misled by evil councillors and claimed, as in the famous *Vindiciae contra Tyrannos*, a divine right to rebel when the ruler broke his contractual obligations to his subjects.[31] Rebels in search of a justification, the league magnates found pamphleteers to defend their revolt. To block the accession of Henry IV to the throne and to justify league pressure on Henry III to persecute the Huguenots, the need for unity of faith was emphasized. When Henry III refused to enforce uniformity, league theorists espoused popular rights residing in the States-General against monarchical sovereignty.[32] Although both groups of rebels were obviously groping for justification for their practical ends (either survival or personal aggrandizement at the crown's expense), their theories generated popular support. Obviously, if the crown were to continue its evolution toward absolutism begun under the last Capetians, it had to win battles both on the field and in men's minds. While Henry IV managed gradually to accomplish the former, political theorists of the late sixteenth century, stimulated by their predecessors' speculations and prodded by the near collapse of royal authority, elaborated the theoretical foundations for royal absolutism. Jean Bodin's *Six Books of the Republic*, which defined sovereignty as the king's undivided possession, was the great breakthrough. By the end of the Wars of Religion royalist pamphleteers had spelled out the traditional, utilitarian, and religious justifications for absolutism. Their arguments, buttressed by the specter of anarchy, succeeded in convincing most of their contemporaries that only strong rule from the center could prevent a recurrence of France's agonies.[33]

Villeroy and Bellièvre, who as royal ministers had to face the consequences of the breakdown of royal authority, were champions of strong royal government. Although they did not theorize on the nature of royal sovereignty, their defense of it approximated that of their more speculative contemporaries: tradition, utility, and religion all required rule by an absolute monarch. When it came to the practical test of their convictions, both ministers generally agreed that no constituted body possessed more than delegated authority that could be withdrawn by the king. However, while Villeroy was willing for the sake of order to override all the traditional checks on royal sovereignty, Bellièvre, although he had no theoretical arguments against absolutism, felt strongly that tradition as interpreted by the parlements should be respected by France's monarchs.

According to Villeroy, "Authority is what maintains states. The destruction of royal authority causes the scorning of laws, and the laws scorned causes license and disobedience, disobedience conspiracy, cabals, and leagues, which have as their special pretexts religion, the public weal, or the service of the sovereign." The two ministers had experienced all of the consequences of the dissolution of royal authority. During the wars of the league, the extremists (the "Sixteen") had even judicially murdered the leading officers of the Parlement of Paris, and Villeroy was on the scene to bewail the fact that "justice has no force or authority." Disobedience had been rampant for decades, during which, as Villeroy put it, "in preference to all consideration of public necessity," everyone pursued his own aims. Leagues had arisen that "trampled on all respect and duties" and defended their "sedition" with "pretexts of religion." As Bellièvre knew at first hand, "where order is not kept all is confused and lost," and in the unstable society of early modern France only royal absolutism could control the centrifugal forces of dissolution. As Bellièvre put it, "kingdoms are like a cowhide; where one steps it yields, where he does not it rises up." What France needed, in Villeroy's view, was a king "so absolute that he can order and dispose of the [unrest] as he pleases." This desire for a strong central authority at home was reinforced by the spectacle of the Dutch republic, which the minister regarded as the antithesis of what a good government should be, "a beast composed of several heads, divided in itself . . . too weak for itself and for its friends."[34] Villeroy, who remembered the days when Henry III had been trapped between Henry of Navarre and Henry of Guise, believed that France needed but one head, her king.

Religion played a major role in justifying royal sovereignty to Villeroy and Bellièvre. They had no doubt that France's kings were divinely ordained to rule, and they probably believed that her sovereigns' decisions were divinely inspired. The clearest proof of the ministers' belief in the divine ordination of kings was their view of regicide, an often-attempted act that ended the lives of both Henry III and Henry IV. It seemed to Villeroy "the most evil act that man can perpetrate," and Bellièvre fully concurred. When he learned of the assassination of Henry III, he cried, "What horror is it that they use the word of God to do the works of the devil? If kings are good, we must preserve them. If they are bad we must endure them. God sends one or the other to punish or console his people." In punishing men like Jean Chastel, who tried to assassinate Henry IV in 1594, Bellièvre begged the king to use "all the rigor of the law to purge the world of these enemies of God, their king, and their native land." A few years later, when preparing the treason trial of the duke of Biron, Bellièvre discussed the merits of a servant's keeping his word to his master in connection with the case of Jacques de La Fin, who, in informing Henry IV of Biron's plot on the king's life, had violated his word of honor as a servant to his master, Biron. For Biron's servant to have done otherwise, Bellièvre concluded, would have been "not a point of honor, but rather a point of corruption."[35]

The ministers did not limit their acceptance of the divine sanction of kingship to France. Foreign rulers, they believed, were similarly ordained. Bellièvre deemed the judicial murder of Mary Stuart a crime, and Villeroy condemned Catholic plots against the life of Protestant James I.[36]

If the ministers had no doubt that kingship was divinely ordained, their letters show to what extent they shared the contemporary view that France's kings were divinely inspired or were semidivine. Bellièvre resigned himself to his dismissal by Henry III by saying, "Since the king's wish has been that I was removed from the service where I was employed, I judge that it was also the will of God." When Villeroy found himself in disagreement with Henry IV, he would fall back on such maxims as "God directs the hearts of our princes" and "God inspires in [our masters] the advice they take and prefer to that of their servants." How seriously the ministers took their own rhetoric is difficult to determine. Since they knew their kings intimately and frequently differed with them on policy matters, the ministers obviously did not believe that every royal decision was either wise or infallible—the disastrous reign of Henry III was proof of that. But Bellièvre and Villeroy did believe that God acted through the kings of France, as Bellièvre put it, "to punish or console his people." When things went badly, as they did for Henry III, "judgments of God that man can neither comprehend nor evade" were responsible. But when things went well, as they gradually did under Henry IV, it was "more from [God's] grace and the king's virtue than from our industry." To the ministers, France's kings were the instruments of an unknowable divine plan, but they were not themselves semidivine; they had human vices and virtues, as the ministers' intimate contact with Henry

III and Henry IV made them aware. To Villeroy and Bellièvre, God acted through France's kings, but France's kings acted not as gods but as wise or foolish men. In this respect the ministers were at variance with less worldly contemporary political philosophers.[37]

The last but not the weakest ideological buttress for royal sovereignty was tradition. In France tradition was embodied in the Salic Law, which decreed that the crown pass through the male line to the reigning monarch's closest male relative. The ultimate test of the ministers' commitment to this fundamental law occurred when Henry IV, a Protestant, became king of France, and Villeroy and Bellièvre, like millions of their contemporaries, had either to accept a heretic as France's hereditary king or to repudiate the law of succession. Their dilemma lasted for eight years, until it was resolved by a compromise, the conversion of Henry IV to Catholicism.

The death in 1584 of the duke of Anjou, Henry III's brother and heir, which left Henry of Navarre as the heir apparent, created the ministers' dilemma. Villeroy saw the difficulty that Anjou's death posed: "Their Majesties and all France are very sad, and not without cause, since the king has no children." For the next five years Villeroy and Bellièvre strove to persuade Navarre to convert, an act "so desirable," according to Bellièvre, "that one would have to be more than a Calvinist to want the contrary." Villeroy frankly stated, "If the King of Navarre does not resolve to embrace the Catholic religion . . . our hurt is without remedy." Bellièvre repeatedly urged Henry III to make almost any promise to secure his heir's conversion, but the king, fearing the league's wrath, was unwilling to tolerate heresy. Navarre, aware that his power base rested in his Huguenot followers' trust and arms, refused all Henry III's overtures. After the Day of the Barricades in 1588, even Villeroy's frantic appeal to Navarre to convert to save the monarchy was unavailing.[38]

Navarre's accession to the French throne on 2 August 1589 set up a sharp conflict between the two ministers' respect for the Salic Law and their Catholicism, and they responded differently. Villeroy refused to consider the law of succession sufficient to legitimize Henry IV, while Bellièvre insisted that it transcended all other considerations. Villeroy from the start held that "a good Christian and a true Frenchman" was duty-bound to support the league until Navarre converted, but he was equally insistent that the league not elect another king. He maintained that Henry IV's conversion to the national faith was "the only remedy for our misfortunes that remained," and this was the goal toward which Villeroy strove for four years. Partially because of his repeated admonitions the league ultimately failed to elect another king. And because of his frequent negotiations with the royalists, whom he constantly reminded that it was a waste of time to speak of peace without conversion, Henry IV eventually conceded that religion as well as tradition legitimized France's kings. Whether Villeroy would ever have been willing to abrogate the Salic Law remains uncertain, but at one point it appeared that he might: "Our laws and customs," he told the league estates, "must not be as dear to us as our religion and the salvation of our souls, so that if we cannot conserve both together, it would be better to be deficient toward men than toward God; and in doing this rather to lose one's goods and life and even the kingdom, than to obey a prince who vows the ruin of our religion."[39] In any case, Villeroy's dilemma was solved when Henry IV decided that Paris was worth a mass.

Bellièvre, who deeply respected tradition, never considered abandoning the Salic Law; to him, Henry IV was France's legal king. But because he was equally convinced that unless Henry IV converted, the king would never regain control of his patrimony and France would never enjoy peace, Bellièvre, too, strove for conversion. To the leaguers willing to violate the Salic Law, Bellièvre replied with an elaborate defense of that fundamental law of the realm. The essence of his position, stripped of its enumeration of historical examples, was, "The surest judgment that we can make for the future is to pattern ourselves on what is past." Convinced that "the hope of change is usually more pleasant than what arises from it," he was convinced that recognition of Henry IV, even before his conversion, was not only necessary to save France from dissolution but also legally permissible. It was on this point that Bellièvre and Villeroy differed. Since both utility and tradition sanctioned Henry IV's legitimacy,

Bellièvre was willing to assume that political reality would eventually lead Henry to buttress his throne with conformity. Proof of Bellièvre's faith in tradition was his willingness to serve the king before his conversion.[40]

The test of the ministers' commitment to royal absolutism was their view of, and behavior toward, the several constituted bodies—the parlements, the States-General, the provincial estates, the assemblies of the clergy and of notables, and the local officials of the various cities—that often claimed the right of exemption from, or participation in, royal authority. Almost without exception, Villeroy and Bellièvre regarded these bodies as instruments of, and not checks on, royal sovereignty.

The States-General, convened when the monarchy wished to gain financial backing and popular support for its actions, did not, during the sixteenth century, serve its intended purpose. Three such gatherings (in 1560, 1576, and 1588) refused to give fiscal or psychological support to the crown. When, instead, they sought a voice in shaping royal policy, Villeroy and Bellièvre were outraged. The States-General of 1576, called to garner support for Henry III's intended war against the Huguenots, refused to grant the taxes necessary to finance the war, demanded basic reforms of the administration, and claimed the right to participate in governmental decisions. When Bellièvre requested the States-General's permission to alienate some of the royal domain in return for reform of fiscal abuses, his pleas were rejected. Villeroy found the delegates who claimed a share in governing the realm "insatiable" and was further exasperated by their subsequent refusal to vote new taxes, even as they called for war against heresy. When the States-General again met in the autumn of 1588, they were completely dominated by the league. Villeroy and Bellièvre, recently dismissed by Henry III, watched in despair as the king was forced to submit to a demand for total war against heresy. To see France's ruler humble himself before his arrogant subjects was to Villeroy a tragic sign of "our impotence in everything."[41]

If the ministers repudiated the actions of previous States-General, they repudiated the legitimacy of that of 1593. The league estates, called to elect a replacement for Henry IV, was, however, a reality with which the ministers had to deal. Villeroy, as an ex officio delegate representing Mayenne's council of state, felt compelled to warn the gathering of the folly of electing a new king. Recognition of Henry IV, if he promised to convert to Catholicism, was, Villeroy warned, France's last and best hope. Bellièvre, who was about to join Henry IV's service, also drafted an address in which he argued that both the Salic Law and the preservation of the state decreed recognition of Henry IV. The king's conversion and latent patriotism evoked by Philip II's heavyhanded attempts to coerce the league estates into electing his daughter queen caused that body to disband in August 1593, eliminating the danger. Bellièvre's resentment lingered, however, for the deputies had broken their promise to send an envoy to Rome to request Henry IV's absolution.[42] The autocratic Henry IV never convened a body that had shown itself unco-operative at best and seditious at worst.

Provincial estates in the *pays d'état* were the bodies toward which France's kings turned for fiscal grants. Although the ministers seldom mentioned the meetings of such bodies, in 1578 Bellièvre dealt with the estates of Normandy, which had been asked to approve new taxes on cloth, wine, and grain to finance Henry III's defense of the realm. However, the estates, using the pillaging of the duke of Anjou's troops on the way to Flanders as an excuse, refused to permit collection of the taxes. Bellièvre, given the task of securing their assent, considered the estates' resistance a "bad example" that had to be eliminated, but by the time he reached Rouen in March 1579, the nobility of Normandy had formed a league to resist collection of the new taxes. Faced with such open resistance, Bellièvre warned the king that he had no choice but to revoke the offensive levies. The minister, foreseeing the danger of such a precedent, asked, "Who will consider the affairs of the king . . . ? If the people abandon the king to the ordinary *aides,* more evil will befall him."[43] Bellièvre's warning proved tragically prophetic.

Because the States-General proved unmanageable, the king occasionally convened an assembly of the realm's notables. Henry III called a meeting of magnates and prelates in November 1583 to gain support for his policy of averting another war with the

Huguenots. When the cardinal of Bourbon, spokesman for the Catholic zealots, demanded an immediate offensive, Henry III silenced him. Villeroy, who opposed war, was delighted that Henry proved to be "full of granite." But the notables' conduct did nothing to enhance Villeroy's faith in such gatherings. Henry IV, who had a profound aversion to consultative assemblies, was finally forced by his fiscal plight in 1596 to consider convening some kind of consultative assembly, reluctantly heeding Bellièvre's warning that only with new sources of revenue could royal armies be kept in the field. Villeroy, who was also apprehensive of an assembly's tractability, agreed that one had to be convened. When the hand-picked prelates, nobles, and burgesses met in December 1596, they granted a new excise tax, after Henry IV had skillfully flattered their egos and dramatized his financial needs.[44] Henry, who had not enjoyed deferring to his subjects, never again called a consultative assembly. There is no evidence that his ministers objected.

When it came to defining the role of the parlements, Bellièvre and Villeroy differed. The secretary considered them merely an instrument of royal absolutism whose function was to record royal edicts without protest. To Bellièvre, however, the parlements had a dual role: to validate the royal will by recording the king's edicts and, just as important, to uphold the traditions and customs of France. Bellièvre was the spokesman for his fellow *parlementaires,* who simultaneously exalted royal absolutism and asked that the king heed their advice.[45]

Bellièvre and Villeroy viewed the role of the parlements differently because they saw the traditional laws and customs of France in a different light. Villeroy took the clear-cut position that customary law was itself a creation of the kings. He spelled out his thinking when he deplored the emperor's seizure of church property in Strasbourg: "Our kings are not accustomed to using such means. They confine their authority and power *within the limits of the customary laws which they themselves made and established* for the conservation and protection of their peoples, from which they deviate unwillingly. And we have seen that every time that they have freed themselves from them, they have suffered for it."[46] On this issue Villeroy represented a line of political thought that deviated from the older medieval theory of limited monarchy as well as from the new theory of absolutism. The former asserted that customary law developed apart from, and was inviolate from, royal sovereignty, while the latter claimed that the king could legitimately replace outmoded customary laws with his new absolute sovereignty. When it came to practice, however, the secretary had no compunctions against the king's overriding custom or innovating. He had no sympathy with attempts by the Parlement of Paris to block the Edict of Nantes and prevent the introduction of the Trentine decrees, both measures that were unprecedented but necessary for the well-being of the monarchy and the church.

When he was made chancellor in 1599, Bellièvre tried to act as the defender of traditional laws and customs by telling the Parlement of Paris, "We must all depend on the judgment of the law and not on the incertitude and will of men." He protested vigorously against the king's arbitrary interference with judicial decisions. Henry's granting great magnates like the count of Turenne immunity from the jurisdiction of the parlement of Rouen also offended Bellièvre's sense of the parlement's powers and France's customs, as did alienation of the royal domain, even after the critical years had passed. In connection with the latter, Bellièvre warned Henry, "Your parlement cannot proceed in the verification of an edict containing the alienation of your domain without breaking all the laws of the kingdom." Finally, by repeated delays in sealing edicts that he deemed offensive to tradition, Bellièvre brought about his own disgrace. He failed to realize that a king who was granted absolute powers could become an arbitrary ruler, leaving men like Bellièvre and his fellow members of the parlements with no theoretical defense for their attempt to limit royal authority. Bellièvre hoped that Henry would heed his admonitions and show more respect for the parlements' advice. Ignored by Henry, the old chancellor might have heeded his own advice of ten years before: "There remains only to carry out what the master announces to be his intention."[47] Bellièvre, who was torn between respect for an older tradition of tempered monarchy and commitment to the new absolutism, found to his dismay that it takes a long spoon to sup with the Devil. So, too, would many others in later generations.

Henry III

Henry III was one of France's most spectacularly unsuccessful kings. Most of his contemporaries probably would have agreed with the papal nuncio, who on Henry III's accession remarked that the "true salvation" of France would be "a king who knew how to be a king indeed. We can look for nothing from this young man." Although students of the period concede Henry III's intelligence, they almost unanimously agree on his political ineptitude. His bizarre conduct, marked by symptoms of manic depression and, allegedly, by sexual perversion, shocked even his contemporaries. Even to his defenders Henry III's finest hour came while he was dying, when he kept intact the succession by recognizing Henry IV.[48]

Bellièvre and Villeroy were aware of Henry III's complex nature. They saw him as a good but tormented man whose misfortune it was to ascend a throne that he was ill-equipped to occupy at a time when France's problems would have tested the wisdom of the ancients. The ministers' view of Henry III as a tragic human being and a well-intentioned but incompetent ruler is probably accurate.

The ministers did not enjoy identical relationships with Henry III. Villeroy was both a trusted adviser and an intimate friend to whom the king could pour out his troubles, but Bellièvre, although respected and relied upon, was never the king's confidant.

To Henry III, Villeroy was both a pillar of strength in his moments of anguish and a sounding board for his infrequent cries of joy. The minister, whose contemporaries knew him to be the king's most trusted servant, helped Henry III endure the grueling responsibilities and the loneliness of power. Henry felt at ease with Villeroy, for he knew that the secretary would serve him "according to my will." He could rely on Villeroy to super-

vise the administration of his realm while he relaxed from his
royal duties and to lighten the pressures of decision making by
determining which matters needed prompt attention and which
could be deferred. The minister could be counted on to come at
whatever hour he was summoned to share a burden or a joy.
When all looked black, Henry could share with Villeroy his
despair that "the bright future that Divine Providence had prepared for us is disappearing." And when the tormented king felt
beside himself "with joy and pleasure," Villeroy was there to
rejoice with him. Most important, Villeroy helped to reduce the
loneliness of power for the Most Christian King, who begged
his servant "always to love me, for I will really be a good master," and to remember "how much I love you."[49]

It was not Bellièvre's friendship but his professional competence that endeared him to Henry III. When "matters of extreme
importance" arose, the king wanted Bellièvre present. If a problem needed analyzing, the king sent Bellièvre "to see at first hand
the state of the country so as to be able to inform me of the
truth on your return." After a successful mission Henry was so
pleased that he wanted to show it by "actions, not by letter or
words." If the minister failed in a task, the king respected his
explanation and assured him that the fault was not his.[50] Bellièvre's competence, combined with Villeroy's companionship,
were two stabilizing influences on Henry III's troubled psyche
and turbulent reign.

The ministers, although they wrote no revelatory memoirs of
the king's character, did, during the course of their long service,
express clear and similar opinions on Henry III's capacities as a
man and as a king.

Villeroy, who was almost constantly at Henry III's side, well
knew the man's strengths and weaknesses. The secretary recognized the king's emotional instability but did not condemn him
for it. As Villeroy told a friend, "The king is a man like any
other; I mean subject to the perturbations and passions of this
unhappy life. And since God has made him our master, he seems
to have a right to be more stubborn in his whims . . . than others."
In Villeroy's opinion, Henry's virtues were his integrity, his
good intentions, and his kindness. Early in the reign Villeroy

defended Henry against blame for France's misfortunes: "We must not attribute them to our good master, who surpasses in integrity and goodness all whom I know in this world." Even after a decade of chaos and royal ineptitude, Villeroy hoped that "finally God will preserve and assist His Majesty, for he has very good intentions in great matters."[51] To those who charged Henry with religious indifference because he hesitated to try to exterminate the heretics, Villeroy angrily replied:

> I do not know what these princes of Guise are thinking of. I know that they are blind. His Majesty embraces the cause of religion with fervor and affection. Everyone knows it and his actions clearly manifest it. If they abuse him they will drive him to despair, and I believe that in the end God will punish those who are the cause of it. I am a good Catholic and as fond of my religion as any man of my sort, but not to endure their rebuking the king and depriving him of his authority on the pretext of piety.[52]

Henry's generosity with his funds as well as his affection moved Villeroy, who praised the king for his "benign and gracious" nature; Henry was, he said, "a good master, without whom I would die of hunger." How could Villeroy not be sympathetic to a master who wrote: "Villeroy, may I speak freely? Yes, for it is to my very affectionate and obliged servant, and because I will at least be relieved in having bared my heart to one who will never do anything but what is necessary for the good of my service."[53] Even when the king dismissed Villeroy without reward or pension, the secretary's momentary bitterness gave way to memories of Henry's earlier kindnesses.

Occasionally the ministers were offended by Henry III's failure to realize that his ministers had their own problems. When Villeroy asked for permission to visit his ailing wife, Henry, who was quick to complain of his own afflictions, refused. "I know that I owe all service and obedience to my king," Villeroy complained to Bellièvre, "but it is also reasonable that he show concern for me and to what I owe someone very close to me." And Bellièvre also complained that he was refused permission to visit his wife on a similar occasion.[54]

Although Bellièvre and Villeroy liked Henry as a man, they did not hesitate to criticize his shortcomings as a king. Some of France's misfortunes they attributed to "a century that engenders only monsters,"[55] but others they knew were the king's fault, like Henry's fluctuation between prolonged lethargy and short bursts of frenetic activity that led to problems being ignored until they became insurmountable and then to rash decisions.

The king's frequent and prolonged withdrawals from the overwhelming problems that confronted him caused the ministers much anguish. His pilgrimages in quest of mental ease or the divine gift of an heir interfered with the normal functioning of government, for the ministers were told not to communicate with him except on urgent business, which was to be presented in summary. Late in 1585, when pressing problems needed resolution, the Venetian ambassador reported that Henry, "totally occupied with his devotions, for many days has not wanted them to speak to him of anything to do with the governing of the kingdom and of the war." Bellièvre, who was in England at the time trying to persuade Elizabeth to spare Mary Stuart's life, complained that "the king will be at his devotions, but it is a good devotion to save the life of his sister-in-law." Even when he was not distracted, Henry III endlessly put off making decisions. To his ministers, who were trying desperately to find answers to France's mounting problems, his indecisiveness was a torment. Villeroy reminded him again and again of the harm such delay could bring to his service, but all too often Henry only "pretended" to, or did not at all, "concern himself with affairs." Villeroy had by then decided that France's sufferings were "as much from lack of resolution as from impotence." "I am very sick of it, but what remedy?" he cried after a two-months effort to persuade Henry to resolve the royal policy toward the Huguenots. Bellièvre, who repeatedly had to beg Henry for instructions for his diplomatic missions, summed up France's plight: "Our master must think closely about his affairs," he wrote Villeroy, "for from what they tell us, there are some who are thinking more than he has ordered them to." As the league succeeded in humbling the monarchy, Villeroy saw the situation all too clearly: "It is ambition which rules us, imprudence which masters us, and irresolution which ruins us."[56]

If Henry III's irresolution exasperated his ministers, his moments of angry activity terrified them. When the king became so annoyed at his sister Margaret, the wife of Henry of Navarre, that he expelled her from court in disgrace, Bellièvre tactfully tried to persuade his master that a reconciliation was vital, since Navarre was likely to be his heir. Bellièvre eventually brought about a reconciliation, but the king's refusal to apologize to Navarre made his task onerous. Successive humiliations by the league so embittered Henry that his ministers feared he might try to retaliate, regardless of the consequences. Bellièvre, who conducted most of the negotiations, reminded the king that "when it is a question of breaking with these men, it must be on a valid issue." Villeroy, although he felt that Henry had "a right to be angry" at Guise's asking him "to play the valet," advised him against retaliation. When Henry moved troops into Paris and it was rumored that he planned to arrest Guise, Bellièvre warned of the danger of war between Catholics. The undoing of Henry's plans by the Day of the Barricades confirmed the ministers' judgment, and his last desperate act, the assassination of Guise, left the ministers appalled: "Nothing that has happened in this kingdom has more astonished me," Bellièvre said, "than the Day of the Barricades and this news."[57]

It was not easy to serve a master who veered between almost catatonic inaction and passionate, desperate activity, but Villeroy and Bellièvre had fond memories of Henry III. Bellièvre was grateful for the king's protection of his property after his dismissal and regretted that he was no longer able to serve his master: "In my opinion, I could have been useful to him." Villeroy, although he was momentarily embittered by exile from court, echoed Bellièvre, regretting that his actions had not been "more fortunate and useful to the king."[58]

HENRY III's sudden dismissal of Bellièvre; Villeroy; his other secretaries of state, Pinart and Brulart; his chancellor, Cheverny;

and his mother, Catherine, on 8 September 1588 was an extraordinary event. A drastic change in the ministers' lives, it severed a psychological relationship in which Henry, his mother, and the ministers were entangled that was one of the most fascinating and tragic features of Henry III's unfortunate reign.

Bellièvre and Villeroy both received handwritten notes from the king ordering them to leave the court and not to return until directed to do so. The stunned ministers appealed to Catherine for an explanation, but she could offer none and confessed that her influence over her son had ended. Bellièvre, torn between "just indignation" and "recollection of the kindness which came before," resolved to "behave in such a way that the king will remain satisfied with my fidelity." Villeroy was relieved to be free of the pressures of life at court, but resented the brusqueness of his dismissal and the rumors that arose questioning his loyalty.[59]

Henry III's treatment of Villeroy and Bellièvre in the following six months showed clearly that for some reason he intended to have nothing more to do with them. Bellièvre appealed several times for a pension promised him, but by December he had abandoned hope of receiving it. Villeroy, whose son Charles had been promised the office of lieutenant governor of the Lyonnais, found his pleas ignored by the king. So hurt and angry was the secretary that he refused offers of intervention on his behalf from several deputies to the States-General as well as from the cardinal of Bourbon. Although leaguers like Mayenne and Guise offered their condolences and Catherine expressed her sympathy, Henry III refused to see the ministers and gave no sign of restoring them to office.[60] After he had been dismissed and his son had joined the league, Villeroy cast his lot with Mayenne. Bellièvre, offered a position by the league but ignored by his former master, withdrew into neutrality at Grignon.

Foreign observers had two explanations. The Florentine Cavriana and the Venetian Mocenigo believed that the king suspected Bellièvre and Villeroy of being too sympathetic to the league. The Englishman Stafford thought that Henry wished to spare his ministers an attack by delegates of the States-General for misgovernment. The ministers themselves were never certain about the king's motives. Bellièvre asked friends at court to uncover them but declined to ask the king himself. Villeroy later concluded that his advocacy of concessions to Guise had led to his dismissal, for he had "feared seeing form and establish itself in this kingdom a Catholic party distinct and separate from the king" and had "advised war against the Huguenots rather than against those of the League." The secretary defended himself, although he admitted that he had "desired and advised the last peace": "Even though I was employed making the treaty," he argued, "I was not eager to grant the articles that were conceded by others."[61]

Earlier students of Villeroy have speculated on the reasons for his dismissal. Nouaillac believed it was because Henry III planned violence against Guise and suspected Villeroy of sympathizing with the league.[62] Sutherland, reasoning from the note to Villeroy in which the king promised to recall him when the moment was propitious, has contended that Henry III planned to dismiss his ministers until after the closing of the States-General and then to recall them. His motive, Sutherland has maintained, was a desire to protect Villeroy from abuse by the delegates. However, after the murders at Blois Henry was unwilling or unable to recall the ministers.[63] This explanation has two weaknesses: it does not account for the king's callous indifference to Villeroy and Bellièvre in the months immediately after their dismissal, or explain why the king changed his mind about recalling them.

That Henry III could have suspected Villeroy, Bellièvre, and Catherine of sympathizing with the league seems highly implausible in light of their faithful service against it. Even Mendoza, who believed Villeroy to be in accord with the league's goals and sympathetic enough to warn Guise had he known that Henry contemplated violence, knew Bellièvre to be a foe of the leaguers. According to Mendoza, "All this Prince's actions contradict themselves to such an extent that the dismissals . . . do not appear to have been the result of a plan decided in advance.[64] That Henry acted irrationally and on the spur of the moment seems the most plausible explanation. The problem then becomes why Henry did so.

The answer seems to lie in the psychological relationship of Henry and his mother and the ministers during the last years of the reign. Their individual and collective responses to the mounting league threat in the years from 1585 to 1588 seem finally to have aroused within the king such a mixture of anger, frustration, and resentment that he turned on those who, in serving him to their utmost, had contributed to his despair and rage.

The responses of the king, his mother, and his ministers to the league's campaigns of coercion followed a rigid pattern. Henry would at first try to ignore the league's threat while his advisers urged him to prepare to meet it. When neglect failed, the king would act belatedly to amass the means to defend the crown and then be compelled to agree to discuss the rebels' demands. Henry would refuse, however, to grant any concession; and when the leaguers increased their pressure, he would respond with threats of forceful retaliation. Villeroy, Bellièvre, and Catherine, who had previously urged the king to prepare for the worst, would panic at the prospect of warfare between Catholics and beg the king to cease his threats and yield to the league's demands. He would finally do so, but begrudgingly and with mounting resentment. The crown's capitulation complete, Henry would try to avoid fulfilling the promises that his advisers deemed necessary to preserve the monarchy. The leaguers, when they realized that the king had no intention of honoring his word, would recommence their aggressions, starting another cycle.

The psychological impact of this pattern was to destroy Henry III's self-esteem and confidence, and pile up rage and frustration. Even before the ceaseless crises of the years from 1585 to 1588, the king was a forlorn, self-punishing, guilt-ridden, and embittered man, who bewailed the errors, weaknesses, and defeats that had filled his first decade of rule. He blamed himself, as well as ill fortune, for France's woes and tried to reconcile himself to failure to win the glory that he had dreamed of when he ascended the throne. Pessimistic about the future, he remarked, "You must all take courage and be drowned in the bark with me."[65] But even his stoicism could hardly have prepared him for the disasters of the next four years. When the ministers and his mother first nagged him to act to forestall disaster, then begged him to restrain himself when his pride and anger drove him to threaten to act forcefully, and finally pleaded with him to give in, Henry III found himself in an increasingly intolerable situation. Signs of the slowly mounting resentment against his servants appeared before September 1588. Ultimately, when he could no longer endure the shame and rage to which his well-intentioned councillors' persuasions had reduced him, the king struck blindly to remove them from sight and mind.

Catherine and the ministers could not, as loyal servants, refrain from urging the listless king to defend himself against his league tormentors. When Henry did not do so, his advisers felt compelled, for two reasons, to counsel concessions: they could not sanction hostilities against the league, for this would have precipitated war between France's Catholics; nor, because of royal military weakness, could they approve the desperate retaliation that the king, in his moments of outrage, planned. Full of the best intentions for France and the king, the ministers and Catherine were bound to act in a manner that brought the crown repeated humiliation and that eroded the self-respect of the master whom they were intent on serving.

The Catholic League, formed in the winter of 1584/85 to coerce Henry III into declaring war on his Huguenot subjects, forced the reluctant king to assent to its demands in 1585, 1587, and 1588.[66] By examining these three occasions and the reactions to them of the king, his mother, and his ministers, the reasons for Henry III's eventual alienation from his principal servants can be discerned.

The league's first campaign of coercion began soon after it was formed, for Guise and his fellow magnates started to raise troops in early 1585 and issued a manifesto on 30 March demanding repeal of all edicts of toleration and calling for war on the Huguenots. Although the leaguers did not directly attack the king, they seized control of all the provinces of northern and eastern France. So great was the imbalance between league forces and the king's (while Guise alone amassed twenty-five thousand infantry and two thousand cavalry at Châlons, the king's attempts at foreign levies were unsuccessful) that Henry III was forced to agree in July 1585 to the Peace of Nemours, which committed the monarchy to lead a war of extermination against the heretics.[67]

Henry and his advisers did not at first recognize the severity of the league threat. The king issued two edicts forbidding the formation of leagues or armed units in France (December 1584 and March 1585), and invited the Guise faction to court; but he did not build up a royal army. By early March, when the fears of Henry and his councillors were aroused, efforts were begun to raise troops. Funds were short, however, and appeals to the provincial nobility went unheeded.[68]

Bellièvre, who at first had sought to raise forces, had no real stomach for conflict and was soon convinced that "it would be better and surer if we were able to end this war with a good agreement." Villeroy urged arming as diligently as possible but agonized over the prospect of war between French Catholics and hoped to avoid "a perpetual and bloody war." And Catherine also leaned toward a diplomatic solution, even as she prodded her son to build up his military resources.[69]

Henry III tried to resist the league just as his councillors began to suggest the opposite. He sought through Bellièvre to persuade his heir, Henry of Navarre, to convert to Catholicism and tried to hire Swiss mercenaries. At the same time, however, he agreed to send Catherine to meet with Guise to sound out his demands. Catherine, when she finally arranged a meeting in May, began to panic at the size of the league's levies, the extent of its demands for pensions and garrison cities for its leaders, and the stubbornness with which Guise insisted on war on the Huguenots. She urged some concessions lest the king lose all control in league-domi-nated areas. Villeroy and Bellièvre were also alarmed and, like Catherine, feared a league attack on Paris. Angered by Guise's in-solence and by rumors of a plot to seize Paris, Henry reluctantly agreed to repeal the edicts of toleration but refused to grant the league nobles garrison cities. He purged the Parisian militia and formed a personal bodyguard, the "Forty-Five"; but when his Swiss levies were prevented from entering France by Guise's superior forces, the king agreed to yield if the leaguers' terms were not too humiliating. The Treaty of Nemours, which proscribed Protestantism in France and granted the league magnates pensions and garrison cities, was abhorred by the king's advisers, but they considered it necessary if war with the league was to be averted. Aware of the king's outrage, Villeroy had been a reluctant negotiator of the crown's debasement.[70]

From July 1585 until January 1587, Henry III tried to fulfill the letter of the Treaty of Nemours without honoring its spirit. He undertook only desultory military action against the heretics but made repeated efforts to convert Henry of Navarre. He kept promising Guise to lead the war against heresy himself, ignored Bellièvre's injunction to build up his forces so that he would not "be at the discretion of others," spent much time at his devotions and pleasures, and tried to ignore the fact that he was caught between league and Huguenot foes. Catherine and the ministers grew alarmed as the king's credit faded. Villeroy, when he learned of Navarre's levying mercenaries in Germany, grumbled, "When we see forty or fifty thousand foreigners in this kingdom, then we will realize our errors." He was unhappy at the prospect of "a very great war" with the Huguenots but conceded, "The stone is cast. . . . We must make the best of it." Catherine, after urging her son to honor the treaty immediately, since he would have to in the end, spent most of 1586 trying to persuade Navarre to convert.[71] For all their nagging, the king's advisers had not by late 1586 succeeded in arousing their master from his lethargy.

In February 1587 the leaguers, infuriated by Henry's procrastination and alarmed by an impending invasion of German mercenaries hired by Navarre, once again lashed out against the king. Guise's relative, the duke of Aumale, seized control of key cities in Picardy from the royal governor, and Guise began sieges of the Protestant-held frontier cities of Sedan and Jametz. Their defense of their aggression was that control of both areas was necessary to prevent an invasion by Navarre's German mercenaries. When he learned of these acts and of a league plan to seize Paris, Henry III considered arresting Guise but, on Villeroy's warning that his forces were diminishing daily, sent Bellièvre to Guise instead. Although Catherine urged Villeroy to persuade the king "to make himself so strong that no other force can do him harm," she favored negotiating. Bellièvre, who had returned from England just as the crisis broke out, exclaimed: "It seems that these princes make up their minds to act as madmen."[72]

Bellièvre, after meeting with Guise—who refused to order Aumale to return the Picard cities, would not cease his attacks on Sedan and Jametz, and wanted more garrison cities for his allies—recommended that the king not try to use force. Villeroy concurred, for he believed the king was too weak to fight on two fronts, and so did Catherine. Henry, however, was so angry that his councillors had difficulty convincing him not to send royal forces against Aumale. Catherine, who was with Bellièvre negotiating with Guise, felt it necessary to ask Villeroy to see that her son not strike against Guise while the talks were in progress.[73]

During May and June, Bellièvre and Catherine arranged the details of a settlement favorable to the league and with some difficulty persuaded the weary king to accept it. The Picard cities remained with Aumale until 1 October, a truce was arranged around Sedan, and Henry III agreed to meet with Guise to plan a joint campaign against Navarre and his German mercenaries. Although Villeroy knew that the leaguers concealed secular ambitions behind a mask of religiosity, he felt compelled because of the imminent Huguenot threat to urge a reconciliation between his master and the arrogant league leader. Guise and the king met at Meaux in early July in an ostensible reconciliation, but the meeting was in fact a triumph for Guise, an ambitious magnate who held his king in contempt. Villeroy, who had promoted the meeting, may have paid the price three months later; in any case, the king made no effort to intervene when his favorite, Epernon, insulted Villeroy in a council meeting.[74]

September 1587 saw the king at the head of a royal army financed in Paris through the efforts of Catherine and Bellièvre. The German invaders had entered France in August and marched toward a rendezvous with Navarre. Henry III seems to have hoped that Guise, in command of a far smaller force, would be defeated by the Germans and that Navarre, who faced an army under the duke of Joyeuse, would suffer the same fate. However, the king's watchful waiting gained him nothing, for Guise won smashing victories against the invaders and at Coutras Navarre led the Huguenots to their first great victory on the open field. Although the king's ministers tried to attribute to him a glorious campaign, Henry III found himself still flanked by his two rivals, whose prestige was enhanced. His efforts to check Guise's harassment of the retreating foreigners only angered the league leader, who continued to demand renewed attacks on heresy. But Henry, never fond of war and short of money, disbanded most of his army and returned to Paris.[75]

The leaguers, who resumed attacks on Sedan and occupied key cities in Picardy in February 1588, also demanded Epernon's disgrace and additional cities for themselves. The king reluctantly promised to begin a spring offensive against Navarre but demanded that Aumale restore the Picard towns, refused to dismiss Epernon, and would not grant the leaguers further garrison cities. Henry III was, as Villeroy put it, "rightfully piqued" and sent Marshal Aumont to recover Boulogne from Aumale; he also ordered Guise to cease attacking Sedan and Jametz. Bellièvre, who delivered the king's response to Guise, found the league chieftain intransigent and concluded that unless Henry withdrew Aumont immediately, as Guise demanded, it would be impossible to placate the league. Henry agreed to withdraw the troops but refused to put his promise in writing.[76]

Henry's mood shifted abruptly when he learned of another league plot to seize both Paris and his own person, and to kill Epernon. "I do not believe that they can do it without offending to the limit my authority and even my person," he told Bellièvre, whom he ordered to warn Guise to cease his machinations; otherwise, Henry said, he would announce to the world that it was the leaguers' aggressions that delayed his campaign against the heretics. Above all, the king warned, Guise was not to come to Paris.[77] To forestall the league plot the king ordered royal troops moved into the northern suburbs of Paris. He spelled out his state of mind to Villeroy:

> I would gladly take all measures in order not to be rebuked or ruined. I can no longer endure anything of this kind, or I would show a very timid courage. I have what I must do

well graven in my heart, I can assure you. I do not want to
be either their valet or in the end lose my authority. . . . I
have only zeal for the Catholic religion. . . . Men will finally
know and recognize it, for I shall no longer hold my peace.
This time M. de Bellièvre must make known to them that it is
mine to demand, for such men think by their falsehoods to
smother us. . . . M. de Guise must not come to Paris without
my permission.[78]

Momentarily elated at his master's firmness, Villeroy wrote Matignon, "The king has declared that he can no longer live as he
has until now. He wants to be obeyed or else to die. It is his resolve, which please God he had begun sooner to execute." Bellièvre, however, was alarmed at the movement of troops into
Paris, for, he said, Guise's reaction showed "greater disaffection
than I have ever seen." The minister remained beside Guise to
try to convince him that Henry III did not wish to go to war.[79]

The king's firmness soon wilted under the persuasions of his
advisers. When Bellièvre arrived back in Paris in early May, he,
Villeroy, and Catherine convinced the king that he should resume negotiations with Guise.[80] But it was too late, and Guise,
displaying to all his contempt for Henry III, rode triumphantly
into Paris, where he was greeted as a hero. The king waited three
days, then ordered his troops into the city. Their rout by aroused
Parisian leaguers on the Day of the Barricades (12 May 1588)
left Guise as "king of Paris" and precipitated the forlorn Henry's
flight to Chartres.[81]

At Chartres he sulked and raged while his mother and ministers worked out the last of a long series of humiliating capitula-
tions by the monarchy. Having lost control even of his capital,
the king heeded his advisers' counsel that everything be done
"to smother this fire before it flames higher." Prodded by Villeroy and Bellièvre, Henry agreed, as his mother advised, to be
one of "those who know how to yield to necessity in order to
save themselves." Catherine and Villeroy negotiated a settlement
by which the king issued the Edict of Union declaring France
to be a Catholic kingdom, promised to convene the States-General, and turned over control of the royal armies to Guise. On
30 July Henry III met Guise and made him lieutenant general

of the realm. Outwardly calm, the king may already have been planning the revenge that he carried out at Blois five months later. His mother and ministers may have failed to discern the depth of his resentment, but two foreign observers did not, for Mendoza warned Guise of a possible assassination attempt and Cavriana prophesied "the day of the dagger."[82]

Although both Villeroy and Bellièvre later claimed that they had had misgivings about recommending capitulation to Guise, they did not in the last month of their service to Henry III indicate any awareness of his resentment toward them. Bellièvre confidently expected to attend the meeting of the States-General at Blois, and Villeroy, although alarmed at being blamed by Epernon for an attempt on the favorite's life, expected to return to court after an August vacation at Conflans.[83] On 8 September 1588, when Henry III's resentment burst forth, both ministers were taken completely by surprise.

In the short run the ministers' and Catherine's policy of concession to the league was not a mistake. First of all, they could not envisage how the monarchy, if it declared war on a large body of its Catholic subjects, could be preserved as a Catholic kingdom. Indeed, Henry III could not himself adopt such a course until the murders at Blois and league repudiation of him as king forced him into an alliance with Henry of Navarre. Second, Catherine and the ministers had to cope with a king who was notoriously unstable. They would have been unrealistic had they trusted in his ability to prepare and carry through a campaign against the league. Even if the ministers and Catherine had not been hampered by religious scruples against war with fellow Catholics and had been blessed with a diligent and resolute king, they would probably have been deterred from resisting the league by the paucity of the monarchy's resources. Thus, for reasons both religious and practical, they believed that monarchy could only be saved by placating the league until Henry of Navarre converted.

In the long run, however, their policy was mistaken, for it had become clear to all three advisers by 1587 that Navarre's conversion could not be counted on and that even if he did convert, there was little likelihood that the leaguers would accept it. At that point the ministers and Catherine would have been better advised to persuade Henry III to ally with Navarre and his Huguenots. Navarre constantly urged such a course, pointing out that the leaguers were using religious pretexts to conceal secular ambitions. Had Catherine, Bellièvre, and Villeroy urged Henry III to strike out at the league, he would probably have done so. In the process he would have forced Catholic *politiques* into an alliance with the king, his legitimate heir, and the Huguenots. Since this was the alliance that eventually saved the throne for Henry IV, its formation earlier might have shortened France's civil wars. If they had been united, the armies of Navarre, the king, and *politiques* like Montmorency might well have crushed the league's forces, for even with Spanish gold, Guise frequently lacked sufficient funds to maintain his levies.[84]

Looking back, it is clear that the effect of the policies that the ministers and Catherine recommended to assure the monarchy's preservation was to defer to less propitious times the inevitable struggle between the crown and the ambitious magnates of the Catholic League.

Catherine de Medici

Catherine de Medici, mother of three kings and the most important personage at their courts, launched the careers of both Bellièvre and Villeroy. Villeroy's appointment as a secretary of state in 1567 was her work, as was Bellièvre's advancement at court during the 1560s.[85] Catherine also supported the ministers' efforts in behalf of the monarchy for more than two decades. What Catherine and the ministers thought of each other is clear from their correspondence, and this knowledge, combined with a comparison of their political styles, permits speculation about Catherine's influence on the ministers' mode of operation.

Bellièvre and Catherine were particularly intimate. While Bellièvre was organizing Henry III's return from Poland, Catherine depended on the minister to assure the king's safe arrival and promised Bellièvre not to forget his "great merit and services." She considered Bellièvre "a man of brains and fidelity" who would "acquit himself worthily, having as he does a great knowledge of [the] kingdom's affairs." If he was at the scene of a crisis, she did not feel compelled to give him advice; "You see all things there better than I do," she once told him. She was always more comfortable, she said, "when I see your news." In Catherine's view, Bellièvre's presence would often "prevent anything worse from happening." She was eager for Bellièvre's advice, whose "accustomed frankness" she appreciated, and often urged him to communicate to the king. Catherine could feel secure that whatever his task, Bellièvre would "omit nothing that one expects from a good and devoted servant." Even if he failed, Catherine was certain that it was not for a lack of "fidelity, affection and dexterity."[86]

Bellièvre returned Catherine's trust in full. He welcomed her "good advice on everything," and missed her when she was absent from court. In his many negotiations Bellièvre reported both to Catherine and to the king. If Henry III threatened to act unwisely, it was Catherine to whom the minister appealed for intervention. When Henry III moved troops into Paris in May 1588, Bellièvre begged her to help "hush up rumors that will perhaps be the cause of the greatest harm that has happened to this kingdom in my memory." If Bellièvre wanted to be released from instructions that he deemed futile, he would turn to Catherine. He was grateful for the queen mother's generosity and good will, which he compared to "the beautiful sun that shines on the strong and weak alike."[87]

Catherine both liked and respected Villeroy. She confided to him matters of which he was "not to inform anyone but the king." If the king ignored Catherine's advice, Villeroy would intercede at her request. Villeroy kept her informed of events at court when she was absent, and she sent her condolences when he was ill and assurances of her support when he was insulted by the duke of Epernon.[88]

Villeroy admired Catherine, whom he saw as the iron will behind a tottering throne. When she was absent from court and troubles mounted, the secretary was eager for her to return to help. When she fell ill at the peak of a crisis, Villeroy missed "her courage and prudence." And on her death, having left each of the two ministers a bequest, Villeroy and Bellièvre could, as Villeroy put it, speak "better than any of her other servants" of Catherine's generosity.[89]

Catherine's most astute biographer, Mariéjol, while honoring her energy and dedication "in maintaining in equilibrium the tottering edifice of the monarchy, in spite of the most violent shocks," has pointed out the limitations of her political wisdom. Catherine's solution to all the realm's problems was "to negotiate always, and in the case of unshakable opposition, to seek to gain time." But her faith in diplomacy was undercut because she tended to underestimate her adversaries, "never suspected the intransigent sincerity of religious passions," and "often saw events not as they were, but as she wanted them to be." Convinced of her own righteousness, the queen mother "ended up by not having any scruples about means. . . . Good words, vague promises, engagements of distant fulfillment, protestations of saintly intentions cost her nothing." Worst of all, Catherine lacked clear strategic goals; as Mariéjol put it, "She lived from day to day."[90]

Both ministers shared with Catherine a belief in the efficacy of diplomacy in solving France's problems. Villeroy once said that conciliation was "the surest route that we can take." If confronted with intransigent opposition, both men shared Catherine's trust that time would eventually provide a solution. When Margaret of Navarre was squabbling with her husband, Villeroy remarked that "since reason has not deterred her, time must provide for it." Bellièvre counseled the duke of Nevers, who was to help Catherine persuade Navarre to convert, to remember that "in negotiations patience and stubbornness can do much." Faced with an uncontrollable situation, Bellièvre said, "We must have patience, for there is no other remedy."[91]

Bellièvre and Villeroy shared Catherine's faith in diplomacy, but their reasons differed. Catherine underestimated her foes because she assumed that her august station, her forceful personality, and her insincere promises would assure their consent to her will. Bellièvre and Villeroy, however, regarded diplomacy as the best approach to France's plight because they believed that other men's commitment to peace, order, patriotism, and reasonable compromise matched their own. Even when the league was attempting to force Henry III into war with the Huguenots,

Villeroy was able to assert that "not only all good servants and ministers of the king, but also all good Frenchmen counseled and desired peace in this kingdom on account of the very great fear that each one has of war." And even in late 1587 Villeroy could express the hope that reason would prevail and make it possible to "appease" the quarrels between Catholics and then to "compose" those with the Huguenots. Bellièvre, in an earlier crisis, had told the king, "Time, and a wise and moderate government of Your Majesty will soothe, if God pleases, the bitterness and defiance that is in the hearts of these people [the Huguenots]."[92]

Both Villeroy and Bellièvre, being, like Catherine, *politiques*, underestimated the depth of religious passion that underlay Huguenot and league enmity toward the monarchy. Bellièvre, for example—who assumed that Henry of Navarre would be able to impose the Peace of Fleix on his followers in Dauphiné, Provence, and Guyenne in spite of Henry's insistence that he could not—failed to see that a political solution would not in itself placate religious fervor.[93] Villeroy understood the religious motivation of the league, although he did not hesitate to flay the hypocrisy of many of its members; but Bellièvre simply could not understand why leaguers placed religious unity above the safety of the state. If in the short run the ministers' *politique* outlook blinded them to the depth of other men's religious feelings, in the long run their faith in the king of Navarre's *politique* viewpoint helped to save France from dissolution.

Compared to Catherine, Villeroy and Bellièvre were scrupulous in the means that they employed to reach their ends. They believed that promises must be honored if diplomacy is to be an effective instrument. In 1585 Catherine and her son promised Henry of Navarre pensions, protection, and the succession if he would convert; at the same time, however, they were yielding to the league's demands for a war of extermination against the Huguenots, and Bellièvre warned Catherine that the dealings with Navarre would have to be in good faith if they were to succeed. When Henry III agreed in 1588 to defer a military expedition against leaguers in Picardy, then appeared about to break his word, Bellièvre warned him, too, that pledges had to be honored if negotiations were to succeed. Villeroy disapproved of the provisions of the Peace of Monsieur (1576) and the Peace of Bergerac (1577) because they granted overgenerous concessions to the Huguenots, but he urged honoring both treaties to the letter. He advocated the same policy when Henry III had to submit to league control by signing the Treaty of Nemours (1585), even though he feared that the treaty had "carried away this crown."[94] Villeroy and Bellièvre advocated keeping one's word, it appears, largely because they believed that to do so was useful. But if there was also an element of honesty (or naïveté) in their dealings with fellow Frenchmen, when frontiers were crossed and foreigners were involved, the ministers were less circumspect in their political morality. They protested against others' Machiavellianism but themselves did not hesitate to use dubiously honorable means to promote France's good.

Although Bellièvre and Villeroy shared Catherine's faith in diplomacy as the best means to solve France's domestic conflicts, this does not prove that the ministers' outlook was acquired from Catherine. As the queen mother's servants, they had to conform to her style of operation, but the difference between the ministers' views and hers on negotiation as the best method of resolving conflict, as well as Bellièvre and Villeroy's greater scrupulosity about political morality, suggests that Catherine only minimally influenced their approach to rule. Far more important in shaping their commitment to government by diplomacy were their temperaments, their faith in reasoned compromise, and their dislike of war. Indeed, the ministers themselves did not consider Catherine their mentor, either during or after their service to her: their political outlook was decisively shaped, according to Villeroy, by "the fine precepts of our late and good master and friend, M. de Morvilliers [the bishop of Limoges]."[95]

Henry IV

Historians have always agreed that Henry IV was a great king, but their estimates of his accomplishments have differed. Poirson, his first scholarly biographer, called Henry the architect of strong but popular monarchy. As he put it, "Richelieu and Louis XIV restricted themselves to re-establishing or developing the work of Henry IV: All goes back to and starts with him." Georges Pagès, on the other hand, saw Henry as the pacifier and restorer of the kingdom, who "accommodated himself to established institutions," and as the last of a line of forceful personalities under whom "the royal power was strong only to the degree that the prestige and will of the king imposed obedience." More recent writers have tended to view Henry IV as the father of bureaucratic absolutism. His use of masters of requests as protointendants and his expansion of the royal bureaucracy in Guyenne are two examples. Even in his death, as Mousnier has pointed out, Henry IV served the cause of royal absolutism: "The knife of Ravaillac helped the triumph of absolutism in France" by convincing Frenchmen that if their kings were to hold France together, it was necessary "to affirm definitively the inviolability of their person, their total independence in secular matters, their complete sovereignty."[96]

To Villeroy and Bellièvre, Henry IV's greatness rested on his willingness and ability to act as a king. In the threadbare Gascon prince become the king of France, the ministers found a hard-working, authoritative, and sagacious leader who at least approximated their ideal of an absolute monarch. Although both men sometimes disagreed with his policies, they respected his judgment and admired his successes. According to Villeroy, "His Majesty is the most sagacious and farseeing of his council. He listens to his servants, takes counsel together with them, but he decides and orders what pleases him. And each one must yield and serve, some murmuring when his commands do not please them. . . . The conduct and direction of the bulk of affairs depend on His Majesty and his will." Six years later, after watching further successes, Villeroy was even more convinced that the king saw "more clearly than all his servants put together." Bellièvre, whose opposition to some of Henry's policies precipitated his fall from grace, did not consider all the king's policies wise, but he respected Henry's aura of authority. Urging Henry to come to Lyons to help him consolidate royal control over the city, Bellièvre told the king, "Your presence, Sire, will reassure those who are Frenchmen at heart, and confound the malice of your enemies." From many negotiations with him during the 1580s, Bellièvre knew that Henry was a stubborn and commanding personage. "I have not the means to force the will of such a prince," Bellièvre admitted when he was unable to convince Henry to accept his wife Margaret back into his good graces. "The caprices of the king of Navarre are strange and sometimes intolerable," Villeroy had told Bellièvre, but when the heretic prince became the Most Christian King, his caprices became royal commands and his forceful personality admirable.[97]

Neither Villeroy nor Bellièvre became to Henry IV the confidant that Villeroy had been to Henry III. The *Vert Gallant* had too many companions, mistresses, children, and hunting dogs to need the companionship of royal bureaucrats. But Villeroy had reason to be grateful for Henry's generosity. When he entered the king's service in 1594, Villeroy was, he said, "so indebted that if the king, in receiving me into his service, had not assisted me with generosity, I would not have enough to live on." Henry, who respected Villeroy's opinions as well as his capacity for work, occasionally dined at the secretary's house but kept their relationship on an impersonal level. The king was at first pleased with Bellièvre, whom he called "one of the most self-sufficient and tested persons in this kingdom, and one of my most trusted servants," but gradually their relationship soured as Henry began to think Bellièvre overtimid in the face of war, and then overbold in trying to delay approval of royal edicts.[98]

The ministers, in spite of their admiration for Henry IV, were highly critical of some of his values. The grounds for their criticism reveal how Villeroy and Bellièvre, despite their prolonged contact with the great nobility, never absorbed its ethical outlook. The gulf between the values of Henry IV—the first gentleman of the realm, whose code of conduct demanded that he live honorably, earn glory, keep mistresses, and pardon his enemies—and that of his ministers was deep. Villeroy and Bellièvre deemed the king's honor less important than France's security, his quest for *gloire* a dangerous threat to his life and France's well-being, his womanizing a pastime that should have been kept entirely apart from matters of state, and his generosity to his foes a threat to his own and France's safety. In essence the ministers, although they were probably only dimly aware of it, rejected the assumption that what was good for the king's *honneur* was good for France.

Henry IV, by virtue of his being king of France, became the exemplar of the standard of conduct called the code of the gentleman, whose chief tenets were *honneur* and *gloire*. *Honneur* was accorded the gentleman who kept his word, was generous to friend and foe, and did not permit others to infringe on his rights. *Gloire* was earned by heroic deeds on the field of battle. Henry IV, temperamentally as well as by virtue of his office, embraced the ideal: "I will leave mistresses, loves, dogs, birds, games and gambling," he told Sully, "rather than lose the least chance and opportunity to acquire honor and glory."[99] He never took such drastic steps, but protection of his honor was always Henry IV's goal.

The quest for *gloire* filled the war years (1589–1600) of Henry's reign. As he explained to Elizabeth I, "I was born and raised in the travail and perils of war: There one plucks glory, the true attitude of all really royal souls, as [one plucks] a rose from the thorns." The king savored battle and constantly tried to earn glory in it. While besieging Paris in 1590, Henry was exultant: "This week either a battle or some deputies must come. The Spanish will join up with the fat duke [Mayenne] next Tuesday. We shall see if he has any blood on his nails." After defeating a Spanish force at Fontaine-Française in 1595, Henry looked forward to continuing the fighting in Franche-Comté. He was fully aware that earning glory meant risking his life. "If you give me an army," he told the Parlement of Paris in 1597, "I will cheerfully risk my life to save you and rebuild the state. If not, I must seek the opportunity, in dying, to give my life with honor." These were not the words of a poseur, for the king acted as he spoke. Henry himself led cavalry charges against the Spanish army at the siege of Rouen in 1592 and in a fracas at Aumale was slightly wounded in the back by an arquebus ball. At Fontaine-Française, the king rashly led a charge against Spanish troops: "I had only two or three hundred horse," he admitted, "although my enemies had all their cavalry together"; "I almost saw you as my heiress," he told his sister. A year later Henry spent the winter in trenches before the city of La Fère. After the Spanish captured Amiens in 1597, Henry insisted on directing the siege himself and fell ill as a result of the rigors to which he exposed himself. He also directed the operations of the autumn and winter sieges of Savoyard fortresses in 1600. Henry IV well deserved his own appellation of "liberator and restorer of this state," but he earned it by risking his life and hence France's future.[100]

To Villeroy and Bellièvre, who profoundly detested war, Henry IV's quest for *gloire* was heroic folly, especially since he had no direct heir. As Henry began the siege of Amiens, Villeroy expressed his feelings with mixed admiration and horror: "The king thinks himself still to be King of Navarre, strong enough to bear the hardships he formerly could. . . . I fear strongly that his body will suddenly grow feeble before his good intentions. But he has such a desire to make some effort to raise the reputation of his affairs that if he had to buy it at the price of his blood, he would respond willingly." For their king, on whose life the state's security depended, to be willing "to stake, even lose all, rather than do anything unworthy of himself" was agonizing. Villeroy was speaking for himself when he wrote, "It angers France greatly to see her king (in the person of whom lies her repose and safety), perpetually exposed to cannonades and harquebusades." Bellièvre tried repeatedly to persuade the king to leave the actual fighting to others. When Henry was about to declare war on Spain, Bellièvre begged him, "Think carefully to preserve your life and health, on which ours depends." On hearing of Henry's victory at Fontaine-Française, Bellièvre, after congratulating him, warned, "Nothing confirms these rebels in their ill-will more than their seeing Your Majesty expose yourself so often and so courageously to all the risks of war." And when Henry began his campaign in Franche-Comté, Bellièvre told the king flatly that he had "lived enough for glory but too little for the extreme need we have for your preservation." Since Bellièvre's pleas had no effect, he ceased making them but could not repress his anxiety. Villeroy, who seems to have resigned himself to Henry's pursuit of *gloire*, still felt "perpetual fear . . . that some accident [might] befall him."[101] Luckily for France, none did.

The code of the gentleman also required one to keep one's word to one's own and others' satisfaction. The difference between Henry's outlook and that of his ministers is shown by their attitude toward keeping treaties. In the Treaty of Greenwich in 1596, the king had promised his ally Elizabeth I not to make a separate peace with Spain. Although Henry soon decided that France needed peace, he was concerned to honor at least the letter of his word. He repeatedly promised Elizabeth that he would observe the treaty in good faith, even as he went ahead with plans for peace. "If I am jealous of my faith and word, I am no less of the conservation of my state," he explained. The stratagem that Henry used to keep his honor intact while making a separate peace was to invite Elizabeth to join the treaty. When she refused, he could honorably order his emissaries to conclude the Treaty of Vervins. Bellièvre and Villeroy, desperately eager for peace and afraid that the king would not sign the treaty unless the English also did, warned him repeatedly that the English wished only to keep France and Spain at war and that France would have "another ten years" of conflict if he waited for the English to support peace.[102] The ministers' alarm indicates that they were uncertain of the extent to which Henry would let concern for his personal honor interfere with France's interests.

Henry IV's many mistresses, although they may have offended the ministers' sense of decorum, did not themselves provoke Bellièvre and Villeroy's criticism. The ministers did, however, oppose the king's injection of private passion into matters of state. Estranged from his wife Margaret during his first eleven years on the throne and without a direct heir, Henry twice seems to have considered marrying one or another of his favorite mistresses, even though such a morganatic marriage would have opened the door to a disputed succession in the recently established and still precarious Bourbon dynasty.

Gabrielle d'Estrées, the king's favorite during the 1590s, had already borne him a son, Caesar, who was made duke of Vendôme. There were rumors that the king intended to marry Gabrielle, but she died in April 1599 from complications in pregnancy. Villeroy and Sully, at least, believed that her death had averted a disaster, and Villeroy, who had long urged remarriage to an eligible princess, grew even more determined that the king "make a choice that turns out to the state's common security."[103] Henry's marriage a year later to Marie de Medici and the subsequent birth of a dauphin eased the ministers' worries.

Soon after Gabrielle's death and before marrying Marie, the king took as his mistress Henriette d'Entragues. So infatuated was Henry that he gave her a written promise that if she bore him a male heir within fifteen months, he would marry her and declare their son dauphin. The birth in June 1600 of a stillborn son to Henriette, followed by Henry's marriage and the birth of the future Louis XIII in September 1601, invalidated the promise. But still enamored of Henriette, whom he had made marquise of Verneuil, the king kept her at court and did not insist on her returning the promise. Even in 1604 when Henry learned that Henriette, her father, and her half-brother had conspired for Spanish recognition of Henriette's surviving son by Henry as heir to the throne, he pardoned her from the sentence of death for treason imposed by the Parlement of Paris and required her only to return the promise.[104]

Although Bellièvre and Villeroy did not go so far as to call Henry IV's court a "bordello," as did one foreign observer, they worried when Henry's passion for his mistresses endangered the dynasty. Bellièvre especially disliked Henriette, whom he called "the king's little whore," and tried to dissuade Henry from making her marquise of Verneuil as well as from legitimizing his bastard son by her. Villeroy also urged her trial for treason and, when the king pardoned her, Villeroy remarked, "His Majesty cannot stop doing good to those who do him harm."[105]

The ministers' rejection of Henry IV's ethical code did not undermine their confidence in him as a leader. In their eyes he was the hero that later generations made of him. On Henry's death in 1610 Villeroy was moved to say, "We have lost our master. He has carried with him the happiness and glory of

France. All our tears cannot suffice to appease the greatness of our affliction and sadness."[106]

The Ministers

Bellièvre and Villeroy developed a strong sense of professional identity in more than forty years of service to the kings of France. As *ministres du roi* they were conscious of having certain qualities and of following a precise code of conduct—of being proficient, unstintingly loyal, quick to defend their prerogatives, careful to maintain close contact with the king, and reconciled to the possibility of dismissal from office.

Bellièvre and Villeroy were proud of each other's skills as well as their own. Bellièvre considered Villeroy "a very far-seeing person," "a wise minister of the king," and "the most necessary and useful servant the king has." Confident of their own ability, the ministers feared that Henry III, after dismissing them, would rely on incompetent councillors. Henry's new servants were, Bellièvre told Villeroy, "very different from you and me, who on similar occasions risked our fortunes to say to our master what we judged to be for his welfare." Bellièvre had enough confidence in his own ability to admit that he sought the office of chancellor and was ambitious, for, he said, "Ambition is praiseworthy that does good for the public."[107]

Nor was the ministers' confidence in their own ability misplaced. Catherine de Medici so trusted Villeroy's judgment that on offering advice she told him, "If it is bad, throw it in the fire, if it is good, show it to the king." Robert Cecil considered Villeroy "one of the best experienced counsellors in Europe," and Chancellor Cheverny described the minister as "an extraordinarily able man." The cardinal legate, Alexander de Medici, said that Villeroy was "subtle and cunning," while an English ambassador termed him "crafty and subtle"; he was, according to a Venetian ambassador, the person "through whose hands all things of importance pass." Even Sully, who in his memoirs was eager to disparage Villeroy's talent, admired his colleague. When Villeroy's cipher clerk sold his codes to the Spanish, Sully, although he claimed in his memoirs that he reprimanded the secretary for carelessness, actually urged Villeroy to pluck up his spirits and resume direction of matters that required his sure hand. Catherine found Bellièvre "a man of brains and fidelity"; the English ambassador, "a good and a wise counsellor." De Thou, although he wished that a member of the Parlement of Paris had been made chancellor, admitted that Bellièvre was best qualified for the post. Late in Bellièvre's life some observers claimed that he had entered his dotage, but these charges are unproven and unlikely, since, although his health had declined, Bellièvre was still carrying out his duties a few months before his death.[108]

To Villeroy and Bellièvre, the test of a minister's honor was his loyalty to his king. Whenever it was questioned, they vehemently defended their integrity. Villeroy held that "honest men are so careful and jealous of their honor that they desire that even their greatest enemies have a good opinion of them."[109]

Four times in his long career Villeroy's honor was jeopardized by attacks on his loyalty. The first crisis occurred in 1582, when a servant of the duke of Anjou accused Villeroy of plotting with the Spanish to assassinate Anjou and William of Orange. The charge was patently absurd, as Henry III assured his secretary, but Villeroy, who would, he said, "rather endure exile from my native land than see my honor in disrepute and subject to such stains and defamation," refused to handle correspondence with the Low Countries until his name was cleared.[110]

The second attack on Villeroy's honor followed his defection to the league, which he defended on the ground of providing for his family's welfare, since the king had refused to guarantee either Villeroy's own safety or that of his property. Villeroy was aware, however, that others would see his actions in a different light and denied that joining the league had made him a traitor to France or a pensionary of Spain: "If at this juncture I have advised war against the Huguenots rather than against the

League, I have not for that been a bad Frenchman, or Guisard or Leaguer, or still less a traitor to my master."[111]

The third attack came when, after Henry IV's conversion, Villeroy abandoned Mayenne and joined the king's service. Villeroy again denied that any concern but the welfare of France and that of his family had dictated his decision to join the league. This time he was especially anxious to clear his reputation, for the *Satyre Ménippée* contained a passage satirizing his league service; there were also rumbles of discontent at former leaguers' receiving royal employment.[112]

In 1604 Villeroy's honor came under fire a fourth time, when his cipher clerk sold his diplomatic codes to the Spanish. Although reassured by his colleagues and the king that his reputation was unsullied, Villeroy insisted that there be a full investigation and public trial (of the traitor's remains, since he had been drowned in the Marne while fleeing toward the Low Countries) "in order that the truth be known and justice done."[113] Self-respect and self-preservation both decreed that a minister's badge of honor—his loyalty—be untarnished.

In Bellièvre and Villeroy's age, when it was a common practice to offer royal servants gifts, the Dutch ambassador sought to reward Villeroy and Sully for promoting a policy of subsidy to the States-General, and the Tuscan ambassador wished to present gifts to them for their part in negotiating a marriage alliance between France and Florence. Bellièvre, who took pride in the fact that he had "lived in this world in the service of four kings," nevertheless disapproved of the practice. When his colleague Brulart de Sillery, with whom he had negotiated the Peace of Vervins, was about to go to Brussels to witness the archduke's oath to it, Bellièvre warned him against accepting gifts. As Bellièvre put it, "When the servant takes, the master is sold, or at least does not regard the servant as he did." Bellièvre was sensitive about his honor, although it was not threatened until near the end of his career. When he was unable to persuade Henry of Navarre to convert in 1585 and Catherine and Henry III thought his efforts dilatory, Bellièvre took pains to point out that the concessions he was empowered to offer were insufficient and that Catherine could hardly expect him to secure Navarre's conversion while she was negotiating with the league for his destruction. Three years later, while Bellièvre was negotiating with the duke of Guise, Henry III uncovered a league plot to seize Paris and himself; lest the unstable king believe that his minister had failed to divulge knowledge of the plot, Bellièvre felt obliged to beg the king to believe him when he said, "If I saw anything here that was against your interest, I would choose death rather than conceal it from you." Because he did not join the league after his dismissal by Henry III, Bellièvre did not face the same fears for his reputation as Villeroy, although even in his retreat Bellièvre found that "those who have held some office, when they live in retirement in their homes, are more exposed to calumnies than others." Bellièvre did, however, fear that Henry IV would think him disloyal and took pains to make known through friends at court his commitment to the royalist cause and his past services.[114]

The only serious threat to Bellièvre's honor occurred in 1602, when, his credit with Henry IV almost expended, the old chancellor was alarmed and hurt by rumors that the king ascribed Bellièvre's opposition to the alienation of parts of the royal domain to personal interest. To these rumors Bellièvre replied that opposition from the Parlement of Paris, not from him, was delaying the alienation: "When it has been a question of setting my hand to the pen for the affairs of Your Majesty," he told Henry, "I have done it more often than six of those whom I have seen handle formerly the seals of France." As for the rumors that he had planned to enrich himself from his office, Bellièvre said, "Sire, I have had the honor to be known to Your Majesty in very great matters. I am badly deceived if he has not always considered me a man who has faithfully served his king." It is doubtful that Henry IV believed the rumors, for in his subsequent repeated orders to Bellièvre to seal royal edicts, he never questioned the chancellor's integrity. But Henry was determined to be obeyed, even if Bellièvre's opposition was based on principle. Rather than brutally depriving Bellièvre of the seals, the king used the pretext of concern for Bellièvre's failing health for giving the seals to Sillery and granted Bellièvre a large pension. Thus the chancellor's honor remained intact to the end, with

Cardinal Du Perron reminding Sillery of "the honor that all France owes to his venerable old age, and his merits and services" and Pierre de L'Estoile referring to Bellièvre in his diary as a man "honored by kings with great offices, in which he had always worthily and virtuously acquitted himself."[115] Bellièvre would have considered L'Estoile's words a fitting epitaph.

BELLIÈVRE and Villeroy were as anxious to defend their prerogatives as ministers as they were to keep their honor unsullied. When Henry III, soon after taking power, denied the secretaries of state the authority to control petitions for royal favors and audiences, Villeroy resented his curtailment of what he considered his legitimate duties. It made him, he said, "A poor servant who is held . . . to obey to the letter what I am ordered to do." Villeroy's resentment subsided, however, when Henry III proved unwilling to sustain the additional burden he had taken upon himself. Only in 1602 did Villeroy express resentment at a threat to his prerogatives. This occurred when he ran afoul of the future duke of Sully, whose customs officials had stopped the Protestant administrator of Strasbourg at the frontier as he was returning home from France and had confiscated his funds and baggage because he had no passport. Villeroy considered the mistreatment of such a dignitary a reflection on his handling of France's foreign relations and ordered the customs officers arrested, whereupon Sully sprang to his officials' defense by countermanding the order. In the end Villeroy seems to have won his case, at least formally, for Henry IV apologized to the administrator and promised that the offending officials would be punished.[116]

Equally sensitive to any encroachment on his prerogatives, Bellièvre must have been pleased early in his mission to Lyons (1594–95), by the king's response to a complaint by the region's military commander, Marshal Alphonse d'Ornano, that Bellièvre's powers were too extensive. The marshal was told that except in military matters he was to co-operate with Bellièvre, who, the king said, "will be able to do me good service there, for the reputation of probity and self-sufficiency in which he is held by all my kingdom." As chancellor, Bellièvre felt threatened by Constable Montmorency's claim to the privilege of presiding over meetings of the *conseil d'état et des finances*, a privilege Bellièvre considered a prerogative of his own office. Reminded by Bellièvre that "our tradition makes no mention of [the constable's] being chief of the king's councils," Henry confirmed the chancellor's prerogative. However, Bellièvre lost his last struggle for power—that with Sully over control of the *conseil des finances*. The conflict was largely inspired by opposing views on the wisdom of hereditary officeholding, but differences of age and temperament also played a part. Bellièvre considered it intolerable that an arrogant younger man far less experienced than he should claim the right to dictate policy to the council. For Sully, whom Bellièvre considered "still wet behind the ears," to treat him as "a clerk of finances" was "unbearable." Until Sully was secure in Henry IV's favor, he had been hesitant to challenge Bellièvre's greater financial experience. In 1599 he had even, in sending two fiscal edicts, written, "I beg you to want to seal them if you find them good. If not, recast them as you please."[117] But when he was certain of the king's support, Sully did not hesitate to lord it over his old colleague.

BELLIÈVRE, who for long periods was removed from the court by his diplomatic missions or by his duties as chancellor, knew that it was important for a minister to have access to his master: as he wrote Du Perron, "When a servant remains a long time without seeing his master, it is to be feared that the master will not take advice and that the servant will not pay enough attention to his good graces."[118] During his struggle with Sully, Bellièvre was seldom able to speak directly with the king and often had to convey his suggestions and complaints by letter, either to the king or to Villeroy.[119] Proximity to Henry IV might not have enabled Bellièvre to sway the king by his arguments, but certainly absence from court did not improve the chancellor's chances.

Fully aware of the precariousness of ministerial office, which they knew was granted, not earned, Bellièvre and Villeroy enjoyed exercising its power and clung doggedly to that power. If they felt, as Villeroy did, that their long service to Henry III deserved better than summary dismissal, they had to admit, as Bellièvre did, that they, like their predecessors, were expendable if they forfeited royal favor. Both men tried to adopt a philosophical attitude to their fall from power. Claiming to have resigned himself to it. Bellièvre maintained that "one who has gotten out of a misfortune and seeks to return to it deserves to be unhappy all his life." Villeroy, who, until a new secretary of state was appointed, had hoped to be recalled to court, bitterly remarked, "If I can remain and live securely in my home, I assure you that I would rather prefer the money than the aforementioned office." For all their professions of detachment and relief at being relieved of public burdens, the ministers craved the power that they claimed to scorn. Bellièvre, indeed, admitted to his cousin, "I have not yet learned that philosophy of saving oneself alone. I must and want to lose or save myself with the public." Four years after his dismissal Villeroy, who told the duke of Nevers that he wanted "nothing more than to spend the rest of my days in patience in my home," was still angling for a call to Henry IV's service.[120]

Bellièvre and Villeroy were men of power—delegated power, it is true—but nonetheless real. They knew their roles and their awesome responsibilities but would not have exchanged them for the world. Bellièvre might claim that his loss of the seals and the end of his struggle against Sully gave him "a great peace of mind," but his contemporaries knew better. At his death one of them remarked that after Bellièvre lost the seals, "the good man was unable to remain content, ambition being the last thing that dies in an old courtier like him." Villeroy might complain of Henry III's ill-treatment of "those who crucify themselves in his service," but he ceased to serve the kings of France only when death stilled his hand. Just before he had entered Henry IV's service, Bellièvre had summed up the isolation and futility of exile from court as well as the satisfaction of being there in a letter to a friend at court: "I am here at [Grignon] as if buried in the clouds, and you live in the light, if anyone still remains so in this miserable France."[121]

3. War and Foreign Policy

War

To the rulers and the nobility of sixteenth- and seventeenth-century Europe, war was an honorable profession.[1] Martial exploits, toward which a nobleman's education and training were directed, justified the existence of his class. This military ethic, rooted in the feudal past, decreed that *honneur* and *gloire* be earned by heroic deeds on the battlefield. To kings and their noble followers war was not an onerous duty but their *raison d'être*. Kings declared war not only to acquire territory and peoples but also to earn glory in battles fought by nobles trained for little else. Contemporary social theorists and imaginative writers did little to refute the glorification of this martial ethic. As Sir George Clark has pointed out, "War was taken for granted as a fixed necessity of human life."[2] It is hardly surprising that Europe's nascent nation states were almost constantly at war.

As royal ministers caught up in the endemic violence of their day, Villeroy and Bellièvre exhibited an ambivalence toward war: as individuals they condemned it on the grounds of humanitarianism, religion, morality, and self-interest, but as royal ministers and patriotic Frenchmen they condoned it on the grounds of the king's honor and the state's interest.

Bellièvre, who spent years traveling about France on diplomatic missions for Henry III and saw entire regions plundered by ill-disciplined soldiers, was horrified by the impact of the civil conflicts: "God knows how our people live; there are not people in Turkey more rudely treated." He pleaded with Henry III to buy off an invasion force of mercenaries, lest they "eat up the people." Villeroy was equally appalled at the murder and assassination that he saw as "the fruits of civil war, from which are exempted more often those who are the cause of it than the innocent." When he entered Paris in 1590, just after the city was relieved from a four-month-long siege, he was greatly moved by the distress of its citizens: "They were not able to look at us, nor we at them, without sighing," he said. Nor was he untouched by the plight of the defeated German mercenaries in Navarre's employ.[3] Neither Bellièvre nor Villeroy ever became inured to the misery of the victims of war.

In the midst of Henry IV's war with the Catholic League, Bellièvre echoed the Prince of Peace: "We have seen few wars in which God was not offended . . . , but in this one that some say they wage in God's honor, I hear of nothing that is not contrary to God's commandments." War was not only unchristian but harmful to Catholicism. When a dispute between the pope and the duke of Lorraine grew heated, Bellièvre feared that it might lead to "a very dangerous war, from which it is impossible that the Catholic religion would not suffer." Villeroy regarded the conflict between the papacy and the Venetian republic as "pernicious to the church and scandalous to the public"; from it, he said, "Only misfortune can come to both parties, the Catholic religion and to Italy." As for the general European war that threatened to develop from the Juliers-Cleves dispute, Villeroy saw it as a catastrophe because it would "reduce all Christendom into two parties, one Catholic and the other Protestant."[4] In his awareness of the folly of injecting religious divisions into secular disputes Villeroy was ahead of many of his contemporaries.

The impact of prolonged warfare on the moral tone of France distressed Bellièvre, who, early in Henry III's reign, complained that "the license of war has given an opening to the complete dissolution and corruption of morals."[5] After another twenty years of civil and foreign war, Bellièvre, on assuming the chancellorship, said, "I feel feeble to combat the great number and variety of monsters that our civil wars have introduced. The corruption of some has aroused the weakness of others to tolerate them. If Cato returned to the world he would say: 'No, I do not know how to endure them, nor they me.' "[6] As the officer responsible for rooting out corruption, Bellièvre's awareness of the problem was acute.

War was not just a horror whose impact others felt; Villeroy and Bellièvre both experienced it at first hand when their family properties were threatened. In 1581 the duke of Anjou's levies on the way to Flanders plundered Villeroy's father's and three of Villeroy's own estates. During Henry IV's wars with the league, foraging troops from both camps supported themselves from Villeroy's manors, causing him to complain of "living only on loans, not having received five hundred écus from all my properties for two years." Bellièvre, whose estate at Grignon was in the midst of campaigns around Paris, was, he said, "forced to have myself guarded in my home at great expense, as if this were a frontier city."[7]

Bellièvre hated "these long wars that have diminished the grandeur that this crown should possess" and felt shame to see "France, queen of the provinces . . . exposed to the opprobrium and injury of petty princes who would once have deemed themselves honored to serve her." Villeroy, at his most depressed, despaired of "a century that engenders only monsters." Even before the civil wars reached their peak, Bellièvre warned Henry III that if they continued, "This kingdom will fall into the same misfortunes as after the war with England [the Hundred Years War]." When the league rebellion added fuel to the fire, Bellièvre concluded, "This miserable kingdom [is] nearing its end if God does not permit us to end this uprising quickly with a good reconciliation." For all his and Villeroy's efforts, however, war continued for another decade, during which, as Villeroy put it, "Our native land is still the theater of all the passions, follies and miseries of the world."[8]

The ministers, whose natural caution was exceeded only by their dedication to the monarchy, preferred to avoid the risks of battle. "War," Bellièvre cried in a moment of exasperation, "is a game of chance. One wins here and loses there. Otherwise no one would want to play with us." Even near the end of the war of liberation against Spain, when it seemed probable that the Spanish would consider peace talks if Henry IV retook Amiens, the ministers hesitated to applaud the king's energetic strategy. Bellièvre feared that Henry, in concentrating his attacks on Amiens, might lose other cities, and Villeroy, who shared his colleague's fears, needlessly reminded him that "the events of war are uncertain."[9]

Still, Villeroy and Bellièvre were not pacifists. Had they been, they could not have survived at court for forty years. When certain conditions prevailed, the ministers were ready, if not eager, to resort to war.[10] According to Bellièvre, "Princes are moved to make war either from necessity or from great utility. There is nothing unjust in necessity. Several [thinkers] have accepted utility as just, and most kingdoms have taken up this commandment." War was unnecessary if there was "no trace of reason to allege it"; "In matters of state we have the maxim that one must not stir up what is not necessary." Moreover, an aggressor is stigmatized by friend and foe alike, which, Bellièvre believed, "Prudence counsels us to avoid."

If Villeroy and Bellièvre could not bring themselves to regard war as useful, they agreed that it was sometimes necessary. (It is true that the ministers considered indirect war against Spain— through subsidization of the Dutch revolt—useful, but open conflict was to be avoided.) War was necessary, first of all, if the king wanted war, for the ministers, even if they disagreed, had no choice but to yield. As Villeroy explained, "We must serve our masters as it pleases them and believe that God inspires in them the counsels that they adopt and prefer to those of their servants." Second, war was necessary when France was attacked and was forced to fight a defensive war. This was the case in 1587, when Navarre's German mercenaries invaded the country. Bellièvre saw that Henry III had no choice but "to repulse force with force," for "once foreign forces are assembled on both sides it will be impossible to negotiate any peace that will not be more harmful than war has been up to now." A third occasion when war was necessary occurred when, late in his reign, Henry III had to choose between fighting the Catholic League or the Huguenots. Bellièvre wanted war with neither but deemed it wiser to side with the league, preferring a war with the Huguenots to "a worse war with the Catholics." The fourth set of conditions that made war necessary occurred when the king's honor was at stake. Among the reasons for Henry IV's declaration of war against Savoy in 1600 was France's interest in recovering a valuable piece of territory in Italy. But Bellièvre and Villeroy both justified it in terms of the king's honor, which would have been besmirched had Henry IV endured any longer the ambition and perfidy of the duke of Savoy. These few examples, which are elaborated below, show how dynastic patriotism, like its modern counterpart, nationalism, made it almost impossible even for men who claimed to "love the public peace in preference to all other things" to keep it.[11]

The ministers, who found justification for war in spite of their aversion to it, were less successful when it came to finding ways of keeping the peace. Indeed, their only attempt to achieve the latter seems to have been Bellièvre's suggestion that the European powers sublimate their internecine hostilities by uniting in a holy war against the Turks. Although this project was favored by the papacy, it was not in France's interest, since it would help the Hapsburgs, and Henry IV carefully avoided committing France to it. During the next century social theorists like Leibnitz, who elaborated projects for perpetual peace that included a holy war against the Turks, overlooked the fact that practical statesmen had long since abandoned the idea of bringing Europe peace through war.[12]

Foreign Policy

Between the 1420s, when Charles VII lost control of most of his realm to the English and their Burgundian allies, and 1792/93, when France's revolutionary republic faced the threat of partition by Europe's conservative powers, France was never more threatened by her neighbors than during the last phase of the Wars of Religion. From 1560 to 1589 the danger to the monarchy was severe—first from Huguenot rebels aided by England, the German Protestant princes, and the Dutch; then from Catholic Leaguers subsidized by Spanish gold—but after the accession to the throne of the Huguenot Henry IV in 1589, the danger became even more acute. Philip II of Spain and the dukes of Lorraine and Savoy intervened openly in the French civil war in an attempt to usurp the crown or plunder the nation of valuable territories. Because of his conversion to Catholicism, his dogged campaigns, and his foes' eventual exhaustion, Henry IV managed by 1598 to repel the threats to France's integrity. But especially before his conversion the outcome had been in doubt.

At a time when it seemed as if all Europe was seeking to profit from France's troubles by seizing part of her territory, Frenchmen grew acutely aware of the virtues of their native land and embittered by their foes' avariciousness. For patriotic Frenchmen like Villeroy and Bellièvre, it was often difficult to decide whether such avowed enemies as Spain were more to be feared than such allies of convenience as England. During the last days of Henry III's sad reign Villeroy exclaimed, "The English from one side and the Spanish from the other throw fuel on the fire that consumes us."[13] Because the ministers dealt with France's rivals for forty years, it is hardly surprising that they developed sentiments that approached xenophobia. Their response to the rivalries of the European state system shows how patriotism and hatred of the enemy sundered the bonds of the *res publica Christiana*.

In an age of almost constant warfare, Villeroy and Bellièvre were torn between their desire to serve the interests of France and their hatred of her enemies. The ministers succeeded in tempering their dislike of foreigners enough to deal with them to France's advantage, but the task was complicated by several factors. Not only was historic French antipathy to Spain and England revived by the resumption of warfare in Bellièvre and Villeroy's day, but the ministers were subject to a siege mentality caused by forty years of civil and foreign war. For example, Villeroy complained in 1603, a year of peace, that Savoy was attacking France's ally Geneva, that Spain was expanding her influence at France's expense in Italy and conducting a placard war against France, and that England was preparing to make peace at France's expense with Philip III. This proved, the secretary said, "Our neighbors want to do us so much harm that we must believe that it is only their impotence that holds them in check."[14] Even during the years of nominal peace after 1598, the ministers were constantly irritated by Spanish aggressions and English suspicions.

In spite of their passionate dislike of France's neighbors, Villeroy and Bellièvre managed to recommend and pursue hard-headed policies predicated on reasons of state. When foes had to be courted or revenge had to be deferred in France's interest, the ministers swallowed their resentment. In doing so, however, they provided at least an unconscious rationale for their amoral politics: since all of France's neighbors—foes and allies alike—appeared to them treacherous and inconstant, the ministers saw no reason why they should not respond in kind in seeking France's advantage. Villeroy and Bellièvre's reasons for believing that France should keep treaties, pay debts, and keep the peace had nothing to do with traditional morality. Therefore, when France's interests dictated ignoring treaty obligations, the ministers felt no qualms about betraying those they believed would as easily betray them. Such acceptance of the tenets of reason of state was hardly new, but it was clearly reinforced by their profound antipathy to France's rivals.

Assessing the ministers' influence in shaping foreign policy is a thorny problem because not only do no records of the verbal exchanges in the royal council exist but the kings also never revealed in writing the rationale for their decisions.[15] The knowns in the policy-making equation—the ministers' opinions, the king's views, and the policies adopted—nonetheless make the ministers' influence reasonably clear. Generally the kings and their ministers agreed on policy. Whether the kings pursued the policies the ministers recommended because they were persuaded to do so or because they arrived at them independently cannot be absolutely determined; however, if there is no evidence of disagreement, it can safely be assumed that the ministers' counsel, at the very least, reinforced the king's predilections and was therefore influential. On those occasions when the king was torn between alternatives and the ministers strongly urged the course that he eventually adopted, their counsel seems to have been important in helping the ruler make up his mind. But often the ministers' advice was ignored.

Two additional factors should be considered. First, Villeroy and Bellièvre did not exert equal weight in shaping foreign policy. Villeroy, who, especially under Henry IV, acted as de facto foreign minister, was consulted more frequently and was better informed. Also, when Bellièvre's overall prestige declined after 1602, so did his ability to influence foreign policy. A second point worth stressing is that Villeroy, who conducted the official correspondence of the kings and sent as well his own despatches to all of France's ambassadors abroad, never attempted in the latter to subvert the king's intention. Villeroy might occasionally complain in his own letters of features of the king's policy, but he never attempted to modify in any significant way the king's instructions. France pursued but one policy *vis-à-vis* her neighbors—that of the king.

On most issues during the reigns of Henry III and Henry IV, the king and his ministers concurred on the basic features of foreign policy. During Henry III's reign the two main goals were to avoid an open confrontation with Spain and to gain the support of England as a check to Spanish might. That the second goal was to be achieved by offering Elizabeth I the duke of Anjou as her consort was agreed upon by Henry, Catherine, and the ministers—all of whom failed to realize that Elizabeth feared France and Spain equally and was determined to prevent both powers from dominating the Low Countries or uniting against her. There were, however, differences between Henry III and his ministers over the first goal, keeping peace with Spain.

In Henry IV's reign a similar consensus prevailed on most issues of foreign policy. The ministers' eagerness to improve relations with Rome was matched by that of Henry IV. As Pagès put it, "There was from [1594] between the pontiff and the king a succession of reciprocal concessions, wherein the church received more than it gave." Urged by Bellièvre "to make known to the pope the respect that [you] bear him, preserving always your dignity and honor," the king followed his minister's suggestion. Although Villeroy was less enthusiastic about Henry IV's twelve-year-long attempt to achieve union with the Protestant princes of Germany, neither Henry nor his advisers had a moment's hesitation about subsidizing the Dutch revolt. It was, according to Villeroy, a "thorn in [Spain's] foot that God has implanted," and Henry also believed, "If [the Spanish] were not checked by fear of my arms and the Dutch war, they would tyrannize all the other princes and potentates who reign here, even to the pope and the Holy See."[16] Keeping peace with Spain, at least until 1610, was also a shared goal, although there was disagreement over the means of doing so.

Only infrequently were the ministers' foreign policy recommendations rejected by Henry III. Most striking was the king's refusal to heed Villeroy's warnings against supporting Anjou's Low Countries adventures. The monarch did, however, let himself be persuaded by Bellièvre and Catherine that financing Anjou's activities abroad would prevent the duke from raising the banner of revolt at home.

The differences between Henry IV and his ministers never arose over the ultimate goals of foreign policy but over the means used to attain them. The ministers, whose byword was caution, sometimes did not dare take the risks necessary to obtain the ends that they and the bolder king sought. Fortunately for France, the royal will prevailed whenever the ministers' timidity clashed with Henry's willingness to take a calculated risk. During the years of open war with Spain (1595–98), for example, the king, Villeroy, and Bellièvre, although they agreed on the necessity of war to secure a tolerable peace, did not agree on the conduct of military operations. Henry saw clearly that forceful campaigning was necessary and kept as much pressure on Spain as his funds permitted him to. Villeroy and Bellièvre, fearful of the risks involved, frequently counseled a military passivity that would have undercut their goal of a victorious peace. By ignoring their overcautious counsel, Henry was able to convince Philip II that Spain could not win the war.

After 1598 Henry, Bellièvre, and Villeroy agreed on the desirability of maintaining peace with Spain while subverting her power by subsidizing the Dutch revolt. They did not agree, however, on how to respond to Philip III's retaliation. Villeroy and Bellièvre were unwilling to face down the Spanish in a series of crises, but Henry IV, certain that Philip "has as much desire and need to live in peace with us as we with him," boldly met Spanish threats with counterthreats. He forced the release of the prisoners in the Rochepot incident by prohibiting commerce with Spain, at the same time accepting papal mediation of the dispute. And when Spain began a tariff war, Henry replied with an embargo on trade with Spain, confident that "in the long run they will receive greater inconvenience than we will." In both situations Villeroy opposed such forceful retaliation. Although Henry IV wanted war with Spain no more than his ministers did, he took these calculated risks against their advice because he was "still less disposed to endure an affront" and because he knew that the Spanish, who could "hardly resist the [Dutch] alone," were unlikely to declare war on France.[17]

Thus, by correctly sensing the political climate in Spain, Henry IV was able both to keep the peace and to defend his honor. That Henry placed peace first and his honor second is revealed by the Biron affair, in which Spain was deeply involved. The king concluded that he had no need to avenge the aggression, since Philip III's ministers rather than the Spanish king himself had intrigued with Biron. In explaining his response to the Rochepot affair to Pope Clement VIII, Henry IV summarized his approach to foreign policy: "As great and powerful princes are rightfully very jealous of their dignity, so too must they be very circumspect and respectful of each other . . . and avoid encounters and accidents that a precipitous and unamended offense draws down on one."[18] Henry was careful not to offend Philip III's honor and equally careful when defending his honor not to draw France into war. If the ministers' advice had been heeded, peace would have prevailed, but not the peace with pride that Henry IV insisted on.

Although no evidence survives to prove that Villeroy and Bellièvre ever persuaded Henry IV to reverse his position on a foreign policy issue, they are known to have helped him twice to decide between alternatives. On both occasions Henry's indecision sprang from his recognition of the virtues of his options. On the first occasion, Henry was persuaded to make a separate peace with Spain rather than to honor treaty obligations with England; on the second he was persuaded to acquiesce in, rather than oppose, the Dutch rebels' truce with Spain.

SPAIN

Villeroy and Bellièvre regarded Spain as the national enemy of France. Although the two powers were openly at war only from 1595 to 1598, their relations were always inimical. During the league episode (1585–95) Spain attempted to secure the crown of France for the Hapsburgs, and after 1598 France fought Spain indirectly by supporting the Dutch revolt.[19] Villeroy and Bellièvre hated and feared the "cursed race of Spaniards" throughout their careers in degrees that varied according to events.[20]

While France was torn by civil war during the first ten years of Henry III's reign, Villeroy and Bellièvre strove by exercising caution to avoid a confrontation with Spain, in spite of Philip II's hostility. They were thwarted, however, by the ambitious duke of Anjou, who from 1576 until his death in 1584 caused France and Henry III, whose brother and heir he was, constant trouble. Anjou's dreams of a throne to match that of his hated brother drove him to seek to exploit the Dutch revolt for his own ambitions, and in seeking election as the rebels' ruler, he implicated his brother, his mother, and France, and caused Spanish antipathy to increase at a time when religious wars in France threatened to overwhelm the monarchy.

Although both ministers initially opposed Anjou's quest for a throne in the Low Countries, they were soon forced to choose between unleashing him there or watching him foment unrest at home. Bellièvre preferred the first course, while Villeroy feared Spanish retaliation if Anjou intervened in the Low Countries. He believed that it would be foolhardy to invite the animosity of Philip II, whose conquest of Portugal could make him as powerful as Charlemagne. Catherine de Medici also supported her younger son, but Villeroy told Henry III that the thought of permitting anyone to arm and become powerful in the kingdom made him "tremble and fear all." Vacillating between approval and repudiation, the king permitted his brother to proceed with his plans.[21]

Both ministers were relieved when, after the failure of a coup against his Dutch subjects in January 1583, Anjou was finally reduced to impotence, but they were outraged by the humiliation of France by Spain that ensued. In 1582 the fleet was defeated that was sent to attack the Azores in order to force Philip II to consent to a marriage between Anjou and the infanta, with the Low Countries as a dowry. Villeroy, who had opposed the venture and warned of Spanish revenge, cursed "the unbearable barbarity" of the victors, who had executed the French sailors as pirates, but warned his master that France was impotent to seek revenge. When Anjou died in June 1584, all that France could show for his six-year adventure was the city of Cambrai and Philip II's increased enmity. Villeroy aptly described Anjou's undertakings as "badly begun and still worse pursued."[22]

Henry III soon paid the price of his ineffectual bellicosity. Philip II, to forestall French aid to England against his armada, subsidized the Catholic League's efforts to force Henry into war with his Huguenot subjects. The king, even in his outrage after the Day of the Barricades, was, as the Spanish ambassador Mendoza crowed, forced "to hand over his authority to [Guise]." Henry protested to Philip II but was too weak to demand Mendoza's recall.[23]

The ministers made no attempt to conceal their resentment of Spain, which was evident to Mendoza, who considered Bellièvre "a friend of Béarn and the Huguenots." If Philip II's wanting "to fish in troubled waters, as Villeroy put it, was outrageous, it was also frightening, and when rumors that Spain was sending an army of invasion across the southern frontier reached court in 1584, Villeroy urgently recommended reinforcing the royal garrisons. Unless he converted to secure the succession, Bellièvre warned Henry of Navarre, "I have no doubt that the king of Spain, by his accustomed subtleties . . . will one day be able to swallow up this kingdom as he has that of Portugal."[24]

The death of Henry III on 2 August 1589 and the succession of the Protestant Henry IV gave Philip II the pretext he wanted for intervening openly in the French civil wars. Posing as the champion of Catholic orthodoxy against heretics and lukewarm *politiques,* Philip financed the Catholic League's efforts to depose Henry IV and twice sent the duke of Parma and his Spanish veterans to the league's assistance. As a reward, Philip asked the States-General of 1593 to elect the Spanish infanta queen of France. These events engendered in Villeroy and Bellièvre a hatred and fear of Spain that they never forgot.

Villeroy, as the chief league diplomat seeking to reconcile French Catholics by Henry IV's conversion, led the fight to prevent Spanish domination of the league. He warned from the start, "The more we put them [negotiations between Catholics] off, the worse it will be." When Philip offered military assistance, Villeroy declared, "If all Catholics were united we would have no need of foreign forces. Being divided, we will sooner or later become the prey of our adversaries." Again and again Villeroy warned Mayenne that to flirt with Spain was to invite Spanish domination, and a letter by him addressed to the duke circulated in late 1589, urging leaguers to seek the conversion of Henry IV rather than the election of another Catholic prince, especially a Spaniard. The latter would assure the extinction of French independence, while Henry's conversion would "deliver the kingdom from war with less peril for the Catholic religion." When conflict between league moderates and extremists flared up in 1591, Villeroy bewailed the extremists' appeals for Spanish aid. This aid, in the form of Parma's army, lifted Henry IV's siege of Rouen in 1592 and by revealing the French monarch's inability to reconquer his kingdom by force, so alarmed Villeroy that he warned Henry's followers that the shaping of France's future was slipping from the hands of Frenchmen. Early in 1593, when the league States-General was debating the election of Philip's daughter as queen of France, Villeroy warned the delegates that such a step would be disastrous, that French unity would not be preserved but shattered, for Spain could disrupt but not rule France. If the infanta were elected, Spain would partition France, leaving the country in ruins. Villeroy realized that Spanish efforts allegedly in behalf of French Catholicism were at heart hypocritical attempts to expand Spanish territory. This was what most outraged Villeroy, who had been trying for so long to be both "a good Christian and a good Frenchman."[25]

In retirement from 1588 to 1593, Bellièvre shared his friend's fear and loathing of Spain. He also believed that Philip's offers of aid to French Catholics had "no other intention to help the French than to hasten their ruin" by partitioning their native land. As he warned a supporter of Henry IV, "We know the power [Philip] has and cannot doubt his desire." Bellièvre reminded both leaguers and royalists that prolonging the civil war would profit only foreigners who hoped to dismember France. By 1592 Bellièvre, who had remained silent in public to protect himself from league depredation, issued two bold warnings against the impending league States-General, for he shared Villeroy's deep fear of the consequences should the Spanish infanta be elected to replace Henry IV. The first warning, in a long letter to Pierre Jeannin, spelled out the threat of such an election to national existence and advised good Catholics to reject Philip II's hypocritical offers of aid and throw their support to the legitimate king, Henry IV. "[It is] more than time that we put an end to our follies," Bellièvre said, pointing out that "he who calls the stronger to his aid makes himself the serf of the stronger." The second warning, in the form of a draft of an address to the league States-General, reiterated in detail the dangers of setting aside the succession.[26]

Franco-Spanish hostilities, which had not been formalized by a declaration of war while Philip II angled for the French throne, became open in January 1595. After converting to the national faith, Henry IV first consolidated his position by welcoming back the leaguers, then declared war on Spain to exploit the resurgence of patriotism produced by his conversion and the Spanish threat. The war of national liberation also served to discredit unregenerate leaguers. Although Henry won several battles against Spain's seasoned troops and able commanders, he was unable to protect France's northern and southeastern frontiers from repeated Spanish incursions. However, the French victory at Fontaine-Française in June 1595 made it impossible for the constable of Castile to save Mayenne from capitulation, and after long sieges, the king had retaken Ardres and Laon in Picardy in the summer of 1594. Rouen also fell before Henry's stubborn siege from December 1595 to May 1596, but the Spanish matched his success by capturing Doulens and Cambrai. Royalist forces slowly repressed Spanish-aided league rebels in Languedoc, Dauphiné, and Provence, but by mid-1596 Henry had exhausted his fiscal resources and had to cease offensive operations. The Spanish seizure of Amiens in March 1597 drew him once more into the open field, this time to defend his honor by retaking the Picard citadel. Only when he had personally overseen the recapture of Amiens (March–September 1597) did Henry agree to listen to peace overtures that papal mediation drew from Philip II.[27] Six months later, after long but generally easy negotiations, the Peace of Vervins on 2 May 1598 ended hostilities on the basis of the situation before the war.[28]

Predictably, the ministers' response to open war with Spain was ambivalent. On the one hand, they were eager for revenge for past wrongs and continued aggressions. Both Villeroy and Bellièvre were outraged at Philip II's urging the pope to refuse Henry IV absolution for his apostasy, for the pope's hesitancy gave league rebels a last tenuous justification for their revolt. So bitter was the ministers' loathing of the Spanish that both men automatically blamed them for Jean Chastel's attempt on the king's life in December 1594. The ministers, on the other hand, were reluctant to fight Spain at a time when their own native land was exhausted from long civil wars. While approving of Henry's declaration of war, Villeroy declared, "France is tired of war. She enjoys her religion, she curses every day those who prevent peace." Bellièvre, even though he knew that the residual league revolt was "fomented by the money and artifices of Spain," did not enjoy his task of extracting funds for subduing it from an already prostrate populace. But until Spain gave signs of wanting peace, France had to fight "the king of Spain's insatiable ambition" so as not to become "subjects of Spanish arrogance." By mid-1597, when peace overtures were in the air, Villeroy and Bellièvre were both in the vanguard of those who pressed Henry IV to accept them. Bellièvre was so relieved by the signing of the Peace of Vervins that he could hardly believe that it was true.[29]

Franco-Spanish relations from 1598 until the outbreak of the

Juliers-Cleves crisis in 1609 resembled a cold war. Both powers avoided open conflict but aided the other's foes. Philip III lent support to internal revolts (the Biron and Auvergne conspiracies), and Henry IV subsidized the Dutch revolt. When hostilities seemed imminent over Spain's mistreatment of the French ambassador in 1601 and imposition of a tariff against French goods in 1603–4, both parties drew back. Competition for allies in northern Italy, although it exacerbated relations, did not bring open war. Only on the eve of Henry IV's death did the crisis over Juliers-Cleves bring France to the verge of war with the Hapsburgs.

Villeroy's and Bellièvre's views on Spain during this twelve-year-long armed truce underwent significant changes, from obsessive fear of Spanish might to contempt for it. Although they still shrank from open hostilities, they became eager to erode Spain's power by aiding her enemies.

The fact that Philip II had overextended Spain's resources gradually became apparent to the ministers. When Philip, "finding himself aged and sick," made peace overtures in 1597, Bellièvre realized that the move was partly motivated by Spain's exhaustion. Villeroy, too, slowly realized that Spanish power was being eroded by overambitious designs. The secretary remarked that while Philip II had been prudent, his son Philip III had misjudged Spain's strength and displayed "great imprudence." As much as Villeroy shrank from open conflict, he was confident that if it broke out, Spain would suffer more from it than France. By 1609, when Philip III was about to abandon his long effort to suppress the Dutch revolt, Villeroy clearly saw that "Spain needs repose as much and even more than [the Dutch] and that the Duke of Lerma and those who govern desire it with a passion." Villeroy's view of Spain was vastly different from what it had been a generation before, when he had feared that Philip II would become more powerful than Charlemagne, but the cautious secretary's memories of Spanish might did not permit him to go as far as Sully, who claimed that "the Spanish . . . are bad only to those who show fear."[30]

Villeroy, who directed France's foreign policy under royal tutelage, always sought to avoid open war with Spain, whose aggression he would meet with vehement protest while counseling moderation to Henry IV. In 1601 Villeroy was alarmed by the Rochepot incident, in which some members of the suite of the French ambassador to Spain, Rochepot, were arrested for killing a Spanish gentleman in a street altercation. Villeroy feared that Henry IV would "never endure the injustice done him" and was uncertain "whether the king of Spain is wise enough to repair it." Henry, however, refrained from more forceful retaliation than imposing a trade embargo until Rochepot's companions were released and recalling his ambassador. A year later, when Villeroy learned of Spanish participation in the duke of Biron's plot to assassinate the king and partition France, he cursed Spanish treachery but counseled against war. Henry IV was eager to discover whether Philip III had had direct knowledge of the plot but unwilling to declare war.[31]

A Franco-Spanish tariff war in 1603/4 was also cause for alarm, for it led Henry IV to impose a total embargo on trade with Spain. Villeroy feared war might ensue and would have preferred that France "scorn rather than imitate or avenge" Philip's actions, even when at the peak of the crisis in May 1604 it was discovered that Villeroy's cipher clerk had sold his codes to Spain. The secretary might have urged drastic reprisals in order to cleanse his name of any taint of connection with the treason, but although the Venetian ambassador reported that Villeroy recommended war, in fact the minister continued to counsel moderation. Like Bellièvre, he did not wish to make public the Spanish ambassador's complicity in the treason, lest the people think France "already at war with the king of Spain." However, the embargo from which French merchants were suffering was also cutting off supplies for the Spanish campaign in Flanders. To Bellièvre's intense relief, Henry IV, more concerned to protect his honor from Spanish affronts than to go to war, eventually agreed to a settlement (October 1604) in which both sides cancelled all tariffs.[32]

The last crisis with Spain, the Juliers-Cleves affair, almost led to a general European war pitting France against the house of Hapsburg. In a disputed succession in the rich duchies of Juliers-Cleves, France backed the Protestant candidates, while the emperor was equally committed to assuring a Catholic succession. Henry IV clearly warned the Hapsburgs that he would fight to assure a Protestant succession. Villeroy also saw the importance of the strategically placed duchies remaining in Protestant hands but sought desperately to avert open war. When his warning that the German Protestant allies with whom Henry planned to take the field were totally unreliable was ignored, Villeroy tried to limit the scope of the conflict by persuading the Spanish archduke to remain neutral. When this maneuver failed Villeroy wearily admitted that war was inevitable,[33] but in spite of his animosity toward and diminished fears of Spain, Villeroy would have preferred to keep the peace. His wish was soon granted, for after the assassination of Henry IV the regent, Marie de Medici, was unwilling to pursue the war during her son's minority and quickly made peace with the Hapsburgs.

Mounting contempt for Spain, shared by both ministers, was not caused by their recognition of Spain's decline—although they feared her less, they still respected her might—but by Spain's constant attempt to veil her secular designs behind protestations of concern for Catholicism. After Spain had posed as the defender of French Catholicism while seeking to usurp the French throne during the league episode, the ministers regarded all Spanish assertions of concern for Catholicism as rank hypocrisy. Villeroy, for example, rejected Philip III's claim that piety had prompted him to aid Irish Catholic rebels against Elizabeth I. And Villeroy, alive to the Spanish secular designs aimed at European hegemony, had nothing but contempt for the Spaniards' claim that they were Europe's best Catholics. The Spaniards' actions, he remarked when he learned of Philip III's efforts to make peace with the Protestant James I, were "real evidence of the continuation of the zeal they have always had and still have for the advancement of God's glory, which they have so usurped and absorbed into their covetousness that they want God to depend on them, and that all those who have other views are held to be schismatics and heretics." Henry IV seems to have shared Villeroy's views, for during the Juliers crisis the king charged, "The Spanish, under this usual cloak of religion, with which they so willingly cover themselves, strive to usurp and invade the inheritance of others." Bellièvre and Villeroy were convinced that the charge of Spanish religious hypocrisy was true because they believed that France, not Spain, was the true defender of Catholicism and that in aiding the league Spain had threatened "to ruin the Catholic religion by ruining the crown of France, the principal support of the Apostolic Holy See." (Richelieu's pamphleteers were to claim that God operated through the French monarchy; Villeroy and Bellièvre were doubtless expressing a widespread conviction that only received theoretical formulation a generation later.) The ministers' belief that Spanish Catholics were hypocrites also provided a perfect rationalization for Catholic France's collaboration with Protestant powers against Spain. Neither minister, even though both were good Catholics, expressed any doubt about the use of heretic arms to defend the French monarchy, the protector of true Catholicism, against "this nation [Spain] lacking all virtue."[34]

The equanimity with which Villeroy and Bellièvre were able to view the two great Catholic powers of Europe at each other's throats, one aided by Protestant heretics, is testimony to the complete fragmentation of Catholic unity. The ministers' rationale for condoning the spectacle must have been shared by many of their contemporaries. When open conflict broke out a generation later at the court of Louis XIII between *dévots*, who sought Catholic unity by friendship with Spain, and *bons Français*, who, with Protestant assistance, sought to weaken Spain, Villeroy's and Bellièvre's outlook triumphed in the policies of the *bon Français* Cardinal Richelieu.[35]

ENGLAND

In dealing with England, Villeroy and Bellièvre were torn by real conflicts. On the one hand, they heartily disliked the islanders for a variety of reasons; on the other, they realized that the English were France's natural ally against Spain. It is to the ministers' credit that they were able to overcome their antipathy and strive for co-operation based on France's national interest.

Anglo-French relations during the reign of Henry III unfolded in two stages. Until 1584 Henry and Elizabeth I flirted with projects for an anti-Spanish alliance that was to be sealed by the queen's marriage to Henry's brother and heir, the duke of Anjou. Agreement was precluded, however, by Anjou's designs on the Low Countries, for Elizabeth feared French encroachment there. After Anjou's death in 1584 and the emergence of the Catholic League, Elizabeth began to subsidize Navarre and his Protestants, her aim being to keep France disrupted by civil war and unable to aid Philip II's impending crusade against England. In this she succeeded, but at the price of alienating the French monarchy.[36]

The ministers were desperately anxious for Anglo-French cooperation against Spain and were embittered by Elizabeth's rebuff. Villeroy deemed a marriage alliance "of marvelous importance to this crown," for it would remove the factious Anjou from France and secure English support in thwarting Spanish ambitions. When Anjou tried to seize control of Flanders by a *coup d'état* in January 1583, Villeroy, while apprehensive of Elizabeth's reaction, still hoped that "our friendship is no less necessary to the English than theirs is to us." When Elizabeth, by aiding the Huguenots, proved that it was not, Villeroy fulminated against her for "tormenting all her neighbors in order better to insure her kingdom's repose." Bellièvre, who was sent to England in the winter of 1586/87 to request clemency for Mary Stuart and an end to Elizabeth's aid to Navarre, came away convinced that the English "fear nothing more than to see an end to our civil wars."[37] The ministers' animosity against the English was only slightly reduced in the next decade, during which Elizabeth helped Henry IV to recover his throne from the leaguers and the Spanish.

English aid to Henry IV, though sporadic, was vital to his success in pacifying France. Between 1589 and 1595, Elizabeth dispatched £200,000 to Henry IV and lost twenty thousand men in his behalf. She then suspended aid until she feared that the French, financially exhausted, might have to abandon the war with Spain. The Treaty of Greenwich in May 1596 promised an English subsidy and two thousand men in return for Henry IV's promise not to make a separate peace with Spain.[38] Two years later, Henry, convinced that Elizabeth wished only to keep her two rivals at war forever, signed the Peace of Vervins.

Neither Villeroy nor Bellièvre ever expressed gratitude for English aid, and they criticized Elizabeth for suspending aid when France needed it most. Villeroy excoriated the English as "neighbors who rest unmoving in the shadow of the fire that consumes us," and Bellièvre was convinced that they wanted to see the French "at open war with the Spaniard in order to rid themselves of him." Villeroy, who put no stock in Elizabeth's promises, opposed the Treaty of Greenwich on the ground that Elizabeth would not deliver the promised aid. Bellièvre feared that the garrisoning of channel ports by English troops might lead to the loss of Calais but deemed fiscal aid too vital to reject. As he warned Henry IV, "One must hold the future in high regard, but one can hope for nothing if the present is lost." Acutely aware, as was Bellièvre, that Elizabeth was exploiting France's misfortunes, Villeroy complained, "What obligation will I have to one who saved me the first day if he abandons me the next, if he helps me only to prolong my illness, not to cure it?"[39]

The ministers' revenge finally came when France began peace negotiations with Spain. Bellièvre, from Vervins, and Villeroy, at Henry's side, kept up a steady stream of arguments for a separate peace. Their repeated charges of hypocrisy against Elizabeth succeeded in overcoming Henry IV's scruples against breaking his word of honor by making a separate peace. When Elizabeth did not avail herself of Henry's offer to secure her a place at the peace table, Villeroy was pleased at this evidence of continued Anglo-Spanish hostility. Bellièvre said the English could not "impute the fault but to themselves," and was amused at the English ambassador's asking him his opinion of the possibilities for an Anglo-Spanish peace, as if Bellièvre were "one of the queen of England's minions."[40]

Between 1598 and the end of Henry IV's reign, he and his ministers sought to use England against Spain. Elizabeth continued her naval war against Philip III until her death, but her successor James I quickly made peace in July 1604. His withdrawal was resented by the ministers, who had hoped to play off England and Spain much as Elizabeth had France and Spain.

Villeroy and Bellièvre both disliked James, the former for his "laziness and nonchalance, and the time he spends on his pleasures," the latter for his "habit of dissimulation." Villeroy was enthusiastic about the duke of Sully's mission in quest of a defensive alliance (May–July 1603), and was pleased when James agreeably, but falsely, promised Sully informal co-operation. Bellièvre, however, so distrusted James that he wrote a memoir opposing any formal alliance, lest James draw Henry IV into war with Spain and then desert him, leaving France to defend her Pyrenean and Flemish frontiers while England remained secure behind her naval barrier. However, James himself had less malevolent designs than Bellièvre imputed. The English king sought only to live at peace with both France and Spain, and refused either to give aid to the Dutch rebels, which Villeroy considered "a signal service to the Spanish," or to ally with France, which the secretary desired "if not in effect, at least in appearance." Particularly after 1607, when the Dutch opened truce negotiations with Spain, Villeroy expected more English co-operation, but when the English remained indifferent to Henry IV's overtures, Villeroy, who trusted them no more than he trusted the Spanish, labeled them "deceivers, the true enemies of France," and accused them of wanting to force the Dutch "to throw themselves completely into their hands." His distrust was confirmed on the eve of a general war in 1610, when James spurned an Anglo-French alliance that Villeroy desperately hoped would force the Hapsburgs to abandon Juliers-Cleves, "the morsel for which they are famished," and the Hapsburgs refused to yield.[41]

Not only was England a traditional enemy, the ravager of France during the Hundred Years War,[42] but English piracy of French shipping continued after 1598, doing, Villeroy charged, "more damage than if we were at open war."[43] Villeroy hated England most of all, however, for her refusal to join France against the Hapsburgs. And this is why, in spite of England's indirect aid to France, he called the English "the true enemies of France."

The fact that England was the arch-Protestant power of Europe did not apparently influence the judgment of the ministers, for they never mentioned heresy as a source of antipathy. Indeed, when English Catholics asked Henry IV for aid in blocking James's accession, Villeroy heatedly rejected their appeal: even if James was an ardent Protestant, Villeroy argued, he was England's legitimate king; English Catholics deserved "compassion" but not support in committing *lèse majesté*.[44] The ministers, convinced that France was the bastion of true Catholicism and reconciled to the permanent triumph of heresy in England, had no qualms about using heretics to diminish the power of hypocritically religious Spain.

THE DUTCH REPUBLIC

The Dutch republic became France's most reliable ally when the two states were thrown together by their shared resistance to Spanish might. In the first of three stages of Franco-Dutch collaboration, Henry III indirectly aided the rebels by sporadically sustaining the duke of Anjou's ambitions for a throne in the Low Countries. Henry's assistance, however, was insufficient to assure his brother's success but enough to offend Philip II, and after Anjou's death in 1584 and the rise of the Catholic League, Henry was forced to stop his aid and in 1585 even to refuse the rebels' offer to elect him their ruler. In the second stage the allies' roles were reversed when Maurice of Nassau's military genius and the diversion of the duke of Parma's Spanish veterans to France to aid the league put the Dutch in a position to help Henry IV, who needed their subsidies to regain his realm. From 1598 to 1609, when France and Spain were at peace, Henry IV returned the favor by dispatching twelve million livres in subsidies to the Dutch. By slowly eroding Spanish wealth and power, the Dutch war for independence was a godsend to France. It was, Villeroy said, a "thorn in [Spain's] foot that God has implanted; at present the Spanish are diverted, occupied and checkmated by the war in the Low Countries."[45]

Villeroy and Bellièvre both saw the wisdom of aiding the Dutch revolt, which they urged their masters to support whenever conditions permitted; but on Anjou's designs the ministers' views differed. Although he sympathized with the rebels' cause,

Villeroy shrank from aiding Anjou for fear of offending Spain, while Bellièvre was more willing to risk Spain's ire in the light of the duke's capacity for promoting unrest at home. But by 1584, when it seemed that Parma's armies might subdue the Dutch rebels and when Philip II began to scheme with the Catholic League, both ministers agreed that aid to the Dutch was vital. Otherwise, as Villeroy put it, Spanish advances "will one day cost us more dearly than we realize today." In retaliation for Spanish aid to league rebels in Languedoc, Villeroy favored acceptance of Dutch sovereignty, which was offered to Henry III in 1584, after William of Orange's death. When the outbreak of the league revolt in February 1585 prevented acceptance, Bellièvre was more disappointed to miss a chance to avenge Spanish arrogance than to lose a heaven-sent opportunity to expand French territory.[46]

In 1598, France was at last free to help the Dutch, to whom Villeroy and Bellièvre warmly urged that an annual subsidy be granted—as inconspicuously as possible to avoid offending the pope. However, both men were against permitting the Dutch to raise troops in France, a measure Henry IV sanctioned as a means of ridding the country of unruly soldiers. The Dutch republic's resident in France, Aarssens, considered both ministers friends of the Dutch rebels' cause, but when it came to open intervention, Villeroy and Bellièvre drew back. Aarssens began appealing for the dispatch of French troops during the Biron conspiracy in 1602, and kept up his campaign until the opening of Hispano-Dutch truce talks in 1607. His appeals, which found a sympathetic audience in the duke of Sully, were stolidly opposed by Villeroy, who urged increasing the annual subsidy but adamantly opposed France's entering the conflict as a belligerent.[47] Henry IV shared Villeroy's views and chose to make the Dutch war of independence France's covert war against Spain.

Weary of their long struggle, the Dutch and Spanish agreed in 1607 to an armistice, apparently shattering France's hopes of permanently disabling Spain with revolt in her rich provinces. Henry IV labeled the Dutch "ingrates," and Villeroy flayed them for having "taken our money in their right hand, and at the same time concluded the bargain [the armistice] and signed it with their left." Henry IV at first tried to bribe and threaten the Dutch to go on fighting but was persuaded by Villeroy to resume his subsidy when promised a defensive alliance. The secretary saw that the rebels would still be France's natural ally even if they made a truce with Spain; to try to thwart the deep-rooted desire of the Dutch for peace would only alienate France's best friends.[48] Because Villeroy was willing to make the best of a disappointing development and able to persuade Henry IV to do likewise, the French obtained a defensive alliance in January 1608, and the Dutch secured a favorable twelve-year truce in March 1609.

The ministers' good will toward the Dutch rebels was inspired primarily by the fact that the Netherlanders were fighting France's battles against Spain. But beyond mere state interest, Villeroy and Bellièvre seem to have felt real affection for the Dutch. Villeroy, who admired their heroic resistance to Spanish tyranny, sympathized with their desire for peace in spite of his annoyance at the 1607 armistice.[49] While he bitterly resented England's refusal to serve France's interests, Villeroy was tolerant of the Dutch rebels' insistence on regarding their own security as paramount. Like the English, neither Bellièvre nor Villeroy ever hesitated to use the patriotism and courage of the Dutch to undermine Catholic Spain. The enormous benefit that France derived from the Dutch revolt must have allayed any qualms that the ministers may have had about championing a rebellion by heretics against their legitimate sovereign.

THE GERMAN PROTESTANT PRINCIPALITIES

During the ministers' tenure French relations with the Protestant princes of Germany were never happy.[50] German Protestant troops twice invaded France in Henry III's reign: in 1576 on behalf of the duke of Anjou and his Huguenot allies, and in 1587 to assist Henry of Navarre. After 1589 the German princes sent Henry IV funds but stopped when he converted. For the rest of his reign Henry IV tried to persuade the princes to ally with him against the Hapsburg emperor, but fear of French ambition and resentment over Henry's delay in repaying their loans caused them to procrastinate. Only in 1610, on the eve of the Franco-Hapsburg war over Juliers-Cleves, did German Protestant fear of Hapsburg power drive them to sign the Treaty of Halle.

The two ministers' views of the Germans changed drastically over the years from fear to contempt. When a German mercenary force invaded France in 1576, Villeroy panicked at the thought of the devastation that the "barbarians" would wreak. Bellièvre, who negotiated their departure for an enormous bribe, was both frightened and angry, especially when he was held as a hostage for payment. Since full payment was never made, both ministers had good reason to fear the Germans' return, and in 1586, when Navarre's agents began to recruit German mercenaries against the league, their fears reached a peak. Bellièvre warned Navarre that this practice would cause him to be detested by the French, while Villeroy, who respected the Germans' fighting prowess, warned that they "do not fight with words." However, internal division and harassment by the duke of Guise's army precipitated the defeat and dissolution of the invading force in 1587, and Villeroy, rejoicing at the mercenary force's being "dissolved and in ruins," could henceforth safely view the German Protestants with contempt rather than fear.[51]

The more than five million livres in aid given Henry IV by such German princes as the landgrave of Hesse and the duke of Württemberg failed to earn the ministers' gratitude[52] any more than did English aid. But when funds from the Germans ceased, Villeroy railed at the ingratitude of the princes who had so quickly forgotten Henry II's assistance in their struggle with Charles V.[53]

After the Peace of Vervins, Villeroy directed Henry IV's attempts to persuade the Protestant princes to join France in a union against the Hapsburgs. France's intended allies were aggrieved when, on appealing for repayment of their loans to Henry IV, Henry concurred in Villeroy's suggestion that French funds were better spent to sustain the Dutch than to pay off German loans. Villeroy, on his side, resented the princes' plea for clemency for the duke of Bouillon, who had taken part in the Biron conspiracy. Since Bouillon was a Protestant and a prince of the

Holy Roman Empire (he ruled Sedan as an imperial fief) Henry IV had to defer bringing him to justice in order not to offend France's potential German allies. Even when war with the Hapsburgs over Juliers-Cleves was almost certain and German Protestant aid finally assured by the Treaty of Halle, Villeroy feared that the Germans would abandon France "in midstream" as they had done in 1595, even though he believed their military forces to be of "low quality."[54] Although Villeroy faithfully sought to secure the princes' support for Henry IV's projects, he considered German Protestants barbaric, timid, and of little use to France.

SAVOY, TUSCANY, AND THE VENETIAN REPUBLIC

Although Henry IV tried to form an alliance against Spain with the independent states of Italy, neither he nor Henry III reasserted the claims of their predecessors to sovereignty over Milan and Naples.[55] France's relations with the duchy of Savoy, the grand duchy of Tuscany, and the Venetian republic were confused and shifting during the ministers' long term of office, but a certain order can be discerned.

Franco-Savoyard relations were almost always inimical. The duke of Savoy, Charles Emmanuel I (1580–1630), was bold, ambitious, and determined to avoid becoming the pawn of either Spain or France.[56] But since Charles wished to increase his domains at the expense of France or her allies, he was a tacit partner of Spain for most of the two ministers' tenure. In the early 1580s and in 1602/3 when he sought to conquer Geneva, Savoy's former dependency and France's ally, he clashed with Henry III and Henry IV. His taking advantage of the French civil wars to usurp the marquisate of Saluzzo in 1588 and his refusal to return it until defeated in war by Henry IV in 1600 poisoned relations between Savoy and France. Embittered by his humiliating defeat, Charles supported Biron's conspiracy and turned more openly to Spain. Denied the dynastic marriage he wanted, he then allied with France in 1610 in the hope of profiting from the impending war with the Hapsburgs.

Although Villeroy and Bellièvre never considered Savoy a major threat to France, they regarded Charles Emmanuel as an obnoxious inconvenience, whose ambition and ill will complicated France's problems. His designs on Geneva in 1582, which could have blocked the passage of Swiss mercenaries to France, alarmed both ministers, for if Savoy controlled the Alpine passes, as Bellièvre explained, France would be able to recruit the Swiss "but at the mercy of the Spanish." Villeroy was enraged by Charles's seizure of France's last transalpine possession, the marquisate of Saluzzo, in 1588, and sporadic forays by Savoyard armies into Provence and Dauphiné during the early 1590s further aroused the ministers' animosity. Although a truce negotiated in 1595 was regularly extended, Henry IV was unable by coercion or bribery to effect the return of Saluzzo. The issue was debated at the peace conference at Vervins, but the Spanish supported Savoy's claims, and rather than delay a general settlement, Henry IV agreed to submit the dispute to papal arbitration.[57]

In 1600, however, Henry IV declared war on Savoy. Not only had the pope declined to serve as arbitrator for fear of offending Spain, but Charles had failed either to restore Saluzzo within three months or to grant compensation as he was bound to do by the terms of the Treaty of Paris (February 1600). Although he knew France's cause was just and resented the duke's "making fun of us," Villeroy was uneasy over the possibility of Spanish intervention; Bellièvre, however, was eager to see Charles's "wings clipped." Both men were pleased when Henry's forces crushed the Savoyards but were less happy with the provisions of the Treaty of Lyons (January 1601). In it Henry agreed to abandon his claim to Saluzzo in exchange for Bresse and some Alpine valleys. Bellièvre would have preferred the return of Saluzzo but conceded that the addition of Bresse would strengthen France's eastern frontier, allow her to control Spain's troop movements from Milan to Franche-Comté, and tighten her contacts with the Swiss. Villeroy acknowledged the merit of his colleague's argument but saw that by abandoning Saluzzo Henry had reduced the likelihood of successful French intervention in Italy. Not only would France have no transalpine staging point for military operations, but Italian confidence in France would be undermined.[58]

Even as the peace treaty of Lyons awaited ratification, Villeroy warned his master, Charles would "always be on the lookout to harm you." The duke's role as one of the "principal authors" of Biron's plot and his profuse denial of his implication after the plot was uncovered confirmed Villeroy's opinion that "the more craftily and softly he speaks, the more we must distrust him." After seven years of peace, when Charles Emmanuel turned to France for a dynastic marriage, Villeroy still suspected the duke's motives. But because Charles's friendship would serve France in Italy when war broke out with the Hapsburgs, Villeroy helped secure the Treaty of Brusol in April 1610.[59]

Among the other independent states of North Italy only two, the grand duchy of Tuscany and especially the Venetian republic, were considered important. Henry III and, until peace in 1598, Henry IV, were too busy with other concerns to pay much attention to the peninsula. When Henry IV finally sought Italian allies, his efforts were unavailing, for they feared Spanish power, from which he was unwilling to give them firm guarantees of protection.[60]

During the years when France was too torn by civil wars to exert any influence in Italy, Bellièvre and Villeroy wished to keep the cautious friendship of states like Venice. Bellièvre hoped someday to restore French influence, a prospect that Villeroy considered threatened by Savoy's intrigues to seize Saluzzo. When the Venetians were the first Catholic power to recognize Henry IV's legitimacy and to lend him funds, Bellièvre grew more optimistic of one day exerting a French presence in Italy. In 1594 he urged Henry IV to reinforce the southeastern frontier garrisons and to keep control of France's last Alpine passes, for, Bellièvre warned, "[Savoy's] putting us completely out of Italy could greatly cool the affection that the rulers of Venice, the grand duke of Tuscany, and other Italian potentates show us."[61]

When peace was restored, Henry IV made an effort to attract Venice and Tuscany into an alliance against Spain. The abandonment of Saluzzo, however, was an inauspicious start, for as Villeroy had foreseen, the grand duke no longer felt he could depend on French assistance against his powerful neighbor in Milan. Villeroy's disappointment at France's failure to create a defensive league with Venice and Tuscany led to his condemnation of "the cowardice of those . . . like the princes and potentates of Italy, who will never recognize the servitude into which they let themselves be led until it is irremediable." The last chance, however slim, of gaining an alliance with Venice slipped away between 1605 and 1607, when the Spanish built a fort in the Valtellina pass to protect their troop movements between the Hapsburg Tyrol and Lombardy. The Venetians—who regarded Spain's presence on territory of their ally, the Swiss Gray League, as a potent threat but did not dare to act alone—appealed for French help. However, although Henry IV had just made a defensive alliance with the Gray League, he was unwilling either to extend military assistance or, as Villeroy and Bellièvre urged, to finance construction of a counterfort in the pass. In the end no action was taken against Spain's belligerent moves, for which Villeroy blamed the Venetians as well as the "lethargy" of his countrymen, sadly admitting that France's quest for Italian partners had failed.[62] Not until Richelieu's day did Villeroy's dream of combatting Spain through Italian allies become a reality.

THE PAPACY

Relations between France and Rome during the reigns of Henry III and Henry IV ranged from lukewarm amity to frigid alienation.[63] Until 1585, relations were fairly cordial, but then the Catholic League emerged and Sixtus V excommunicated Henry of Navarre, compounding Henry III's problems. When Navarre became king, the papacy led the effort to depose him and even after Henry IV's conversion waited for two years before absolving him of his former apostasy. This hurdle cleared, relations improved rapidly. Although they were prevented by Spanish domination of Italy from pursuing an openly pro-French policy, Clement VIII and Paul V sought whenever possible to bestow favors on France to gain her support as a counterweight against Spain.

Villeroy and Bellièvre viewed the papacy as a power whose friendship could serve the political purposes of the French monarchy. The best of all possible worlds, Villeroy said, would see "the king of France in a position to create the popes."[64] But if this was out of the question, he and Bellièvre at least expected the pope's spiritual assistance against France's enemies, and when it was not forthcoming the ministers grew impatient, even angry.

Sixtus's excommunication of Henry of Navarre made more difficult the task of persuading the heir to convert to save the throne. And when Sixtus made no secret of his sympathy for the league, Bellièvre, who hoped that the pope would welcome Navarre back into the church, predicted, "If the pope is not wiser, he will lose us and we him." The minister's prediction nearly came true, for by 1591 the pope was sending men and money to the league, and Bellièvre was blaming him for Henry III's murder of Guise, on the ground that the pope's failure to support Henry had driven the king to that desperate act. So profound was Bellièvre's estrangement from Sixtus's successors for aiding the French monarchy's foes that the minister went so far as to assert that Frenchmen owed a higher loyalty to their king than to the pope. As for Clement VIII's procrastination in lifting the ban of excommunication after Henry IV's conversion, Bellièvre declared that it threatened to create "the most dangerous schism Christianity has ever had," a French church cut off from Rome. "Most Catholics," he claimed, accepted the sincerity of Henry's conversion, and the two ministers agreed that papal delay in lifting the ban only prolonged league resistance. But in 1594 Clement refused to receive the king's emissaries requesting absolution: "The pope alone," Bellièvre commented, "could bring a remedy to this harm [schism] with which Christianity is threatened, but it seems that his ears are completely deaf to our complaints, and his eyes completely bound in order not to see our miseries." When Jean Chastel made an attempt on Henry's life in December 1594, Bellièvre claimed that if absolution had been granted, "the pretext these wretched assassins use would cease" and told Henry that nothing could be expected from Clement "until he hears in Rome of the terror of your arms." However, Clement, himself dreading a schism of French Catholics, was preparing a bull of absolution that Villeroy and Bellièvre rejoiced to see granted in September 1595.[65]

Once France was back in the fold, the ministers made every effort to increase French influence in the Curia and to maintain amicable relations with the pontiffs. The popes in turn favored the interests of the French monarchy when they could. Neither France nor the pope was always satisfied, but the deep alienation of the league years was soon over.

The successful efforts of the cardinal legate, Alexander de Medici, to mediate the war with Spain (1596–98) helped to gain France's good will, as did Clement's dissolution of Henry IV's barren marriage to Margaret of Valois in 1599; by the latter act the pontiff had, as Villeroy put it, "given life to the kingdom." Although the secretary was disappointed at the pontiff's speed in creating new French cardinals, he was grateful for papal mediation of the Rochepot incident and the Franco-Spanish tariff war. Since their new queen was also a Medici, Bellièvre and Villeroy were overjoyed by the election of Pope Leo XI in April 1605 and shed "hot tears" on his death a month later. His successor Paul V (1605–21) met the ministers' approval until he backed the emperor's claim to the right to determine the Juliers-Cleves succession.[66]

In return for papal beneficence the ministers sought to promote projects favored by the popes. The introduction of the decrees of Trent (with restrictions to protect Gallican liberties) was among these until Gallican and Huguenot opposition became too great. Papal interest in the Jesuits' return to France prompted Villeroy's and Bellièvre's efforts toward that end. And between 1605 and 1607, when Rome and Venice came close to war in a dispute over the autonomy of religious orders in the republic, Villeroy guided the French diplomats who helped mediate the conflict.[67]

Villeroy and Bellièvre regarded the pope as primarily a political rather than a spiritual leader and believed that his power should be employed to advance the interests of French Catholicism in particular rather than those of Catholicism in general. This aspect of the ministers' Gallicanism was a natural extension of their belief that God acted through the French monarchy. It was also a sign of the complete fragmentation of Catholic unity.

Bellièvre's and Villeroy's views of foreigners have a decidedly modern cast, for they, too, tended to blame foreigners for internal problems and to use their hatred of them as an outlet for fear and frustration. Dislike and even hatred of other powers in Europe were the products of the ministers' intense patriotism and of foreign aggression against France. The cold war psychology that permeated the ministers' thinking was both the cause and the effect of their chronic inability to see virtue in foreigners and extreme reluctance to acknowledge gratitude for foreign assistance. Xenophobia, which is usually considered a concomitant of modern nationalism, was not far beneath the surface of the ministers' thinking. A tendency to stereotype also marked their views of foreigners, causing Villeroy and Bellièvre to speak of "the Spanish" and "the English" as if all Spaniards and all Englishmen were alike; however, in an era when kings were absolute the actions of a people were effectively those of its ruler. The ministers' secular outlook is also striking, for the conviction that the will of God was served by the French monarchy's prosperity was the only religious element in their view of foreign policy.

Three features of the ministers' world view—their patriotism, their antipathy to war, and their xenophobia—governed their policy decisions, but patriotism was the primary influence. As much as they disliked war, Villeroy and Bellièvre were willing to condone it when France's interests dictated engaging in hostilities. They also suppressed their hatred of Spain and England in order to keep the peace they desired and to protect France from the afflictions of war. Only after 1598 did the ministers enjoy the luxury of seeing France at peace, although helping to subvert the power of the Hapsburgs.

Bellièvre and Villeroy are entitled to some of the glory that Henry IV's foreign policy brought to their master. But most of the glory rightfully belongs to Henry, who avidly sought it, and who, unlike his ministers, was never too cautious to take the risks necessary to obtain his ends.

4. Society and the Economy

The Nobility

On the conscious level, at least, Villeroy and Bellièvre accepted the values of a hierarchical society in which birth was the criterion of worth. As long as the *noblesse d'épée* fulfilled its primary function of fighting for the king, the ministers were willing to grant it its traditional privileges. They deferred to its members, to whom they hoped to marry their offspring; accorded its members pensions and privileges; and forgave its transgressions against the crown it claimed to sustain. In this respect the *gens de robe* Bellièvre and Villeroy did not differ from their noble colleague Sully, who wished the nobles to "enjoy all the privileges of their fighting function, but only within the royal administration and under strict control."[1] But if Villeroy and Bellièvre were unable to conceive of a social order different from that which medieval society had bequeathed them, they were impatient with its flaws. Chief of these was the nobility's unwillingness to perform its assigned tasks, for rather than defending the king, many nobles, including the great magnates of the realm, sought to control him and to aggrandize their own power at his expense. Even this did not persuade the ministers that a recasting of the social order was necessary, but it did convince them that power had to be reassigned within the traditional framework. Almost imperceptibly and only half consciously Bellièvre and Villeroy arrived at the *ancien régime*'s solution to the problem of how to retain the traditional social hierarchy and yet make it work—that of protecting the nobility's privileges and excluding it from real political power.

Even though he was frequently in contact with great magnates in state affairs, Bellièvre was extremely flattered when the dukes of Nevers and Luxembourg visited him, as was Villeroy when Sully, long his colleague, deigned to dine at his table. Villeroy, moreover, hoped to marry his son into the family of the duke of Joyeuse, Henry III's favorite. His plans came to nothing because of Epernon's jealousy, but many years later the son married the daughter of the duke of Créquy. Bellièvre may also have hoped to ally his family with the nobility, but his son Nicholas married into another *robe longue* dynasty, the Brularts.[2]

Even when the ministers disliked a great noble, they addressed him in deferential, if not fawning, terms. In spite of the duke of Montmorency's intrigues with Navarre against Henry III, Villeroy was always concerned to keep his favor. Bellièvre, too, was careful to congratulate Montmorency on his elevation to the office of constable. When they became involved in disputes with great nobles, as Villeroy did with the duke of Epernon, the ministers remained self-effacing even when they were clearly in the right. After Epernon's unjustified public attack on Villeroy in Henry III's council in 1587, Bellièvre meekly told the duke, "Your dignity requires that you be the one who repairs by gentleness and humanity what bitterness has spoiled between you two." Villeroy, who privately was contemptuous of Epernon for being "puffed up with favor at the king's side," publicly, though the aggrieved party, played the humble suitor.[3]

The crown's practice of paying great nobles pensions, partly to keep their loyalty and partly to permit them to live in a manner befitting their rank, seems not to have been questioned by the ministers. Villeroy regretted that Henry III's chronic lack of funds meant that "even the services of princes cannot be rewarded," while Bellièvre frequently urged Henry III to dispense the expected pensions to magnates like the duke of Nevers, the prince of Condé, and Henry of Navarre. The ministers were not even averse to giving indemnities and pensions to rebellious league nobles in return for submission to Henry IV. Although Villeroy grumbled at Mayenne's bargaining, he was eager to buy off his revolt, as was Bellièvre, who had to secure the Parlement of Paris's approval of the reconciliation (the Edict of Folembray). Indeed, Villeroy defended the practice of buying off rebel nobles on the ground that pensions were cheaper than military campaigns.[4] Since Villeroy and Bellièvre themselves received large pensions from the crown, it might be argued that they could hardly oppose their being given to nobles. But it should be remembered that whereas the ministers were paid for loyal service, the nobles were, in effect, bribed to be loyal.

The ministers were reluctant to offend the honor of individual nobles or their families. When the duke of Biron was convicted of plotting against Henry IV's life, Bellièvre suggested a private execution to spare the family humiliation, and both he and Villeroy, anxious that the traitor's family not suffer for his transgressions, urged Henry IV to permit Biron's son to inherit his father's property. The duke of Bouillon refused for four years to beg the king's pardon for his part in Biron's plot, but Villeroy, who believed the duke should merely be made to "humble himself," in 1606 negotiated his submission. Although Villeroy recommended execution for Bouillon's followers, he and Bellièvre favored the pardon that the duke eventually received.[5]

Aware that the nobles were "more accustomed to handling the sword than the pen," both ministers expected them to wield the former in defense of the realm. During the civil wars Villeroy advised Henry III to pay his men at arms, whom the secretary deemed the principal instrument for keeping the peace. Villeroy feared "the entire and final destruction and ruin of our nobility, and as a result, of our crown" when Henry III considered opposing German mercenaries invading France with the nobility alone. A similar concern for the nobility is revealed by Bellièvre's fear that the duke of Anjou would lead his noble followers to destruction at the hands of the duke of Parma's Spanish veterans.[6] However, the nobility's refusal to perform its assigned tasks and its massive opposition to the crown in the civil wars gradually changed the ministers' attitude.

The ministers slowly, and only half-consciously, decided that the nobility was best excluded from positions of real political power. Their outlook was shaped by several factors. First of all, as the accounts of contemporaries and the ministers' own infrequent reference to the presence of magnates at council meetings indicate, their masters Henry III and Henry IV both began to restrict the great nobles' role in policy matters. Second, the ministers, beneath their public deference to the privileged caste, seem to have felt considerable antipathy to the irresponsible and

self-seeking behavior of the nobles. Villeroy and Bellièvre's confidence in the hereditary elite was shaken by princes who acted
like "madmen" and assaulted the throne during the league wars
and by the treachery of so trusted a servant as Biron in betraying
Henry IV. Rather than directly attacking the nobles' right to
political power, however, the ministers applauded their masters'
initiative in excluding the nobles from the inner councils and
sought to promote the role of their own class, the *gens de robe*,
in the royal administration. Villeroy's pleasure at the exclusion
of the nobility from Henry III's councils is testified to by Mornay, to whom, when the Huguenot pointed it out to Villeroy,
the secretary is said to have replied, "What do you want? Do
they not deserve it?" Among many other signs of the ministers'
desire to see their own class occupy key positions of power in
the royal administration was Bellièvre's suggestion that the *conseil des finances* be staffed with *robins*. It is probable that Villeroy and Bellièvre welcomed Henry IV's refusal to allow Sully
to persuade him to introduce more of the nobility into his councils.[7] Clearly Villeroy and Bellièvre regarded the *officiers*, or bureaucrats, rather than the nobility, as the buttress of the new
absolute monarchy.

The Bureaucracy

The need for a bureaucracy able and willing to enforce France's
kings' theoretical claims to absolute sovereignty was recognized
by both the kings and their principal servants. At issue, however,
was not only how such a loyal, honest, and efficient class of bureaucrats was to be created and maintained but also how much
power its upper echelon, the *noblesse de robe*, should have *vis-à-
vis* the crown.

Villeroy and Bellièvre, having tacitly concluded that the *noblesse d'épée* was an unreliable instrument of monarchical authority, quite naturally saw their own class, the bureaucracy,
as best qualified to be the crown's loyal servants. From his first
days with Henry III until the end of his service under Henry IV,

Bellièvre strove to convince his masters of the importance of an able and loyal bureaucracy. Although his efforts were partially inspired by a desire to further the interests and authority of the *noblesse de robe*, Bellièvre's major concern was the good of the monarchy, which he believed was crippled by the corruption and incapacity of its officials. As early as 1575, soon after he became superintendent of finance, Bellièvre proposed that fiscal bureaucrats be picked for their ability, trained for their profession, well paid to reduce the temptations of corruption, and given a respected place in society. "Evil and corruption have penetrated so far," Bellièvre maintained, that sweeping reforms were necessary, and he recommended that inspectors be appointed to examine the accounts of fiscal officials, who, if irregularities were uncovered, should be given the chance to divest themselves of their ill-gained riches.[8]

Unfortunately for France, the civil wars and Bellièvre's preoccupation with negotiations prevented him from attempting to implement his program. In any case, Bellièvre repeatedly warned Henry III that unless his officials were paid, their loyalty could not be assured; but the funds to do so were lacking. Indeed, in 1581 funds were not even available to pay the judges of the *chambre mi-partie* of the parlement of Bordeaux, the tribunal promised to the Protestants of Guyenne in the Treaty of Fleix. When the league rose, the loyalty of the officials was strained not only by their being unpaid and tempted to peculate but by religious considerations as well. Numerous provinces, along with their officers, defected to the rebels. Although the bureaucracy eventually proved to be the monarchy's mainstay against the league, it rallied to the king to defend its own offices as well as his authority only after royal authority broke down over much of France.[9] And the fact that an official ultimately remained loyal did not mean that he was either able or honest.

Bellièvre tried to implement his reform program for the bureaucracy when he was made chancellor, the officer theoretically in charge of the entire royal administration. He was determined to root out the endemic corruption that the civil wars had worsened and at the same time to protect the integrity of the *noblesse de robe* from royal authority. As a result, he lost royal favor, and the opportunity to reform the fiscal bureaucracy passed to Sully, the new superintendent of finance. But when Sully twenty-five years later put into effect Bellièvre's suggestion that investigatory commissions be used to uncover fraud in fiscal officials' accounts, the chancellor was not pleased. He tried to take over the direction of a commission's investigation in 1605, perhaps because he knew that Sully used such bodies less as an instrument of fiscal reform than as a means of extorting restitution of ill-gotten gains from corrupt officials; Bellièvre's intention had been to root out the corrupt officials and train reliable replacements, not to accept corruption as a way of life and to profit from it. The *paulette*, which made royal offices hereditary, appalled Bellièvre not only because it would cause the price of offices to rise, depriving able men of the chance to acquire them, but because members of a hereditary officer class would, as he put it, be not "officials of the king, but officials of their purses."[10]

Bellièvre attempted, in spite of royal indifference, to protect the quality of the *robins*. He urged Henry IV to use extreme care in selecting men for the parlements, for, he said, "Most seek to aggrandize themselves at the expense of the king and the public." When the king's appointee as first *président* of the parlement of Toulouse, Nicholas de Verdun, asked to be permitted to retain his post as a *président* of the Parlement of Paris for three years, Bellièvre warned that such plural officeholding would erode the quality of the courts. In establishing French judicial and administrative systems in Chambéry after its capture from Savoy in 1600, he recommended that Henry IV appoint only able men and that he do so by regular procedures. However, although Bellièvre warned the members of the Parlement of Paris of the deleterious effects of nepotism, he spared no effort to have his son Albert appointed to the *cour des aides*.[11]

Bellièvre's efforts to persuade Henry IV to reform the ranks of the bureaucracy failed for reasons of which Bellièvre was fully aware: "Money speaks, and reason and honor are mute." The sale of offices was too profitable in the short run to abandon; the monarchy was willing to tolerate corruption as long as corrupt officials could periodically be forced to disgorge their illicit gains.[12]

Bellièvre's attempts to enhance the power of the upper reaches of the bureaucracy, the *noblesse de robe*, were no more successful than his efforts to purge the bureaucracy of abuses. His protests against Henry IV's arbitrary intervention in judicial cases were overruled or—as was the case with his most important suggestion, that the king's councils be reformed—ignored. In 1601 Bellièvre suggested that the *conseil d'état* be reduced from a hundred-odd members to eight, to be drawn from the *noblesse de robe*, and that the offices be rotated frequently. At the same time he made another suggestion that would have had farther-reaching implications, that a special *conseil des finances* be created that would meet thrice-weekly and be staffed by *robins* like Pierre Jeannin, Brulart de Sillery, Hurault de Maisse, Villeroy, and of course, the future duke of Sully. As Villeroy intimated it would be, this suggestion—which would not only have assured Bellièvre's mastery of the council against Sully's attempts to control it but would also have made the council a preserve of the *robins*—was ignored by the king. Bellièvre apparently tried to press the matter, which Villeroy promised him would be considered when he came to court, but the king did not open the proposal to discussion. It was about this time that Bellièvre began to complain of declining influence.[13]

The irony of Bellièvre's campaign to strengthen and purify the bureaucracy was that those who opposed him, Henry IV and Sully, succeeded in one of his aims through the *paulette*. Because it made royal offices hereditary and therefore more desirable, it caused the royal bureaucracy to expand at the expense of local and provincial officials, thus increasing the monarchy's control over its subjects although corruption was not checked.[14]

If Villeroy did not champion increased power for the officials, he was aware of the importance of their loyalty. Indeed, he considered prompt payment of their salaries essential to the success of his program for the pacification of the Midi in 1580. He also opposed the duke of Mayenne's request for a six-year suspension of the *taille* in Dauphiné, since it would leave the king without funds to pay his servants. Although Villeroy refused to support Bellièvre when the latter's reforms met with Henry IV's disapproval, the secretary was nonetheless concerned about the officials' caliber and in 1582 had urged Henry III to select a man of ability as *président* of the parlement of Bordeaux rather than to sell that vital position in Huguenot-dominated Guyenne to the highest bidder. By the time of the regency, Villeroy was reminding Marie de Medici that the bureaucracy was the monarchy's principal support.[15]

Whether the product of venality and hereditary office, as proved to be the case, or of careful selection and inculcation of habits of loyalty, as Bellièvre advocated, the officials' loyalty was crucial to the success of royal absolutism. That the crown had this loyalty was shown during the crisis of Marie de Medici's regency, for when the clergy pressed the royal government to resume the offensive against Protestantism and the nobility demanded pensions and the restoration of their lost powers in the provinces, it was the officials who sprang to the defense of monarchical authority at the States-General in 1614. Thus was the stage set for the absolutism of Louis XIV.[16]

The Clergy

Clerical reform in France lagged largely because leadership was lacking, for the Concordat of Bologna of 1516, which gave the crown control over appointments to bishoprics and abbeys, meant that the great clergy were more often royal favorites than men of piety. Abuses were rampant even before the wars broke out, and two generations of chaos only accelerated the deterioration of the clergy's integrity. The wars also undermined the clergy's traditional loyalty to the crown. When Henry III refused to assume leadership of the campaign to exterminate heresy, many of the clergy considered Guise and the Catholic League the true defenders of the faith. And on Henry IV's accession, unlike their secular peers, most of the clergy could not easily adopt a *politique* position—as did Bishop Gondy of Paris and the future

Cardinal d'Ossat—and accept a heretic king. Never before had the union between throne and altar been so precarious, and it would not be so threatened again until the Revolution.[17]

The ministers were concerned not with the clerics' sacerdotal function but with their role in secular society. As good royal Gallicans, both men held that the church and its clergy should be loyal servants of the crown. As Villeroy put it, the clergy should not only be appointed by the king but should, in turn, serve the crown, lend it moral (and fiscal) support, and avoid stirring up unrest among the Huguenots. Villeroy and Bellièvre therefore approved of such clerics as Cardinal Du Perron, whom they helped obtain the red hat; Cardinal d'Ossat, Henry IV's able diplomat and Villeroy's friend; Jean Morvilliers, bishop of Orléans, their mentor as royal servants; and the bishops who in 1593, in the face of papal admonition, absolved Henry IV of his apostacy and accepted him into the Gallican church. According to Bellièvre, however, four-fifths of the great clergy supported the league. The ministers were on the alert for anti-Gallican sentiments in the nuncios. Villeroy, for example, warned Henry III, "The nuncio wants to make it customary to control the actions of Your Majesty in the disposition of abbeys by attributing to himself and his successors some authority over them." Bellièvre had nothing but contempt for the cardinal of Plaisance, the nuncio who sought to persuade the league States-General to elect the Spanish infanta queen of France. He bristled if even a prospective nuncio's sympathies were anti-French, opposing the appointment of the cardinal of Mantua because "his opinions were not too firm during our disorders." On the other hand, a papal emissary who served France—like Cardinal Legate Alexander de Medici, who between 1596 and 1598 helped to arrange Franco-Spanish peace talks—was "wise and well-intentioned," and Cardinal Bufalo, who helped mediate the tariff war with Spain (1604), was also respected.[18]

The ministers expected the clergy to serve the monarchy not only as individuals but collectively, and they held that the clerical assemblies that since 1562 had made *dons gratuits* to help sustain the monarchy were rendering the Most Christian King no more than his due. When, as was frequently the case, the assemblies bickered over the amount of the *don gratuit* or tried to secure concessions in return, the ministers were piqued. In 1579, after requesting the assembly of Melun to reaffirm its *don gratuit*, Bellièvre admonished that body of clerics, "If obedience towards the king was lost in all of the rest of the kingdom, we would hope to find duty in you." Villeroy expected the same loyalty six years later, when the king asked the clergy for a special subvention of 100,000 écus to sustain his impending war against heresy, and was outraged when the clerics hesitated to make the grant even though it had been authorized by the pope. In 1596 Henry IV was desperately seeking funds for his war against Philip II, and Bellièvre addressed another tightfisted clerical assembly to request an extension of the *don gratuit*, arguing that fiscal hardship was a small price to pay to escape Spanish domination. When the clerics asked for the right to nominate the great clergy in return for their gift, Bellièvre complained, "The ecclesiastics are making themselves the protectors of the pope's authority."[19] Such ultramontane sentiments were to Bellièvre a threat to royal Gallicanism.

Clerical reform, as long as it did not impinge on royal control of the church or disrupt the newly won religious peace, was sought by both ministers. Villeroy seems to have been especially aware of the prevalence of abuses within the Gallican church. Himself the patron of a small convent in which he tried to impose discipline and a high level of spirituality, the secretary was appalled by corrupt religious orders "in which the disorders that increase at a glance are ready to crush the church of God in this kingdom." He proposed to France's ambassador in Rome that, since the existing religious orders were under the control of worldly prelates, the pope consider founding a new order that would better exemplify the renewed spirit of Catholicism.[20] Villeroy also hoped to reinvigorate the French church by introducing the decrees of the Council of Trent and by permitting the Jesuits to return.

The Trentine decrees had remained unpublished in France for several reasons.[21] Gallicans opposed them because the king's appointive power would have been nullified and because some of the abuses they were intended to reform were lucrative. Huguenots considered the decrees the words of Antichrist. Villeroy and Bellièvre, although sympathetic with the decrees' thrust toward reform, had to consider the political implications as well: mounting Gallican and Huguenot dissatisfaction on the one hand, deterioration of the monarchy's relations with the papacy on the other. Ultimately, political considerations outweighed the decrees' religious benefits.

In 1585, when a commission appointed to study the matter of introducing the decrees into France recommended delaying until Gallican opposition subsided, Villeroy complained that the commissioners had "done nothing for themselves nor for the service of the king and the good of the church." Not only did the delay offend the pope, who was being asked to sanction the alienation of church property to finance the crown's wars, but necessary clerical reforms were put off. Eleven years later, as a condition of absolution, Henry IV promised to introduce the decrees, but only after the Edict of Nantes was issued, pacifying the Huguenots and offending the pope, did the king make an effort to do so by calling a meeting of the *présidents* of the Parlement of Paris in April 1600 to sound out their views. Henry IV was prepared to accept the decrees in so far as they did not infringe on royal control of the church, but the parlement was so hostile to the plan that it was abandoned, to Bellièvre and Villeroy's disappointment. However, when in 1605 an assembly of the clergy called for publication of the Trentine decrees, Villeroy dismissed the idea for fear that "Huguenots will profit from it."[22] To the royal ministers, internal stability was more important than a spiritually elevated clergy.

The Society of Jesus—expelled from the jurisdiction of the Parlement of Paris in 1595 on charges of teaching the doctrine of tyrannicide that had allegedly inspired Jean Chastel to attempt to assassinate Henry IV—fared better than the canons and decrees of the Council of Trent. Just after Chastel's attempt, the ministers professed to believe the charges and to approve the expulsion, but soon Villeroy was advocating the Jesuits' return, suggesting to Henry IV that if they proved their loyalty in the provinces, they should be restored to the parlement's jurisdiction. Not only would the order's return please the pope, but "piety and good letters" would once more be taught France's youth. Papal pressure increased, and by 1603 Henry agreed to the Jesuits' return if they swore loyalty to him and promised not to interfere with the activities of the diocesan authorities. When the general of the order agreed to these restrictions in January 1604, Villeroy was elated that the soldiers of the pope had agreed to serve the first warrior of France and told the king that he hoped the Jesuits would "live and serve the king and the public so well that His Majesty has occasion to favor them and bestow more on them." Bellièvre apparently did not share Villeroy's enthusiasm. At least there is no evidence that he pressed for the Jesuits' return, and the papal legate, who repeatedly urged him to support their reinstatement, reported that Bellièvre did not like them.[23]

In spite of Villeroy's efforts to foster reform among the Gallican clergy, he grew alarmed when some orders actually tried to clean house. He feared that Franciscan friars expelled for lack of zeal would become Huguenots and take refuge "under the shelter of the edict that we observe." The secretary, who favored priors who would maintain discipline "as much by prudence and gentleness as by rigor," applauded a royal edict suppressing the Confraternity of Our Lady of Compassion, composed, Villeroy claimed, of "certain Capuchins who are more passionate than religious." Nor, as long as there was no risk of serious friction, did he oppose the request of other Capuchins for royal assistance in reforming some of their houses. Villeroy's apprehension over religious reform was no doubt prompted by the memory of the zeal of the leaguers, whose fanaticism, he had feared, would "consume and destroy our religion."[24] Villeroy honestly wanted to see the church reformed, but only if domestic tranquility were not disrupted. He welcomed the introduction of the Trentine decrees until it became clear that opposition would be bitter, then dropped the issue. He accepted the Jesuits only when it was evident that opposition to their reinstatement would be minimized by placing them under severe restrictions. And he wanted reformed religious orders as long as no one was driven from the church. It was not from the efforts of such compromisers with the world that the Catholic Reformation was to triumph in France.

Bellièvre, who, unlike his colleague, never showed much concern for clerical reform, actively sought ecclesiastical benefices for his offspring and relatives. It is not surprising that he did not attack the evils of nonresidence and pluralism to which he contributed—by helping a nephew obtain a benefice at Saint-Chapelle from Henry III and by openly pulling strings to obtain his son Albert a succession of benefices, among them the archbishopric of Lyons.[25] Even if Bellièvre had felt constrained to support clerical reform, it is doubtful that he, a *robin* dynast, would have seen any contradiction between such support and his family's benefices.

Given Villeroy and Bellièvre's view of the clergy as an instrument of the state and of France as the repository of true Catholicism, they would doubtless have found Richelieu's France a mirror of their own vaguely formulated ideal had they lived into his era.

The Peasants

French peasants, whose lot had gradually improved since the Hundred Years War, suffered severely from the Wars of Religion. Their plight varied from region to region, but few escaped foraging troops, famine, and disease. Royal taxation in the form of the *taille* fell most heavily on the hapless peasantry. Moreover, in regions in which civil war was endemic, taxes were collected by all of the combatants. The result was that many small proprietors were forced to mortgage and then to sell their lands to wealthy bourgeois. The peasants (and the marginal rural nobility) were the real losers in the religious wars.[26]

Villeroy and Bellièvre, who were seigneurial proprietors as well as royal servants, were aware of the peasants' plight. Like their contemporaries, the ministers regarded the peasant as the monarchy's basic exploitable commodity, but their humanity as well as their desire to protect the state's main source of income motivated their attempts to ameliorate the misery of society's lowest order. During the civil wars Bellièvre repeatedly urged Henry III to repress the brigands and looting bands of soldiers who afflicted the peasants. Villeroy bewailed the misery that leaguers and royalists alike imposed on France's helpless countrymen, and was active in founding hospitals for the victims of war and famine. In their frequent appeals for an end to the wars, both ministers spoke of the misery that these conflicts brought to the common people.[27]

The protection of their own estates and peasantry was uppermost in both men's minds. Bellièvre, in retirement at Grignon, who spent much of his time trying to shield his holdings from royalists and leaguers alike, appealed for relief from billeting troops and from the *taille*, which he claimed his tenants could not pay. Villeroy, some of whose estates in Touraine were confiscated when he joined the league, tried to prevent the royalists from seizing the remaining ones, with singular success, thanks both to his own efforts and Bellièvre's interventions. After the war was finally over, Bellièvre, who was supervising the Spanish evacuation of Picardy, recommended that French troops be present in order to protect the French peasantry.[28]

Concern for the peasants diminished when peace was restored after 1598, but Bellièvre was still compassionate. When famine threatened in the Midi in 1604, for example, he urged the king to permit grain to be brought in from adjacent regions. And when Irish refugees in Paris were about to be resettled in Brittany, Bellièvre asked Henry IV to spend 1,000 écus on food for them lest they spread disease among "the poor men of the country side."[29]

If the ministers persistently tried to spare the peasants the ravages of war, they were less energetic in their efforts to relieve them of the burden of royal taxation. Only during the last stages of the war with Spain (1595–98) did Bellièvre at least admit that taxation was exceeding the peasants' capacity to pay. Not only were "the richest reduced to necessity," he warned Henry IV, but "the little people [were reduced] to mendicancy." So desperate was the situation around Lyons that Bellièvre reported, "The poverty of the peasants is more powerful than the force of the soldiers, and they will chase [the collectors of the *tailles*] off by force." Because of the rural population's misery, Bellièvre appealed to the Assembly of Notables for new sources of revenue, but once France enjoyed peace, he opposed any diminution of the *taille*.[30]

Both men claimed to have suffered a drastic decrease in income between 1589 and 1593, but it is not known whether it was caused by the ravages of war or Bellièvre and Villeroy's attempts to alleviate the peasants' burdens by reducing their fees and services.[31] However, the ministers voiced their complaints so bitterly that their loss of income appears to have been involuntary. That they felt compassion for the peasants is proven, but that their charity began at home seems unlikely.

The Huguenots

During Villeroy and Bellièvre's tenure as royal ministers the fortunes of French Calvinism underwent many vicissitudes. From a low point of power and a peak of alienation after the Saint Bartholomew's Day massacre, the Huguenots organized nationally and began a concerted drive to secure full toleration. Their fortunes reached their height in the 1580s and 1590s, when the "Huguenot state" was able first to thwart Henry III's and the league's efforts to crush it, then to provide the Protestant Henry IV's main support, and finally to compel the converted king to grant it legal and religious equality by the Edict of Nantes. The edict of toleration transformed the Huguenots into a permanent minority by denying them effective means of proselytizing. The monarchy, on the other hand, had the honors and offices with which to encourage the conversion of lukewarm Huguenots. After 1598, Calvinism's relative decline began.[32]

Villeroy and Bellièvre, who played key roles in these events, had to choose between toleration of a sect they abhorred and endless civil war which they detested. As good Catholics they had no desire to see a "pretended" reformed religion established, but as good Frenchmen they were appalled at "the extremity of the misery into which this miserable France is plunged and almost submerged on account of division in the matter of religion."[33] The ministers' gradual reconciliation of the demands of conscience with the necessity of politics—that is, the acceptance of practical toleration—was doubtless representative of an entire generation's inner struggle.

The motives for the ministers' eventual willingness to tolerate heresy within the realm of the Most Christian King were multiple. First of all, toleration was necessary to assure the safety of the state. As Bellièvre put it, if religious warfare continued it would be impossible to enforce "the obedience that is due kings and without which kingdoms cannot exist."[34] Second, the ministers realized that attempts to repress heretics only provoked Huguenot persecution of Catholics. Last, Bellièvre and Villeroy assuaged their consciences in the belief that once peace was secured, peaceful conversion would redeem many of those who had strayed from Rome.

The prime impetus for both men's acceptance of toleration was their desire to preserve the monarchy. Between 1574 and 1598 they saw public opinion was so polarized that the monarchy, denied the loyalty of both its heretic and of its most zealous Catholic subjects, was unable to govern large areas of the realm. Although Bellièvre's commitment to toleration emerged earlier and was more deep-rooted than Villeroy's, both men strove to pacify France by placating the heretics.

The disasters of Henry III's reign taught the ministers their first lessons in toleration, and as early as 1576, when Henry III was debating whether or not to begin war with the Huguenots, Bellièvre urged a peaceful accommodation. Villeroy, however, was willing to go to war if the States-General granted funds, and a year later he objected to the generous provisions of the Peace of Bergerac on the ground that concessions would lead to further Huguenot demands. But after 1580, when the War of the Lovers proved that the crown could not defeat its heretic subjects, Villeroy joined Bellièvre—not in advocating toleration but in abandoning any hope of forcefully repressing heresy. Bellièvre went further and was in favor of special courts in the parlements (*chambres mi-parties*) for the Huguenots so that they would receive justice. By 1585—when the monarchy was caught between the Catholic League, which demanded all-out war against heresy, and Huguenot rebels—both ministers were trying desperately to avoid a renewal of war with the Huguenots. Bellièvre's analysis of the situation was realistic: "If some say that the best way would be to exterminate them [the Huguenots], you can see the progress that we have made in this war, and can judge the difference between facts and desires." Villeroy agreed that to attempt to root out heresy was folly because the Huguenots would receive foreign Protestant aid, and the result would be "a perpetual and bloody war." He regarded the Peace of Nemours (July 1585) proscribing Protestantism in France as a tragedy. Only when the league's pressures became unbearable and the Huguenots' foreign allies were about to invade France in 1587 did the ministers reluctantly concede that war against the Huguenots was inevitable. Otherwise, Bellièvre maintained, "Instead of our having a war with the Huguenots, we will have a more troublesome war with the Catholics." Both ministers had by 1589 learned their first lesson in toleration, that war could not exterminate the heretics and only weakened the monarchy. Bellièvre, who had gone further in his studies than his colleague, drew up a memoir on the subject in which he pointed out that experience had proven, not only in France but in the Low Countries as well, that those who tried "to chase the new religion from kingdoms by force"[35] always failed.

During the first decade of Henry IV's reign, Villeroy and Bellièvre worked out their rationale of religious toleration. To preserve the monarchy they were willing to make concessions—as few as possible—to the Huguenots. In return they demanded the absolute loyalty of the heretics to the interests of the monarchy. Bellièvre again took the lead, asking Huguenots to see the futility of religious conflict and to accept the notion that religious differences could be settled through compromise. To Villeroy, who was less eager to condone toleration, Bellièvre argued that no stable peace was possible until the Huguenots were permitted full religious rights. He hoped that the Edict of Mantes (August 1591), which gave the Calvinists extensive liberties in the areas they controlled, would content them, but when they demanded more, he accepted the broader guarantees of the Edict of Nantes.

Villeroy, who had reluctantly countenanced the liberties granted by Henry IV, was infuriated by the slackening of Calvinist support after the royal conversion and called down "misfortune on those who fail [the king] in his need," when the Huguenots refused to send aid to Henry's siege of Amiens in 1597. Villeroy also resented the Huguenot appeal to Elizabeth I for assistance in securing further concessions, but his commitment to toleration was unshaken:

> If those who have published their complaints had as well represented the favors and gifts they have received from His Majesty, and which they have enjoyed everywhere in great tranquility since his accession to the throne, and of the way they have conducted themselves towards the Catholics where they are the masters, the queen would not pity their fate and condition as she does. . . . They live in such liberty that I believe that there are few cities in this kingdom where they do not preach almost publicly and known to everyone. I do not want for that to excuse the rigors which some parlements and officers use towards them, but at the first complaint, His Majesty will attend to it as best he can. [The Huguenots'] seeking remedies to their complaints without him renders [the Catholics] more licentious, to the great regret of His Majesty, who I attest before God does what he can for the preservation of both [religions], as a good prince must. But if it is lawful for one [group] to have recourse to foreign princes, what will the others do? And if our neighbors and friends greet and favor them, what will become of the monarchy? We will . . . return to greater confusion than ever.

In spite of his apprehension at the thought of giving the heretics garrison cities with which to defend their new liberties, Villeroy was nevertheless ready, for the sake of peace, to approve the provisions of the Edict of Nantes.[36]

Having learned to live with religious pluralism in order to preserve the state, for the rest of the reign Bellièvre and Villeroy tried to avoid controversy between the two religions, while opposing any extension of the Huguenots' political powers. In 1602, for example, when a Huguenot synod called the pope Antichrist,

Villeroy opposed the royal retaliation demanded by the nuncio on the ground that it would give "our Huguenots too much opportunity to complain." Nor did the duke of Bouillon's refusal to seek a royal pardon for his part in the Biron plot, as much as it angered the secretary, prompt him to recommend repression, for he believed that should the duke's Huguenot followers be aroused, "the Spanish will obtain by means of the Huguenots what they have not been able to obtain from the Catholics"—the disruption of France. Villeroy agreed that Henry's raising an army to humble Bouillon in 1606 was necessary, but he dreaded "an upheaval of which this kingdom has no need." Although Villeroy welcomed the outcome of the Mornay–Du Perron debate in 1600, in which the Huguenot "pope" was bested in a public disputation by the Catholic controversialist, he did not like to see issues debated publicly that only aroused men's passions. When it came to permitting the Huguenots to hold political assemblies, Henry IV and his ministers were uneasy; a gathering of heretics was too reminiscent of the civil wars, and Villeroy was always relieved when such meetings were over.[37]

Bellièvre and Villeroy tolerated heresy to protect Catholics in Huguenot territories from persecution. During his travels about France in behalf of Henry III, Bellièvre saw at first hand the plight of Catholics under Huguenot control, like those in the countryside around the Protestant citadel of Montauban, who were treated "with a cruelty that one cannot see even among the Turks on the frontier of Hungary." Belliévre's experience had taught him that religious wars "have brought diminution rather than increase to the Catholic religion."[38]

The ministers' acceptance of toleration was made easier by their realization that the stabilization of the religious situation in France would make it possible for Catholicism—bolstered by the reform of the clergy, the proselytizing of the Jesuits, and the monarchy's power to grant pensions and offices—to make severe inroads in heresy's ranks. Accordingly, Bellièvre wished Henry IV to make "all efforts possible to attract all his subjects to [Catholicism]," and Villeroy hoped that more Huguenots would follow the example of the son of Calignon, the chancellor of Navarre, and convert. Bellièvre, who considered such defections "the most desirable thing we can ask of God," hoped, "God will take pity on us and in the end grant us the grace to reunite us all in the Catholic religion."[39]

That Bellièvre and Villeroy practiced the toleration they preached is shown by their relationship with the Huguenot "pope," Philip de Mornay. Mornay respected both ministers—Villeroy as a prudent man and a faithful servant of the crown, Bellièvre as a reasonable man willing to keep the peace during Henry III's reign and a suitable emissary to the Huguenots in the negotiations leading up to the Edict of Nantes. Such praise would hardly have come from Mornay had he considered either minister a bigoted Catholic. His respect was reciprocated by both Bellièvre and Villeroy. The former, who was a judge at the Mornay–Du Perron debate, regretted the Huguenot's humiliation but felt compelled to vote against him when he was shown to have made errors of scriptural interpretation. Villeroy met Mornay twice, in 1590 and 1592, to negotiate a settlement of wars between Henry IV and the league and was confident that Mornay, though a rigid Calvinist, shared his own concern for the good of France.[40] Mutual respect and common humanity helped to bridge the gulf between the faiths for Bellièvre and Villeroy, as it no doubt did for many of their contemporaries.

There is an ambivalence about the ministers' view of religious toleration. Did concern for public order and the security of the state secularize their outlook toward politics? Did they as *politiques* place politics above religion? In one sense, the ministers placed the welfare of their faith on a par with that of the monarchy. They swallowed the bitter pill of toleration because it alone assured the survival of the French monarchy—the true receptacle of Catholicism and inseparable from it, for without the Most Christian King there would be no French Catholicism (Gallicanism), and without Catholicism there could be no Most Christian King. In another sense, however, Villeroy and Bellièvre at least unconsciously drifted toward a secular view of the state, for they eventually concluded that religious homogeneity, although highly desirable, was not absolutely essential for a nation's political unity, and after 1598 acted on the assumption that the Huguenots would remain loyal subjects of the crown as long as they were guaranteed their liberties. In the ministers' minds as well as in the law a single faith was no longer necessary to preserve the law and the crown. This shift of attitude, the product of the grim lessons of religious civil war followed by ample evidence of the utility of toleration, brought Villeroy and Bellièvre to the threshold of the modern world.

The Economy

The economic policies of Henry III's and Henry IV's governments were aimed at solving two perennial problems, that of amassing sufficient funds to finance its activities and that of extending royal control to all areas of the economy potentially remunerative to the monarchy.[41] These two problems, fiscal and regulatory, were intimately related, for mercantilist controls were intended to foster economic growth, which, in turn, provided more revenue. The fiscal problem was endemic and was ameliorated only late in Henry IV's reign.

When Henry III ascended the throne of a nation torn by religious strife, Bellièvre prophetically remarked, "If we had some money . . . we would have fewer enemies." The king's prodigality, combined with his loss of control over large (taxable) areas of France, left the monarchy impoverished just as its problems reached their peak. Henry IV's reconquest of his realm was retarded by a perennial shortage of funds; "All will go well if I have some money," he complained. Even though Sully managed to amass a considerable surplus in the royal treasury after 1598 by means of fiscal expedients, some of which were "thoroughly disreputable," the hoard was quickly dissipated by the regency government in buying off its internal foes.[42] The monarchy's responsibilities, real or imagined, exceeded its ability to siphon off the national wealth to support them.

The problem of economic regulation, or mercantilism, although hardly new, received much attention. Kings had been trying to foster and then to tap economic growth since the twelfth century, but only by the late sixteenth and early seventeenth centuries were mercantilist regulations actively promulgated and at least partially enforced through subsidies to key industries, royal monopolies, and prohibitions against the export of unfinished materials. Thus, although mercantilism still awaited theoretical formulation by men like Barthélemy Laffemas and Antoine de Montchrétien, its tenets were practically operative.

Bellièvre, first as Henry III's superintendent of finance (1574–82) and then as a member of Henry IV's *conseil des finances* (1595–1607), was deeply immersed in France's economic problems. Although he always favored traditional but efficient financial policies, before 1598, when the monarchy's survival was in the balance, he tolerated such fiscal abuses as alienation of the royal domain, the sale of offices and titles, and the suspension of interest payments on government bonds. But when peace was restored his pressure for fiscal reform brought him into conflict with the king and the new superintendent of finance, Sully.

During the religious wars Bellièvre conceded regretfully that funds had to be found regardless of the means employed. The Swiss mercenaries, "one of the foundation stones of this crown," had to be paid, pensions had to be made available to buy the nobility's loyalty, league rebels had to be bought off (if only momentarily), and royal officials' salaries had to be paid. To obtain the necessary funds, Bellièvre resorted to fiscal measures that obtained short-term benefits at the price of further erosion of the monarchy's resources and credit. In 1578 he therefore asked the Parlement of Paris to approve alienation of parts of the royal domain, and in 1587 he hired Swiss mercenaries with promissory notes; but he recognized the folly of such measures. In 1575, soon after being made superintendent, he advised Henry III to eliminate unnecessary expenses, pay his fiscal officials so as to assure efficient collection of taxes, minimize the sale of offices, and cease alienating the royal domain. To burden future revenue with debts to the Swiss distressed Bellièvre: "This nation is not accustomed to paying with letters rather than money." But when the clergy proved laggard in granting a *don gratuit* to help repel an expected invasion of Protestant mercenaries in 1586, Bellièvre conceded, "We must find [funds] elsewhere, in advance." It must have gone against the grain a year later for him to have to borrow 200,000 livres on anticipated revenue from the royal domain.[43]

In November 1594, when Bellièvre took office under Henry IV and was made a member of his *conseil des finances,* the crown's finances were even more precarious. Bellièvre was aware of the awesome task that awaited him and his fellow councillors: "The debts of the kingdom are so great, the people so poor, the disorders so great, the insolence of some so limitless, the freedom to abuse the finances by those who are in charge so deep-rooted, that . . . the one charged with the finances runs a risk of not being trusted." As the king's proconsul in Lyons from June 1594 to August 1595, the minister had become familiar with the state's fiscal problems, for during the first ten months he had had to spend 174,000 écus to defend the region and had collected only 50,000 écus in taxes. ("The sergeants of the *taille* receive only blows," he told the king.) He had managed to secure the remainder only by loans and extraordinary taxes, and by permitting the garrison troops "to pay themselves with the sword" at the peasantry's expense. So dire had Bellièvre's fiscal plight been that he had been granted permission to sell part of the royal domain in Languedoc to defend the Lyonnais. After this experience and the failure of the king's offensives against Spain because it was "impossible to satisfy the expense," Bellièvre admitted that although such expedients were evil, in a state of war it was necessary "to increase the receipts as best we can." Therefore, because there was no alternative, he borrowed funds from financiers at exorbitant interest rates. But even these sources were insufficient, and Henry IV had to cease campaigning by mid-1596 for lack of money. Thanks to the Assembly of Notables—which in December 1596 granted a new excise tax (the *pancarte*) on all goods entering towns and suspended officers' salaries for a year—Henry managed to keep his armies in the field long enough to dishearten the equally hard-pressed Philip II.[44]

Direction of the finances after 1598 was assumed by the future duke of Sully, who as superintendent, breathed "fresh life into the old regulations" and managed to balance the budget and even build up a considerable surplus in the royal treasury. By keeping the *taille* high, selling offices prodigally, and extorting payments from fiscal officials by threatening investigation by a *chambre de justice*, Sully raised the state's income from 20 million livres in 1600 to 33 million livres in 1610. Because Sully's regime restored the monarchy's solvency, Henry IV—who had little knowledge of, or interest in, finance—gave him a free hand. Having long called for efficiency, Bellièvre might have been expected to praise Sully, but by attempting to organize and lead resistance to the superintendent in the *conseil des finances*, the aging minister fell from royal favor.[45]

Bellièvre's opposition to Sully's policies was based on both personal and philosophical differences. Bellièvre resented being ordered about like "a clerk of finances" by a man "still wet behind the ears."[46] The duke's aristocratic arrogance and high-handed manner offended the cautious and temperate old *robin*. More than differences in generation and temperament were involved, however. Bellièvre objected strongly to Sully's continued sale of fiscal and judicial offices, because he feared that it would undermine the loyalty of the royal bureaucracy. It was even more dangerous, Bellièvre was convinced, to make such offices hereditary; not only would the monarchy lose control of its officials, but the price of offices would mount, and ambitious, deserving men would be hard pressed to secure them. Bellièvre's opposition to what came to be called the *paulette* seems to have been based equally on concern for the monarchy and for his own class, the *robins*.

He began his campaign against Sully's fiscal policies on principle and ended it in petty attempts to discredit his triumphant rival. In December 1602, when Sully urged Henry IV to establish the *droit annuel*, a yearly payment to the crown of one-sixtieth of an office's value in return for the hereditary rights, Bellièvre fought the proposal, but Henry, who wanted immediate revenues above all, backed the superintendent. For the next two years Bellièvre tried to organize support within the *conseil des finances*, but his efforts were doomed to failure because the king favored Sully, whose victory was signaled by the Edict of the Paulette in December 1604. After having tried repeatedly to delay Sully's policies by refusing to seal royal edicts, Bellièvre was reduced in 1605 to trying to discredit his rival by proving corruption in his financial administration. So far eclipsed was Bellièvre's influence by then that Henry IV merely ordered him to drop the matter until Sully himself could direct an investigation.[47]

The quarrel between the two ministers revealed sharply divergent philosophies of government and finance. Sully's only goal was to build up the monarchy's finances; he cared little for the social implications of his policies. Bellièvre also wanted fiscal solvency and urged the king to keep the *taille* as high as possible without causing unrest.[48] But the chancellor objected to the effect of hereditary and venal officeholding on the *robins*, whom he regarded as the monarchy's principal servants. Since the *robins* served loyally in return for the privilege of holding office, Bellièvre believed that to expand their numbers and ignore their advice as Henry and Sully did would undermine the very foundations of the monarchy. When Henry IV had to choose between monarchical authority tempered by the *robins*' advice and Sully's concept of royal absolutism, the choice was not difficult.[49]

Unlike Bellièvre, Villeroy showed little interest in fiscal matters, over which he had no power. Indeed, when appealed to for help in obtaining salaries or pensions, he would reply, "In matters of finance I have neither credit nor power, for which I am more unhappy for my friends than for myself." The sole standard by which Villeroy seems to have judged fiscal policy was political —whether or not it secured the state sufficient income. He not only failed to object to the existing system or to the expedients that so alarmed Bellièvre; he even seems not to have understood Bellièvre's alarm at the implications of the *droit annuel*. Although Villeroy sympathized with Bellièvre's resentment of Sully's high-handed manner, he urged his friend to give in and seal what later became the Edict of the Paulette, for Sully had promised quick profits, which Villeroy considered necessary if France's foreign policies were to be financed. Eventually Villeroy grew irritated by Bellièvre's continued efforts to obstruct fiscal edicts.[50] What mattered to the secretary—and to Henry IV and Sully— was revenue, not how it was raised.

Bellièvre and Villeroy, like their colleague Sully, subscribed
to the conventional wisdom of mercantilist theory. They favored
protecting domestic industry from foreign competition—French
woolen manufacture, for example, from English imports. Bellièvre also condemned the outflow of specie for foreign manu-
factures and luxuries,[51] but Villeroy, at least, did not always
practice the bullionist theory that his colleague preached, for he
asked the French ambassador in Venice to procure tapestries
there for him.

There were two blind spots in Bellièvre and Villeroy's economic vision. In spite of the visible profits that Spain and the
Dutch Republic were garnering from the Americas and the
Indies, the ministers showed no interest in securing France an
entree into the New World. And even when Henry IV was
briefly interested in obtaining commercial privileges in the East
Indies for French merchants. Villeroy remained indifferent. However, even Sully opposed overseas colonization—on the grounds
that the French had "neither the perseverance nor the required
foresight." The ministers also failed to understand, as did most
of their contemporaries, that the astronomic rise of prices in their
era, one of its most striking phenomena, was due largely to the
influx of New World bullion. Bellièvre and Villeroy were, of
course, aware of the importance of American treasure to Spain's
aggressive designs. Villeroy rejoiced when he heard that the English had seized a Spanish treasure fleet in 1582, and Bellièvre told
Henry IV that most of Philip II's gold was "used against your
kingdom." But they saw no connection between the circulation
of Spanish bullion in France and the rapid rise in prices. Neither,
it seems, did Sully.[52] The ministers may have ignored the price
revolution because at their level of income even a fivefold increase in the price of wine would not have been onerous. Moreover, the ministers, like men before and since, tended to pass over
what they did not understand.

Villeroy and Bellièvre nevertheless had acute insights into
other aspects of the economy. Bellièvre was fully aware of two
reasons for the slow growth of French industry and commerce.
He saw that the practice of proliferating royal offices, although
it brought immediate income from their sale, burdened the treas-

ury with salaries. His claim that "one-half of the *tailles* are employed for the payment of the [officers'] salaries" may be exaggerated, but these payments did drain off state funds that might otherwise have been used for economic expansion. He also saw that the purchasers of offices, whose price rose rapidly, were diverting their capital from productive enterprises: "Trade is forsaken," he lamented. "An infinite number of those who could serve in war and agriculture and in those activities in which the kingdom was growing rich, consume their capital and would pursue offices." Bellièvre's warnings were prophetic, for private capital for commercial and industrial ventures in France was always wanting under the *ancien régime*. Villeroy also saw that foreign commerce was a means not only of increasing national wealth but also of promoting international amity. He opposed Henry IV's tariff war with Spain because he believed that trade was "the bond that maintains society and public amity"[53]—an insight that Colbert, who believed that trade was to be fought for rather than engaged in, disastrously lacked.

# 5. Conclusion

BELLIÈVRE AND VILLEROY strove throughout their lives to create a stable and ordered society. To achieve this essentially conservative goal, they adopted means that, when implemented by their successors, were to lead to significant changes in the social structure and political system of France and in the Weltanschauung of Frenchmen. Like many men who live in troubled times, Villeroy and Bellièvre looked back to a better past while preparing for a different future.

They denounced the violence, irresponsibility, and selfishness of their contemporaries. When Richelieu suppressed dueling, when the Catholic reformers cleansed the church of abuses, and when Colbert rooted out corruption, they were applying remedies that the ministers (and many of their contemporaries) had long called for.

If Villeroy and Bellièvre correctly assessed polarization of public opinion and the monarchy's fiscal and military weakness as the principal reasons for the crown's inability to keep order, they were not always able to solve the problems that they understood so well. The endemic fiscal weakness of the monarchy was, it has been claimed, inevitable, given the limited wealth of a preindustrial society and the martial ambitions of France's kings. Retrenchment, efficiency in tax collection, and the end of such self-defeating expedients as alienation of the royal domain and the massive sale of offices—the solutions that Bellièvre recommended—would have served Henry IV just as under Colbert's direction they did Louis XIV. Although Bellièvre and Villeroy made no concrete suggestions for reforming the army, they saw that prompt payment was the key to its reliability. Bellièvre suggested a plan for reorganizing the king's councils, and never ceased to advocate the creation of an honest and reliable bureaucracy. The ministers, then, not only knew the weaknesses of Renaissance monarchy, but also proposed reforms, which in essence were implemented by subsequent generations.

In applying the theory of royal absolutism to the governing process, Bellièvre and Villeroy showed a delicate sense of the possible. The king might claim that his will was law, but until the machinery to enforce such arbitrary rule existed, the ministers—and Henry IV as well—knew that the tacit consent of powerful subjects, even if gained through compromise, was necessary for effective rule. Neglect of this dictum was to bring Mazarin face to face with the Fronde.

Dynastic patriotism, on which the polity depended, was all too rare in the ministers' day. They understood its importance in holding France together in the face of internal revolt and foreign aggression, and had a clearer concept of France than most of their contemporaries. Their own example of patriotic fervor and their use of the latent patriotism of their contemporaries to unite France against external foes strengthened this vital bond of polity.

War, which was to the *noblesse d'épée* a métier, was to the ministers an abomination. They were temperamentally opposed to war and hated its evil effects on men, morals, and nations. They had no grand design for keeping peace, but they did have specific proposals for preventing war, at least until the clarion call of patriotism or "necessity" drowned out the voice of reason. To condemn war in a court in which *gloire* was sacrosanct, was courageous as well as clearsighted.

When the ministers surveyed the European state system, they were dimly aware that the forces of dynastic patriotism had pulled asunder forever the old Christian commonwealth. Their vision of international relations encompassed both the beginnings of a state system consciously based on secular dynastic interests and the last gasp of a state system bound together by Christian unity. Villeroy and Bellièvre appeared to view foreign-policy issues strictly on grounds of reason of state, but there was in fact a religious basis to their outlook. By defining France as Europe's Most Catholic Nation, they justified her co-operation with heretic powers against the Catholic Hapsburgs. Subconsciously at least, Villeroy and Bellièvre believed *gesta Francorum, gesta Dei.*

Survival in office was no mean feat in such turbulent times as theirs. Pressures from without created tensions that the ministers withstood through close co-operation and the mutual reinforcement of friendship. To understand a royal master's strengths and weaknesses, whims and passions, was vital when power depended entirely on royal favor. To be more than ciphers, the ministers had to persuade as well as execute. Although it is impossible to prove the degree to which Bellièvre and Villeroy actually influenced the decisions of Henry III and Henry IV, the ministers' suggestions were often accepted, and in the eyes of their contemporaries their frank and often bold advice made them model ministers to absolute monarchs.

When Villeroy and Bellièvre turned to the organization of society, they accepted the hierarchical form that was the legacy of the Middle Ages but subtly shifted the concept of the functions of the hierarchy's components. The nobility, they tacitly concluded, could no longer be trusted to act as the instrument of royal rule, a conclusion that under Louis XIV led to the nobility's political emasculation. To replace the nobility the ministers looked to the clergy, who had long served the state with their talent and funds, and to a new group, the royal officials, whom they desired to make the principal instrument of royal rule. Although the great mass, the peasantry, was to continue, according to the ministers' concept, to be society's beast of burden, Bellièvre and Villeroy wisely saw that the lot of the peasant had to be improved. Bellièvre and Villeroy's concept of the roles of the elements of society was not revolutionary, but it was enlightened, and it defined those roles much as did their successors until the Revolution swept away the old hierarchy.

In accepting religious toleration the ministers, along with other *politiques,* made a leap forward. And once the leap was made, they labored to see that peace based on toleration was maintained, even if it meant abandoning the idea that religious diversity is a threat to political unity, a concept that Louis XIV could not grasp.

The ministers' economic views were, with few exceptions, in

accord with the mercantilism of their day. Bellièvre's great insight was to see the harmful effects of hereditary and venal officeholding on the supply of investment capital for commerce and industry. Villeroy's was to realize, unlike most of his contemporaries, that commerce was not only a cause of war but also a force for international unity.

Bellièvre's and Villeroy's stature in their times is attested to by their retention as royal ministers by one of France's ablest monarchs, Henry IV. Their historical reputation was earned by intelligence and dedication. They not only understood their times but suggested paths for the future that their successors either followed or should have followed. They also so devoted their lives to the service of France and her kings that it would be ungenerous to disagree with Bellièvre, who, in a rare moment of self-pity, exclaimed, "I have lived too much for others and too little for myself."[1]

Appendix

Notes

Bibliography

Index

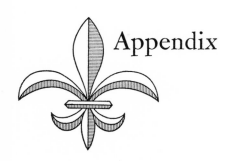

Appendix

Chronological List of Events

FRANCIS I, 1514–47; HENRY II, 1547–59; FRANCIS II, 1559–60

1529	Birth of Bellièvre in Lyons
1543	Birth of Villeroy
1559	Peace of Cateau-Cambrésis. Death of Henry II

CHARLES IX, 1560–74

1562	Outbreak of civil war
1562–73	Bellièvre ambassador to Swiss Confederation
1567	Villeroy appointed a *secrétaire d'état*
1568–69	Villeroy with Henry, duke of Anjou, on campaigns against the Huguenots
1570	Peace of Saint-Germain. Bellièvre appointed a *conseiller d'état*
1572	Massacre of Saint Bartholomew
1573–74	Bellièvre ambassador to Poland

HENRY III, 1574–89

1574	Civil war renewed
1576	Bellièvre in negotiations with Huguenots and their German Protestant allies. Peace of Monsieur
1577	War with Henry of Navarre. Peace of Bergerac negotiated by Villeroy
1578–79	Restraint of duke of Anjou in the Low Countries attempted by Bellièvre and Villeroy
1580	War of the Lovers. Peace of Fleix negotiated by Villeroy and Bellièvre
1581–82	Pacification of the Midi attempted by Bellièvre
1582	Salcedo affair

1583–84	Reconciliation of Henry and Margaret of Navarre by Bellièvre. End to disorders in the Midi sought by Bellièvre
1584	Catholic League formed
1585	War threatened by Catholic League. Peace of Nemours negotiated by Villeroy and Catherine de Medici. Henry of Navarre's conversion to Catholicism sought by Bellièvre
1586–87	Elizabeth I urged by Bellièvre to spare life of Mary Stuart. War against Henry of Navarre pursued by Henry III
1587	Placation of Guise and Catholic League attempted by Bellièvre. Villeroy attacked by duke of Epernon
1588	End to Guise's aggression against crown sought by Bellièvre. Day of the Barricades. Henry III's capitulation to the league negotiated by Villeroy and Catherine. Villeroy and Bellièvre dismissed
1589	Henry III and Henry of Navarre in alliance against Catholic League. Henry III assassinated

HENRY IV, 1589–1610

1588–93	Bellièvre in retirement at Grignon. Villeroy principal Catholic League negotiator with royalists
1590	Paris unsuccessfully besieged by Henry IV. Intervention by Spain
1591–92	Henry IV unable to clear realm of Catholic League and Spanish forces
1593	League States-General. Conversion of Henry IV. Henry IV joined by Bellièvre
1594	League abandoned by Villeroy. Villeroy appointed a *secrétaire d'état*
1594–95	Bellièvre on mission in Lyons. War on Spain declared by Henry IV
1595–97	Villeroy with Henry IV on military campaigns. Bellièvre active in financing war against Spain
1596	Catholic League dissolved
1597	Amiens recovered by Henry IV. Peace overtures made by Spain

1598	Peace of Vervins negotiated by Bellièvre, directed by Villeroy. Edict of Nantes
1599	Bellièvre appointed chancellor
1600	War with Savoy
1601–3	Bellièvre in conflict with Henry IV and Sully
1604	Tariff war with Spain. Hoste Affair. Seals lost by Bellièvre
1606	Submission of duke of Bouillon negotiated by Villeroy
1607	Death of Bellièvre
1607–9	French mediation of Twelve Year Truce between Spain and Dutch republic supervised by Villeroy
1609–10	Juliers-Cleves dispute
1610	Henry IV assassinated

LOUIS XIII, 1610–43 (MARIE DE MEDICI REGENT, 1610–17)

1610	War with Hapsburgs abandoned
1614	Last States-General meeting until 1789
1616	Villeroy dismissed by Concini
1617	Villeroy returned to power by Louis XIII. Death of Villeroy

Notes

Abbreviations

CCC	Cinq Cents Colbert, Bibliothèque Nationale
CSP	Great Britain, *Calendar of State Papers*
Desjardins	Desjardins, ed., *Négociations*
Dupuy	Fonds Dupuy, Bibliothèque Nationale
ER	Sully, *Mémoires des . . . royales œconomies*
FF	Fonds Français, Bibliothèque Nationale
F. It.	Fonds Italien, Bibliothèque Nationale
HMC	Great Britain, Historical Manuscripts Commission
LCM	Catherine de Medici, *Lettres*
LM	Henry IV, *Lettres missives*
Mornay	Mornay, *Mémoires*
NAF	Nouvelles Acquisitions Françaises, Bibliothèque Nationale
Négociations	Jeannin, *Négociations*

1. The Men and Their Times

1. The early history of the Bellièvre family has been studied in Kierstead, *Bellièvre*, pp. 9–24 passim.

2. See Sutherland, *Secretaries*, pp. 150–51; Kierstead, *Bellièvre*, pp. 14, 17–18.

3. Kierstead, *Bellièvre*, pp. 24–32.

4. Sutherland, *Secretaries*, pp. 151–57.

5. Quoted in Nouaillac, *Villeroy*, p. 270.

6. Quoted in Sutherland, *Secretaries*, p. 156.

7. Bellièvre to Nevers, Oct. 1586, FF 3372, fol. 218. Villeroy to Bellièvre, 23 Oct. 1590, FF 15909, fol. 333.

8. Bellièvre to Villeroy, 28 Oct. 1594, FF 15893, fol. 201; Bellièvre to Loménie, 15 Aug. 1603, FF 15894, fol. 574. Bellièvre to Henry III, 25 June 1576, FF 15890, fols. 427–30. Bellièvre to Casimir, 11 and 22 Aug. 1576, Dupuy 502, fols. 108–10; FF 15890, fol. 448. Catherine to Bellièvre, 8 Aug. 1576, *LCM*, 5:212. Walsingham to Wilson, 2 Sept. 1578, *CSP, Foreign* [1578–79], p. 71. For a sparse account of these negotiations, see Kierstead, *Bellièvre*, pp. 41–45. Bellièvre to Montmorency, 5 Aug. 1584, FF 15891, fol. 361.

9. Bellièvre to Elizabeth, [Jan. 1587], FF 15892, fols. 79–81; his reply, however, may never have been sent. Elizabeth to Henry III, Jan. 1587, *CSP, Foreign* [1586–87], p. 184. Bellièvre to Henry IV, 7 Sept. 1594, FF 15912, fol. 44. Idem, 9 Nov. 1594, FF 15912, fol. 130. Idem, 11 Dec. 1594, FF 15912, fols. 160–61. Bellièvre to Villeroy, 28 Oct. 1594, FF 15893, fol. 201.

10. Villeroy to Bellièvre, 28 Nov. 1580, FF 15905, fol. 530. Villeroy was even afraid to enter Paris when Mayenne was absent (Villeroy, *Mémoires*, p. 160). Villeroy to Bellièvre, 29 Apr. 1589, FF 15909, fol. 252. Idem, 17 Aug. 1591, FF 15909, fol. 407. Villeroy to Nevers, 22 Mar. 1597, FF 7784, fol. 295; Villeroy to Montmorency, 24 Mar. 1597, FF 3548, fol. 49. Villeroy to Fresnes, 22 Nov. 1600, FF 23196, fol. 171. Villeroy to Montmorency, 22 Mar. 1601, FF 3581, fol. 5. Idem, 6 Mar. 1603, FF 3208, fol. 69.

11. Villeroy, *Mémoires*, p. 162. Bellièvre to [Revol], 21 Mar. 1593, FF 15893, fol. 100. Villeroy to Bellièvre, 23 Nov. 1590, FF 15909, fol. 338.

12. Mendoza to Philip II, 2 Aug. 1589, quoted in Baguenault de Puchesse, "Philippe II," p. 45.

13. Henry forbade the count of Soissons to duel with Sully [late Aug. 1603], *LM*, 6:157–58. "Discours de ce qui se passa lundy xxvi d'octobre au logis de Mons. le Chancelier a la chambre du conseil entre Mons. d'Espernon et le sr. de Rosny," FF 3456, fols. 44–45; Contarini, 31 Oct. 1598, F. It. 1747, fols. 128–29; Du Maurier to Mornay, 21 Nov. 1598, Mornay, 9:185. Villeroy to Mornay, 8 Nov. 1597, Mornay, 7:387. Sully, *ER*, 2:334–42. Bellièvre to Sillery, 14 July 1600, FF 15894, fol. 405. Villeroy to Montmorency, 7 Sept. 1600, FF 3591, fol. 140.

14. Sir Edward Stafford, the English ambassador to France, considered Bellièvre "the honestest plain man that this State hath . . ." (Stafford to Walsingham, 25 Oct. 1584, *CSP, Foreign* [1584–85], p. 117); Villeroy he considered "not to be covetous . . ." (Stafford to Walsingham, 17 July 1584, *CSP, Foreign* [1583–84], p. 621. Staf-

ford to Walsingham, 18 and 23 Sept. 1584, *CSP, Foreign* [1584–85], pp. 69, 72; Morosini, 12 Oct. 1584, F. It. 1733, fol. 476; Busini to Vinta, 2 Oct. 1584, Desjardins, 4:532. Cheverny to Nevers, 7 Apr. 1588, FF 3407, fol. 63. Nouaillac, *Villeroy*, p. 285.

15. Henry IV to Bellièvre, 1 Aug. 1602, *Lettres . . . 1581–1601*, p. 28. Bellièvre to Henry IV, 11 July 1602, FF 15894, fol. 530; Villeroy to Bellièvre, 18 July 1602, FF 15896, fol. 324. Villeroy to Servières, 1 Aug. 1602, FF 16912, fol. 49. See also Villeroy to Béthune, 1 Aug. 1602, FF 4017, fol. 84.

16. Louis d'Orléans to Bellièvre, 18 Apr. 1603, FF 15900, fols. 440–41. Bellièvre and Sillery to Villeroy, 26 Feb. 1598, Mornay, 8:105. Villeroy to Bellièvre, 17 Apr. 1603, FF 15896, fol. 404. Nouaillac, "Retraite," pp. 142–45, 150.

17. Mariéjol, *Daughter*, pp. 164–71. Thou, *Histoire*, 10:24; Giovannini, 26 Dec. 1604, Desjardins, 5:550. Villeroy to Bellièvre, 26 Oct. 1588, FF 15909, fol. 205. Idem, 1 Mar. 1589, FF 15909, fol. 239. Villeroy was a proud father when he bade his son good-by (Villeroy to Bellièvre, 11 June 1605, FF 15896, fol. 511). Giovannini, 14 Nov. 1604, Desjardins, 5:546.

18. For a good account of his family interests, see Kierstead, *Bellièvre*, pp. 137–47. Sillery to Bellièvre, 17 Nov. 1599, FF 15900, fol. 102; Kierstead, *Bellièvre*, p. 145. Villeroy to Bellièvre, 8 Apr. 1606, FF 15896, fol. 530. Nouaillac, "Retraite," pp. 142–45. Bellièvre to Henry IV, 22 Sept. 1590; Bellièvre to Fresnes, 28 Sept. 1590, FF 15892, fols. 295, 296–97.

19. Villeroy to Jeannin, 8 Dec. 1607, *Négociations*, p. 230. Bellièvre and Sillery to Montmorency, 2 Oct. 1598, FF 3574, fols. 59–60. Villeroy to Henry IV, 17 Nov. 1599, FF 23195, fol. 434; Villeroy to Boissise, 24 Nov. 1599, FF 4128, fol. 124; Nouaillac, *Villeroy*, p. 287. Bellièvre to Catherine, 10 Sept. and 8 Dec. 1588, FF 15892, fols. 175–76, 220.

20. Villeroy, *Mémoires*, pp. 152, 213; Villeroy to Fleury, 18 Apr. 1592, Mornay, 5:300. Bellièvre to the duke of Nemours, 27 July 1594, "Lettres," p. 316. Nemours to Bellièvre, 28 July 1594, ibid.

21. Mariéjol, *Catherine*, p. 372. Dodu, "Henry III." Villeroy described his failing health (Villeroy to Maisse, 16 Mar. 1584, FF 16092, fol. 208). Henry almost died of bladder stones in 1603 (Villeroy to Bellièvre, 22 May 1603, FF 15896, fol. 408; Cavalli, 25 May 1603, F. It. 1752, fol. 57).

22. Villeroy to Brulart, 6 Oct. 1584, CCC 9, fol. 159. Pruili, 28 Aug. and 30 Sept. 1606, F. It. 1755, fols. 85, 118. Villeroy to Maisse, 30 Mar.

1585, FF 16092, fols. 353–54; Villeroy to Joyeuse, 4 Jan. 1607, FF 6633, fol. 64.

23. Bellièvre to [?], Dec. 1592, FF 15893, fols. 44–45. Bellièvre to Cardinal de Medici, 26 Oct. 1597, FF 15893, fol. 458. Bellièvre to [?], Dec. 1592, FF 15893, fols. 44–45.

24. During the Assembly of Notables at Rouen, Henry IV hunted while Villeroy and Bellièvre dealt with the delegates (Henry IV to Montmorency, 15, 17, and 20 Nov. 1596, *LM*, 4:659–61; William Lilly to Essex, 13 Dec. 1596, HMC, *Salisbury*, 6:519); Bellièvre, when he wished to discuss the impending peace talks with Spain, dined with the king, whom he found to have "hunting on his mind" (Bellièvre to Villeroy, 27 Dec. 1597, FF 15893, fol. 467).

25. In her study of the secretaries of state during the years from 1547 to 1588, N. M. Sutherland reveals the existence of general co-operation and harmonious relations between the twelve secretaries but finds only one potentially close relationship, that between Claude Laubespine, Catherine de Medici's favorite secretary, and his brother-in-law Villeroy. These two men "would undoubtedly have formed a strong, unique and remarkable partnership in the state" (*Secretaries*, pp. 157–58) but were prevented from doing so by Laubespine's premature death. Orest Ranum's study of Richelieu and his *créatures*—the secretaries of state Chavigny and Sublet de Noyers, and the superintendents of finance Bullion and Bouthillier—proves that Richelieu's subordinates co-operated with each other but also shows that Chavigny and Sublet "did not always remain on good terms" (*Richelieu*, p. 88); moreover, both men's relations with Bullion revolved not around friendship but around their desire to remain in Bullion's good graces (ibid., p. 161).

26. Nouaillac, *Villeroy*, pp. 281–300.

27. Ranum, *Richelieu*, pp. 27–44.

28. Stafford to Burghley, 17 Nov. 1586, *CSP, Foreign* [1586–88], p. 146. Mendoza to Philip II, 11 May 1586, *CSP, Spanish*, 4:574.

29. Villeroy to Bellièvre, 14 Jan. 1591, FF 15909, fol. 354.

30. Idem, 26 June 1576, FF 15904, fol. 166. Villeroy to Mauvissière, 28 June 1576, CCC 472, fol. 43. Bellièvre to Montmorency, 5 Aug. 1584, FF 15891, fol. 361. Villeroy to Bellièvre, 16 Apr. 1584, FF 15907, fol. 417. Idem, 21 July 1584, FF 15907, fol. 516. Idem, 9 Mar. 1581, FF 15906, vol. 1, fol. 245. Bellièvre to Villeroy, 27 and 28 May 1587, FF 15892, fols. 119–22.

31. Villeroy to Bellièvre, 17 June, 1574, FF 15903, fol. 75. Bellièvre to Epernon, [Nov. 1587], FF 15892, fol. 137. Sutherland, *Secretaries*,

p. 238. Villeroy to Bellièvre, 3 Aug. 1582, FF 15906, vol. 2, fols. 729–30. Villeroy to Henry III, 31 Aug. 1582, FF 6628, fol. 123. Bellièvre to the duke of Anjou, [Oct. 1582], FF 15891, fols. 299–300. Villeroy to Bellièvre, 5 and 26 Oct. 1588, FF 15909, fols. 188, 205. Idem, 28 Sept. 1588, FF 15909, fols. 178–79. Idem, 6 Jan. 1589, FF 15909, fol. 226. Villeroy to Nevers, 7 Apr. 1589, FF 3629, fol. 129. Bellièvre to Villeroy, 11 Mar. 1589, FF 15892, fol. 329.

32. Idem, 28 Aug. 1584, FF 4736, fol. 231. Idem, 23 Dec. 1586, FF 15892, fol. 57. Villeroy to Bellièvre, 24 Dec. 1587, FF 15908, fol. 534. Idem, 8 June 1582, FF 15566, fol. 13; idem, 10 Dec. 1587, FF 15908, fol. 529.

33. Bellièvre to Villeroy, 2 Jan. 1590, FF 15892, fol. 359; if any were sent, none has survived.

34. Villeroy to Bellièvre, 12 Mar. [1589], FF 15909, fol. 241. Bellièvre to Villeroy, 18 Nov. 1590, FF 15892, fol. 387. Bellièvre to [?], [1591], FF 15892, fol. 487; Bellièvre to [?], 21 Mar. 1593, FF 15893, fol. 100. Idem, [1591], FF 15892, fols. 487–88. Villeroy to Bellièvre, 23 Nov. 1590, FF 15909, fol. 338.

35. Villeroy to Bellièvre, 2 Jan. 1590, FF 15909, fol. 282. Idem, [early 1590], FF 15909, fol. 284. Bellièvre to Villeroy, 26 Mar. 1592, FF 15892, fol. 20. Bellièvre to [?], 12 Apr. 1592, FF 15893, fol. 24.

36. Villeroy to Bellièvre, 24 Mar. 1589, FF 15909, fol. 247. Bellièvre to Cheverny, [1590], 13 Jan. 1591, FF 15892, fols. 357, 440. Villeroy to Bellièvre, 19 Jan. and 14 and 17 Aug. 1591, 3 and 7 Jan. 1592, FF 15909, fols. 355, 405, 407, 440, 441. Idem, 13 Feb. [1591], FF 15909, fol. 366. Idem, 6 and 13 Feb. 1591, FF 15909, fols. 365, 366. Idem, 17 Feb. 1591, FF 15909, fol. 373. Idem, 12 May 1591, FF 15909, fol. 382.

37. Villeroy to Bellièvre, 12 Mar. 1589, FF 15909, fol. 241; "it seems to be that if we wait until all is lost before doing what we must for the general welfare, we will answer for it before God, and that He will also reproach us for shame, not to mention the fact that we will be a party to the evil that will not spare those who remain patiently in their homes any more than, and perhaps less than, the others." Bellièvre to Jeannin, 7 Mar. 1589; Bellièvre to Mayenne, 29 May 1589, FF 15892, fols. 327, 335. Bellièvre to Jacques Faye d'Espesses, 14 July 1590; Bellièvre to Cheverny, July 1590, FF 15892, fols. 289–90, 373. When Henry IV's Protestant adviser, Mornay, heard of Bellièvre's nomination, he opposed it, perhaps from jealousy, since he had earlier in the year treated with Villeroy (Jacques Faye d'Espesses to Bellièvre, 17 Aug. 1590, FF 15909, fol. 317). Bellièvre to Faye d'Espesses, 12 Aug. 1590, FF 15892, fols. 375–76. Ibid., fol. 375. Bellièvre to Henry IV,

[late 1590]; memoir, [late 1590], FF 15892, fols. 400, 402–10. Villeroy
to Bellièvre, 14 Jan. 1591, FF 15909, fol. 354. Bellièvre to [?], [1591],
FF 15892, fol. 484.

38. Mornay to Buzanval, 28 Sept. 1594, Mornay, 6:92. Bellièvre to
Gondy, [early 1593], FF 15893, fol. 119. Villeroy to Mayenne, 2 Jan.
1594, Villeroy, *Mémoires*, pp. 254–55. Henry IV to Brèves, 20 Mar.
1594, *LM*, 4:119. Villeroy to Bellièvre, 9 Apr. 1594, FF 15910, fol. 84.
Bellièvre to Villeroy, Oct. 1594, FF 15912, fol. 124.

39. See Kierstead, *Bellièvre*, pp. 76–89. Villeroy to Bellièvre, [early
1595], FF 15910, fol. 374. Villeroy to Bellièvre and Sillery, 1 May
1598, Mornay, 8:418. Bellièvre and Sillery to Villeroy, 12 May 1598,
Mornay, 8:510.

40. "If you were beside the king we would be relieved of the trouble of writing so much…" (Villeroy to Bellièvre, 29 May 1601, FF
15896, fol. 317). See Kierstead, *Bellièvre*, pp. 124–34.

41. Villeroy to Bellièvre, 29 Nov. 1602, FF 15896, fol. 375. Idem,
8 Dec. 1602, FF 15896, fol. 379. Idem, 13 Dec. 1602, FF 15896, fol. 377.
Idem, 19 Mar. 1603, FF 15896, fol. 390. Idem, 15 May 1603, FF 15896,
fol. 407.

42. Badoer, 7 and 21 Jan. and 17 Feb. 1604, F. It. 1752, fols. 178, 187,
205; Giovannini, 28 Dec. 1603, Desjardins, 5:519; Bufalo, 29 Dec. 1603
and 10 Jan. 1604, *Correspondance*, pp. 632, 642. Giovannini, 26 Feb.
1604, Desjardins, 5:525. Villeroy to Bellièvre, 22 Oct. and 5 Nov.
1605, FF 15896, fols. 523, 528. Bellièvre to Villeroy, 30 Apr. 1604,
NAF 5129, fol. 56. See below, p. 114. Bellièvre to Cardinal Du Perron,
1 Jan. 1605, FF 15894, fol. 607. Villeroy to Bellièvre, 8 Apr. 1606, FF
15896, fol. 530. Villeroy to Jeannin, 19 Sept. 1607, *Négociations*, p.
150.

43. Sutherland, *Secretaries*, pp. 153–54. Kierstead, *Bellièvre*, pp. 13,
24–25.

44. Mastellone, *Reggenza*, p. 125. Bellièvre to Villeroy, [Aug.]
1598, FF 15894, fol. 149. Cardinal de Medici to Clement VIII, 28 Dec.
1596, Leo XI, *Lettres*, p. 98. Kierstead, *Bellièvre*, p. 25. Bellièvre to
Gregory XIV, [1591], FF 15892, fols. 491–537. Brulart to Bellièvre, 19
Feb. 1583, *LCM*, 8:419. Mattingly, *Diplomacy*, pp. 204–5.

45. Villeroy to Bongars, 20 Apr. 1597, Anquez, *Henri IV*, p. 48.
"Un escrit contre la convocation des prétendus estats de la Ligue," FF
15893, fols. 68–96 passim. Bellièvre to [?], Nov. 1593, FF 15893, fol.
108. Bellièvre to the bishop of Evreux, Sept. 1599, Dupuy 194, fol. 87.
Bellièvre to Epernon, 20 July 1594, FF 15912, fol. 8. "Touchant les
divisions de la Chrétienté," FF 15892, fol. 11. Bellièvre to [?], 24 Feb.

1591, FF 15892, fols. 442–44. Bellièvre to Henry III, 18 Nov. 1581, FF 15891, fol. 270. Bellièvre to Catherine, 29 Aug. 1583, FF 15891, fol. 316. Bellièvre to Henry IV, 29 Apr. 1596, FF 15893, fol. 340.

46. Bellièvre to [?], [early 1589], FF 15892, fol. 307; Bellièvre to Jeannin, 7 Mar. 1589, FF 15892, fol. 327. Bellièvre to [?], 18 Oct. 1606, FF 15894, fols. 611–12. Bellièvre to the bishop of Evreux, 3 July 1600, Du Perron, *Ambassades*, p. 244. Sutherland describes Villeroy's chateau in *Secretaries*, pp. 154–55. Villeroy to Mauvissière, 21 June 1582, CCC 472, fol. 107. Villeroy to Brèves, 18 Sept. 1606, FF 3541, fol. 11; Sutherland, *Secretaries*, p. 155. Villeroy to Montmorency, 6 June 1608, FF 3605, fol. 9. Sutherland, *Secretaries*, p. 155. Villeroy to Saint-Sulpice, 27 May 1578, Cabié, *Guerres*, p. 405.

47. Mornay to Montaigne, 18 Dec. 1583, Mornay, 2:394. Bellièvre to Du Haillan, 17 Apr. 1593, FF 20480, fol. 163. See Ossat's letters to Villeroy in Ossat, *Lettres*. Villeroy wrote Du Perron before the debate with Mornay: "Having God and the king with you, all other assistance is superfluous..." (Villeroy to Du Perron, 5 Apr. 1600, *Ambassades*, p. 77). Villeroy to Sillery, 17 June 1599, FF 15777, fol. 233. Sutherland, *Secretaries*, p. 155.

48. Hexter, "Education," pp. 65–70. Wiley, *Gentleman*, chap. 6. Stone, *Crisis*, pp. 303–31. Mousnier, *Séguier*, 1:21–183, especially pp. 180–82.

2. The State and Government

1. Major, "Renaissance Monarchy," p. 112.
2. Pagès, *Monarchie*, pp. 3–13.
3. Major, "Renaissance Monarchy," pp. 112–24.
4. Villeroy to Maisse, 30 Mar. 1585, FF 16092, fols. 353–54. Villeroy to Bellièvre, 26 Feb. 1581, FF 15906, vol. 1, fol. 198. Bellièvre to Mayenne, 16 Jan. 1576, CCC 8, fols. 20–21. Villeroy to Bellièvre, 3 Mar. 1581, FF 15906, vol. 1, fol. 290. Villeroy to Maisse, 20 Dec. 1585, FF 16082, fol. 454. Bellièvre to Henry III, 15 Dec. 1587, FF 15892, fols. 131–32. Villeroy to Maisse, 14 Feb. 1586, FF 16093, fol. 26.
5. The roles of Villeroy and Bellièvre in the diplomacy of the period are discussed in Sutherland, *Secretaries*, and Kierstead, *Bellièvre*.
6. See Nouaillac, *Villeroy*, pp. 159–264.
7. Villeroy and Bellièvre approved this policy.
8. "Réponse de Henri IV aux remonstrances du Parlement sur le

rétablissement des jésuites," 24 Dec. 1603, *LM*, 6:182–85. Henry IV to [Biron], 14 and 31 May 1602, *LM*, 5:594, 602–3. Henry IV to Sully, 3 Nov. 1602, *LM*, 5:689. Villeroy to Béthune, 15 Jan. 1603, Henry IV, *Correspondance*, pp. 343–44. Henry IV to [Bouillon], 18 Nov. 1602, *LM*, 5:696–97. Henry IV to La Force, 5 Sept. 1605, *LM*, 6:513. Henry IV to Sully, 1 Apr. 1606, *LM*, 6:596.

9. Bellièvre to Revol, Mar. 1592, FF 15893, fol. 22. Villeroy to Bellièvre, 12 Mar. [1592], FF 15909, fol. 376. Villeroy to Maisse, 12 Apr. 1586, FF 16093, fol. 45.

10. Bellièvre to Catherine, 6 Jan. 1581, *LCM*, 7:456. Villeroy to Bellièvre and Sillery, 16 Feb. 1598, Mornay, 8:80. Villeroy to Bellièvre, 12 Dec. 1576, FF 15904, fol. 375. Bellièvre to Henry III, 9 Mar. 1581, FF 15891, fol. 163. Bellièvre to Bishop Gondy, [1592], FF 15893, fol. 64. Villeroy to Béthune, 28 Aug. 1602, Henry IV, *Correspondance*, p. 279. Villeroy to Brèves, 22 Mar. 1609, FF 3541, fol. 29. Bellièvre to [?], 21 Sept. 1583, FF 15891, fol. 308. Villeroy to Montmorency, 30 July 1600, FF 3591, fol. 115.

11. Mousnier, "Conseil du roi," p. 40. Pagès, "Conseil du roi." See the Venetian ambassadors' reports: Moro, 18 May 1582, F. It. 1732, fol. 330; Dolfin, 15 Mar. 1585, F. It. 1734, fol. 5; Cavalli, 6 Sept. 1600, F. It. 1749, fol. 105.

12. See Mousnier, "Sully." Bellièvre to Villeroy, 31 May 1603, FF 15894, fols. 563–64.

13. Mornay to Navarre, 9 Mar. 1584, Mornay, 2:554. Stafford to Walsingham, 27 Feb. 1584, *CSP, Foreign* [1583–84], p. 370. Morosini, 18 May 1582, F. It. 1732, fol. 330. Wolf, *Louis XIV*, pp. 164–65. Morosini, 7 Feb. 1577, *CSP, Venetian*, 7:555. Mornay to Navarre, 20 Feb. 1584, Mornay, 2:532. Stafford to Walsingham, 10 Apr. 1585, *CSP, Foreign* [1584–85], p. 410; Dolfin, 29 June 1585, F. It. 1734, fols. 147–48. Stafford to Elizabeth, 22 Jan. 1587, *CSP, Foreign* [1586–87], p. 193; Dolfin, 7 May 1587, F. It. 1736, fol. 55. Stafford to Elizabeth, 5 Apr. 1588, *CSP, Foreign* [1586–88], p. 583; Mocenigo, 6 May 1588, F. It. 1737, fol. 55; Stafford to Elizabeth, 8 May 1588, *CSP, Foreign* [1586–88], p. 604; Mendoza to Philip II, 8 May 1588, *CSP, Spanish*, 4:277.

14. Giovannini, 8 July 1600, Desjardins, 5:430. Foscarini, 9 and 14 Feb. 1610, F. It. 1761, fols. 225–26, 227; Aarssens to Mornay, 13 Feb. 1610, Mornay, 10:544; Pecquius to the archduke, 10 Feb. 1610, Aumale, *Condé*, pp. 355–56. Sillery to Villeroy, 23 and 26 Apr. 1602, FF 15577, fols. 131, 136. *ER*, 2:525–30. Contarini, 12 Feb. 1600, F. It. 1748, fol. 194; *ER*, 2:323–25.

15. Ragazzoni to Cardinal Rusticucci, 8 and 25 Nov. 1585, *Ragaz-zoni*, pp. 471, 482.

16. Henry IV to Bellièvre, 19 Feb. 1604, *LM*, 6: 199.

17. See a rather harsh critique of early institutional historians in Ranum, *Richelieu*, pp. 4–5, 45–46. A papal legate described the dispersion of the ministers: "The king does not settle down either in a stable residence or in Paris. It follows that all the councillors are dispersed, some being in the country, part with the king, and part in Paris" (Cardinal de Medici to Clement VIII, 10 Sept. 1596, Leo XI, *Lettres*, p. 73). The locations of the ministers, as indicated by the addresses of the correspondence, prove that they could not have met regularly in a council.

18. Sutherland, *Secretaries*, pp. 39–43. Bellièvre to Villeroy, [summer 1597], FF 15893, fol. 453. Sully to Jeannin, 26 Feb. 1608, *Négociations*, p. 282. Villeroy to Bellièvre, 17 July 1604, FF 15896, fol. 465. See Mastellone, *Reggenza*, pp. 123–67, and Tapié, pp. 11–64. Ibid., pp. 65–298. Ranum, *Richelieu*, pp. 10–44. Wolf, *Louis XIV*, pp. 134–35; "Each of the cardinals had developed a 'team' made up of relatives and friends who were dependent on him, and who worked with him to manage the government of the kingdom as well as the king or regent." Ibid., pp. 135–67.

19. Vaissière, *Henri IV*, p. 376.

20. Hanotaux, *Richelieu*, pp. 540–41. Hauser, *Modernité*, pp. 41–42. Drouot, *Mayenne*, 1: 127–32; 2: 183–88, 367–73, 484–85. Mattingly, *Diplomacy*, p. 140. André Duchesne, *Les antiquitez et recherches de la grandeur et majesté des roys de France* (Paris, 1609), p. 128, quoted in Mousnier, *Assassinat*, p. 227.

21. Drouot, *Mayenne*, 2: 455. Mariéjol, *Henri IV*, pp. 41–43. Braudel, *Méditerranée*, pp. 1066–67. See Porshnev, *Soulèvements*. Mousnier, "Recherches." See Kossman, *Fronde*.

22. Stafford to Walsingham, 25 Oct. 1584, *CSP, Foreign* [1584–85], p. 117. Idem, 24 Mar. 1587, *CSP, Foreign* [1586–88], p. 255. Aarssens to the States-General, 15 Aug. 1599, Buzanval, *Lettres*, p. 262. Henry of Navarre to Bellièvre, Nov. 1584, *LM*, 1: 692. Bellièvre to Bouillon, 22 June 1592, FF 15893, fol. 40. Villeroy to Bellièvre, 14 Aug. [1591], FF 15909, fol. 405.

23. Bellièvre to Nevers, 5 Nov. 1593, FF 3987, fol. 21. Villeroy to Bellièvre, 24 Aug. 1593, FF 15910, fol. 46.

24. Villeroy to Bellièvre, 14 Jan. [1591], FF 15909, fol. 354.

25. Bellièvre to Nevers, 20 Sept. 1586, FF 3372, fol. 214. Bellièvre to Henry IV, 2 Jan. 1595, FF 15912, fols. 167–68. Villeroy's "Avis de

1611," CCC 17, fol. 40. Villeroy to Joyeuse, 15 Feb. 1606, NAF 2750, fol. 141.

26. Bellièvre to Nevers, 20 Sept. 1586, FF 3372, fol. 214. Bellièvre to Morvilliers, 19 June 1576, FF 15890, fol. 417. Bellièvre to Villeroy, 3 Dec. 1586, NAF 5128, fol. 95. Villeroy to Maisse, 13 Sept. 1585, FF 16092, fol. 416.

27. Bellièvre to Catherine, 12 July 1574, FF 4736, fol. 83. Bellièvre to Cheverny, 7 Dec. 1588, FF 15892, fol. 218. Villeroy to Maisse, 15 Dec. 1597, quoted in Kermaingant, *Boissise*, 1:146–47. Bellièvre to Villeroy, 30 June 1597, FF 15893, fol. 454. Henry IV to Sillery, 13 Dec. 1597, *Lettres*, ed. Galitzin, p. 251. Bellièvre and Sillery to Villeroy, 26 Feb. 1598, Mornay, 8:102.

28. Bellièvre to Henry IV, Sept. 1600, FF 15894, fol. 371. Nouaillac, *Villeroy*, pp. 452–60. Bellièvre to Villeroy, 10 Aug. 1595, FF 15912, fols. 260–61. Villeroy to Bellièvre, 22 June 1583, FF 15907, fol. 121; Villeroy to Maisse, 23 July 1583, FF 16092, fol. 121.

29. Mariéjol, *Catherine*, pp. 253–57. Bellièvre to Sillery, 28 June 1600, FF 15894, fol. 403.

30. Villeroy to Nevers, 13 June 1588, quoted in L'Epinois, "Réconciliation," p. 79. Bellièvre to [?], 1 Aug. 1589, FF 15892, fol. 339. Villeroy to Henry IV, 7 Nov. 1601, Dupuy 89, fol. 60. Villeroy to Nevers, 15 Oct. 1589, FF 3977, fol. 312. "Advis de M. de Villeroy à M. le duc de Mayenne," Villeroy, *Mémoires*, p. 223. Ibid., p. 208. Mocenigo, 7 Feb. 1594, F. It. 1742, fols. 127–28. Villeroy to Mornay, 26 Dec. 1594, Mornay, 6:127. Bellièvre to [Sillery], 23 July 1599, FF 15894, fol. 317.

31. Allen, *History*, pp. 302–31.

32. Mesnard, *XVIe siècle*, pp. 371–85.

33. See Church, *Constitutional Thought*, especially chaps. 4, 6.

34. "Avis de 1611," CCC 17, fol. 40. Villeroy to Bellièvre, 27 Nov. 1591, FF 15909, fol. 427. Villeroy to Maisse, 24 Apr. 1587, FF 16093, fol. 157. Bellièvre to Villeroy, 22 Mar. 1587, FF 15892, fol. 116. Bellièvre to Nevers, 10 Nov. 1594, FF 3622, fols. 137–38; Villeroy to Mornay, 26 Dec. 1594, Mornay, 6:127. Bellièvre to Buhy, 21 June 1590, FF 15892, fol. 369. Bellièvre to Henry IV, 22 June 1601, Dupuy 194, fol. 94. Villeroy to Nemours, 3 Dec. 1609, FF 3651, fol. 40. Villeroy to Jeannin, 24 Aug. 1607, *Négociations*, p. 133.

35. Villeroy to Bongars, 27 Dec. 1594, FF 15591, fol. 355. Bellièvre to [?], 1 Aug. 1589, FF 15892, fol. 339. See Mousnier, *Assassinat*, pp. 201–8. Bellièvre to Henry IV, 2 Jan. 1595, FF 15912, fol. 167. Memoir on the trial of Biron, 1 July 1602, FF 15894, fol. 174.

36. Bellièvre to Elizabeth, [Jan. 1587], FF 15892, fols. 79–81. Villeroy to Béthune, 1 Aug. 1602, FF 4017, fol. 85.

37. Bellièvre to Catherine, 30 Sept. 1588, FF 15892, fol. 191. Villeroy to Bellièvre and Sillery, 16 Feb. 1598, Mornay, 8:80. Villeroy to La Boderie, 20 Mar. 1610, CCC 475, fol. 355. Bellièvre to [?], 1 Aug. 1589, FF 15892, fol. 339. Villeroy to Maisse, 13 Sept. 1585, FF 16092, fol. 416. Villeroy to Mornay, 26 Feb. 1596, Mornay, 6:460. Church, *Constitutional Thought*, chap. 6.

38. Villeroy to Maisse, 12 June 1584, FF 16092, fol. 239. Bellièvre to Nevers, 20 Sept. 1586, FF 3372, fol. 214. Villeroy to Maisse, 4 Jan. 1586, FF 16093, fol. 3. Bellièvre to Catherine, 27 May and 3 June 1585, FF 15891, fols. 403, 411. See, e.g., "La réponse du roi de Navarre à Henri III," [Jan.–Feb.] 1588, Mornay, 4:183–85. Villeroy to the king of Navarre, 12 May 1588, FF 3430, fols. 60–68.

39. Villeroy to Bellièvre, 14 Aug. [1591], FF 15909, fol. 405; Villeroy to [?], 25 Sept. 1589, FF 3409, fols. 23–24. Nouaillac, *Villeroy*, pp. 175–76. Villeroy, *Mémoires*, p. 208. Villeroy to Fleury, 27 Mar. 1592, Mornay, 5:249. "Harangue faicte par M. de Villeroy, pour estre prononcée en l'assemblée des prétendus estats de Paris, 1593," *Mémoires*, p. 242.

40. Bellièvre to Jeannin, 13 Dec. 1592, "Lettre." Bellièvre, Chauvigny, Bourges, Schomberg, and Revol to Messrs. de la Ligue, 23 June 1593, FF 15893, fol. 125. Bellièvre to Biron, 13 May 1592, FF 15893, fol. 30.

41. Major, "French Renaissance Monarchy." Thou, *Histoire*, 5:355. Villeroy to Bellièvre, 12 Dec. 1576, FF 15904, fol. 375. Villeroy to Saint-Sulpice, 30 Jan. 1577, Cabié, *Guerres*, p. 328. Villeroy to Bellièvre, 26 Oct. 1588, FF 15909, fol. 205.

42. See States-General, *Procès-verbaux*. Ibid., p. 21. "Harangue . . . ," Villeroy, *Mémoires*, p. 254. "Un escrit contre la convocation des pretendus estats de la Ligue," FF 15893, fols. 68–96. Bellièvre to Nevers, 24 Aug. 1593, FF 3985, fol. 101.

43. Mariéjol, *Catherine*, p. 292. Déclaration du roy, 13 Mar. 1579, FF 15905, fols. 4–6. Bellièvre to Matignon, 24 Nov. 1578, FF 3389, fol. 91. Bellièvre to Henry III, 10 Mar. 1579, FF 15891, fol. 36. Bellièvre to Matignon, 1 Apr. 1579, FF 3291, fol. 161.

44. Villeroy to Hautefort, 2 Nov. 1583, FF 15566, fol. 168. Villeroy to Bellièvre, 22 Nov. 1583, FF 15907, fol. 270. He promised in a declaration of 4 Aug. 1589 to convene a States-General within six months, but never did so. Henry IV to Bellièvre, 20 and 24 May 1596, *Lettres . . . 1581–1601*, pp. 215, 217. Bellièvre and the constable [Mont-

morency] to Henry IV, 26 June 1596, FF 15893, fol. 351; Henry IV to Bellièvre, 26 June 1596, *LM*, 4:609. Villeroy to Bellièvre, 27 July 1596, FF 15910, fol. 347. Henry IV to the Assembly of Notables, Nov. 1596, *LM*, 4:657.

45. Mastellone, *Reggenza*, p. 109.

46. Villeroy to Bongars, July 1598, cited in Anquez, *Henri IV*, p. 62 (italics added).

47. Bellièvre to the Parlement of Paris, [1599], FF 15894, fol. 389. See Kierstead, *Bellièvre*, pp. 108–12. Bellièvre to . . . , 8 Oct. 1603, FF 15894, fol. 577. Bellièvre to Henry IV, 20 Aug. 1602, FF 15577, fol. 273. Bellièvre to Montmorency, 30 Sept. 1595, FF 3552, fols. 17–18.

48. Pastor, *History*, 19:523. See Mariéjol, "Réforme," pp. 212–37. Dodu, in "Henri III," collects the contemporary evidence and offers an attempt at a psychological analysis. Lafue, *Henri III*, p. 294.

49. Stafford claimed that it was Villeroy "upon whom the King reposeth the whole weight of the state . . . ," Stafford to Walsingham, 17 July 1584, *CSP, Foreign* [1583–84], p. 621; Mendoza to Philip II, 24 Dec. 1586, *CSP, Spanish*, 3:689. Henry III to Villeroy, n.d., NAF 1246, fol. 25. Idem, NAF 1245, fol. 89. Idem, NAF 1243, fol. 47; NAF 1246, fols. 36, 79. Idem, NAF 1246, fol. 63. Idem, FF 3385, fol. 8. Idem, NAF 1245, fol. 87. Idem, NAF 1243, fol. 149. Idem, NAF 1244, fol. 103.

50. Henry III to Villeroy, n.d., NAF 1245, fol. 91. Henry III to Bellièvre, 29 Apr. 1584, FF 15907, fol. 429. Henry III to Villeroy, n.d., NAF 1244, fol. 40. See, for example, Henry III to Bellièvre, 7 Sept. 1578, FF 15905, fol. 137.

51. Villeroy to Nevers, 9 Sept. 1583, FF 3350, fol. 131. Villeroy to Saint-Sulpice, 25 Feb. 1578, Cabié, *Guerres*, p. 393. Villeroy to Maisse, 11 Sept. 1587, FF 16093, fol. 192.

52. Villeroy to Matignon, 14 June 1587, *LCM*, 9:216 n. 1.

53. Villeroy to Nevers, 9 Sept. 1583, FF 3350, fol. 131. Villeroy to Henry III, 19 Sept. 1586, FF 6631, fol. 76. Henry III to Villeroy, 14 Aug. 1584, *Archives*, ser. 1, 9:228.

54. Villeroy to Bellièvre, 10 Apr. 1581, FF 15906, vol. 1, fol. 344. Idem, 29 Apr. 1584, FF 15907, fol. 427.

55. Villeroy to Saint-Sulpice, 25 Feb. 1578, Cabié, *Guerres*, p. 393.

56. See Martin, *Gallicanisme*, pp. 215–17, for an account of Henry III's religious devotions. Henry III to Villeroy, n.d., NAF 1243, fol. 47; NAF 1246, fol. 36. Idem, NAF 1246, fol. 79. Dolfin, 20 Dec. 1585, F. It. 1734, fols. 349–50. Bellièvre to Brulart, 18 Dec. 1585, FF 4736, fol. 425. Henry III to Villeroy, [1579], *LCM*, 7:77, n. 1. Villeroy to

Henry III, 21 Feb. 1580, FF 15562, fol. 147. Villeroy to Hautefort, 1 Oct. 1583, quoted in Sutherland, *Secretaries*, p. 242. Villeroy to Bellièvre, 23 Mar. 1581, FF 15906, vol. 1, fol. 288. Villeroy to Nevers, 29 Sept. 1581, FF 3974, fol. 24. Villeroy to Bellièvre, 6 Apr. 1581, FF 15906, vol. 1, fol. 335. Bellièvre to Henry III, 21 June 1576, FF 15890, fol. 420; Henry often left much to Bellièvre's discretion: Henry III to Bellièvre and La Guiche, 28 Mar. 1588, FF 15909, fols. 62–63. Bellièvre to Villeroy, 28 Aug. 1584, FF 4736, fol. 229. Villeroy to Matignon, 24 May 1587, quoted in Sutherland, *Secretaries*, p. 275.

57. Bellièvre to Henry III, 26 Aug. and 4 Sept. 1583, FF 15891, fols. 312–15, FF 6629, fol. 71. See Garnier, "Scandale," pp. 153–89, 561–612. Bellièvre to Brulart, 20 Apr. 1588, FF 3402, fol. 8. Villeroy to Matignon, 19 Mar. 1588, FF 3356, fol. 78. Idem, 28 Apr. 1588, *LCM*, 9:334 n.1. Villeroy to Bellièvre, 5 July [1589], FF 15909, fol. 438. Bellièvre to Catherine, 25 Apr. 1588, FF 3402, fol. 11. Bellièvre to [?], [early 1589], FF 15892, fol. 307.

58. Bellièvre to Jacques Faye d'Espesses, 4 Sept. 1589, FF 15892, fol. 285. Bellièvre to Villeroy, Oct. 1589, FF 15892, fol. 345. Villeroy to Bellièvre, 8 Feb. 1589, FF 15909, fol. 235.

59. Villeroy, *Mémoires*, pp. 128–29; copy of the king's note in Bellièvre's hand, 7 Sept. 1588, FF 15892, fol. 174. Bellièvre to Catherine, 10 Sept. 1588, FF 15892, fols. 175–76; Villeroy to Bellièvre, 28 Sept. 1588, FF 15909, fol. 179. Catherine to Bellièvre, 20 Sept. 1588, *LCM*, 9:382. Bellièvre to [?], [late Sept. 1588], FF 15892, fol. 235. Bellièvre to Brulart, 26 Sept. 1588, FF 3420, fols. 71–72. Villeroy to Bellièvre, 28 Sept. 1588, FF 15909, fol. 178. Idem, 5 Oct. 1588, FF 15909, fol. 188.

60. Bellièvre to Catherine, 10 Sept. 1588, Bellièvre to [?], 1 Oct. 1588, FF 15892, fols. 175, 222–23. Bellièvre to Faye d'Espesses, 27 Dec. 1588, FF 15892, fol. 234. Villeroy to Bellièvre, 26 Oct. 1588, FF 15909, fol. 205. Villeroy, *Mémoires*, p. 135. Ibid., pp. 135–36; Villeroy to Bellièvre, 6 Jan. 1589, FF 15909, fol. 226. Villeroy, *Mémoires*, p. 135. Catherine to Villeroy, 1 Dec. 1588, *LCM*, 9:391–92.

61. Cavriana, 13 Sept. 1588, Desjardins, 4:822–23; Mocenigo, 7 and 15 Aug. 1588, F. It. 1737, fols. 197, 211. Stafford to Walsingham, 11 Sept. 1588, *CSP, Foreign* [1588], p. 178. Bellièvre to Nevers, 4 Oct. 1588, FF 3336, fol. 103. Bellièvre to Mayenne, 27 Oct. 1588, FF 15892, fol. 207. Villeroy, *Mémoires*, pp. 130–33. Villeroy to Nevers, 26 Apr. 1589, FF 3422, fol. 37. Villeroy to Bellièvre, 6 Jan. 1588, FF 15909, fol. 227.

62. Nouaillac, *Villeroy*, pp. 140–45.

63. Sutherland, *Secretaries*, pp. 300–303.

64. Mendoza to Philip II, 9 Aug. 1588, Croze, *Guises*, 2:356–57. Mendoza to Philip II, 20 May 1587, *CSP, Spanish*, 4:86–87. Idem, 24 Sept. 1588, Croze, *Guises*, 2:372–73.

65. Henry III to Villeroy, 14 Aug. 1584, *Archives*, ser. 1, 9:228–35. Ibid., p. 234.

66. The most complete account of these events can be found in Saulnier, *Bourbon*.

67. Mariéjol, *Catherine*, p. 371.

68. Saulnier, *Bourbon*, pp. 113–14, 117. Ibid., p. 113. Ibid., p. 119; Bellièvre to Catherine, 5, 7, and 15 Apr. 1585, FF 15891, fols. 391, 393, 395.

69. Bellièvre to Catherine, 3 Apr. 1585, FF 15891, fol. 389. Villeroy to Maisse, 30 Mar. 1585, FF 16092, fol. 353. Idem, 11 May 1585, FF 16092, fol. 371. Catherine to Villeroy, 20 Apr. 1585, *LCM*, 8:259–60.

70. Kierstead, *Bellièvre*, pp. 46–48. For Catherine's negotiations, see Mariéjol, *Catherine*, pp. 371–76. Catherine to Villeroy, 3 June 1585, *LCM*, 8:311. Villeroy to Maisse, 8 June 1585, FF 16092, fol. 386; Bellièvre to Catherine, 9 June 1585, FF 15891, fol. 414; Catherine to Brulart, 7 June 1585, *LCM*, 8:313. Saulnier, *Bourbon*, p. 129. Mariéjol, *Catherine*, p. 376. Saulnier, *Bourbon*, p. 132. Henry to Villeroy, [June 1585], NAF 1244, fol. 128. Villeroy, *Mémoires*, p. 110; Thou, *Histoire*, 6:462.

71. Villeroy to Maisse, 1 Mar. 1586, FF 16093, fol. 31. Bellièvre to Nevers, Oct. 1586, FF 3372, fol. 218. Dolfin, 20 Dec. 1585, F. It. 1734, fol. 349. Bellièvre to Catherine, 25 Aug. 1586, FF 15892, fol. 3. Villeroy to Maisse, 4 Jan. 1586, FF 16093, fol. 3. Idem, 5 July 1585, FF 16092, fol. 395. Idem, 4 Aug. 1585, FF 16092, fol. 402. Mariéjol, *Catherine*, pp. 381–90.

72. Saulnier, *Bourbon*, p. 173. Sutherland, *Secretaries*, p. 274. Villeroy to Maisse, 28 Feb. 1587, FF 16093, fol. 142. Catherine to Villeroy, 14 Mar. 1587, *LCM*, 9:194. Bellièvre to Villeroy, 22 Mar. 1587, FF 15892, fol. 116.

73. Bellièvre to Henry III, 21 Apr. 1587, FF 4734, fol. 165. Villeroy to Maisse, 11 Apr. 1587, FF 16093, fol. 153. Catherine to Bellièvre, 14 Mar. 1587, *LCM*, 9:193. Henry III to Bellièvre, 18 Apr. 1587, FF 15908, fol. 384. Bellièvre to Henry III, 21 Apr. 1587, FF 4734, fol. 165. Catherine to Villeroy, 16 May 1587, *LCM*, 9:203–4.

74. Mariéjol, *Catherine*, pp. 390–91. Bellièvre to Nevers, 9 June 1587, FF 3398, fol. 107; Villeroy to Maisse, 18 June 1587, FF 16093, fol. 171. Saulnier, *Bourbon*, p. 178. Villeroy to Matignon, 24 May 1587, Sutherland, *Secretaries*, p. 275. Villeroy, *Mémoires*, p. 116.

Guise to Mendoza, 4 July 1587, Croze, *Guises*, 2:294–95. Villeroy to Maisse, 3 July 1587, FF 16093, fol. 174. Sutherland, *Secretaries*, pp. 280–82, gives the details of the incident.

75. Mariéjol, *Catherine*, pp. 391–92. For a colorful account of the war of 1587, see Mattingly, *Armada*, pp. 146–71. Villeroy to Maisse, 5 Dec. 1587, FF 16093, fol. 216; Bellièvre to Henry III, 15 Dec. 1587, FF 15892, fol. 131. Villeroy to Bellièvre, 24 Dec. 1587, FF 15908, fol. 534. Bellièvre to Henry III, 15 Dec. 1587, FF 15892, fol. 132.

76. Instructions to Bellièvre, 27 Feb. 1588, FF 15892, fols. 145–46, 149–50, 151–52. Villeroy to Matignon, 19 Mar. 1588, FF 3356, fol. 78. Henry III to Bellièvre, 16 Mar. 1588 (2), FF 15909, fols. 50, 55–56. Bellièvre to Henry III, 20 and 25 Apr. 1588, FF 3402, fols. 1–2, 14–15. Bellièvre to Brulart, 20 Apr. 1588, FF 3402, fols. 8–9. Henry III to Bellièvre, 22 Apr. 1588, FF 15909, fol. 80.

77. Saulnier, *Bourbon*, pp. 188–89. Henry to Bellièvre, 23 Apr. 1588, FF 15909, fol. 70. Henry III to Bellièvre, 26 Apr. 1588, FF 15909, fol. 84. Idem, 23 Apr. 1588, FF 15909, fol. 70.

78. Henry III to Villeroy, [late Apr. 1588], NAF 1246, fol. 27.

79. Villeroy to Matignon, 28 Apr. 1588, *LCM*, 9:334. Bellièvre to Henry III, 26 Apr. 1588, FF 3402, fol. 22. Bellièvre to Brulart, 30 Apr. 1588, FF 3402, fol. 30.

80. Villeroy, *Mémoires*, p. 116; Thou, *Histoire*, 10:319; Stafford to Elizabeth, 8 May 1588, *CSP, Foreign*, [1588], p. 604.

81. Mattingly, *Armada*, pp. 218–44.

82. Catherine to Villeroy, 15 and 26 May 1588, *LCM*, 9:340, 354. Idem, 23 May 1588, *LCM*, 9:348. Catherine to Bellièvre, 2 June 1588, *LCM*, 9:368. Mendoza to Philip II, 9 Aug. 1588, Croze, *Guises*, 2:356. Cavriana, 1 July 1588, Desjardins, 4:795.

83. Bellièvre to Miron, 29 Aug. 1588, FF 15892, fol. 173. See Sutherland, *Secretaries*, pp. 292–94. Villeroy to Bellièvre, 27 Aug. 1588, FF 15909, fol. 132.

84. Villeroy to Matignon, 8 Feb. 1587, FF 3356, fol. 61; Bellièvre to Nevers, 13 Feb. 1587, FF 3398, fol. 63; Catherine to Bellièvre, 1 Mar. 1587, *LCM*, 9:189. Navarre to Catherine, [July 1585], *LM*, 2:98; "Manifeste au clergé, à la noblesse et au tiers-état de France," 1 Jan. 1586, *LM*, 2:172. Saulnier, *Bourbon*, pp. 137, 161, 168–69.

85. Sutherland, *Secretaries*, p. 160. Kierstead, *Bellièvre*, p. 29.

86. Catherine to Bellièvre, 5 July 1574, *LCM*, 5:298. Idem, 25 July 1574, *LCM*, 5:299. Catherine to Morvilliers, 13 Dec. 1575, *LCM*, 5:310. Catherine to Henry III, 15 Mar. 1579, *LCM*, 6:303. Catherine to Bellièvre, 14 Nov. 1575, *LCM*, 5:307. Idem, 1 Mar. 1587, *LCM*, 9:189.

Idem, 15 Dec. 1578, *LCM*, 6:178. Idem, 7 Feb. 1581, *LCM*, 7:347. Idem, 27 June 1588, *LCM*, 9:375. Idem, 28 Sept. 1578, *LCM*, 7:39. Catherine to Bellièvre and La Guische, 28 Mar. 1588, *LCM*, 9:333.

87. Bellièvre to Catherine, late June 1574, *LCM*, 5:37 n. 1. Bellièvre to Villeroy, 30 Mar. 1581, FF 15891, fol. 191. Bellièvre to Catherine, 25 Apr. 1588, FF 3402, fol. 11. Idem, 26 Mar. 1588, FF 3403, fol. 31. Idem, late Dec. 1588, FF 15892, fol. 262.

88. Catherine to Villeroy, 1 Dec. 1586, *LCM*, 9:99. Idem, 23 Aug. and 21 Nov. 1579, 18 Dec. 1587, *LCM*, 7:101, 198; 9:316. Idem, 10 Oct. 1579, *LCM*, 7:163; Villeroy to Henry III, 28 Jan. 1579, NAF 5128, fols. 61–62. Catherine to Villeroy, 16 Apr. 1585, *LCM*, 8:256. Idem, 4 May 1585, *LCM*, 8:273. Idem, 5 Oct. 1587 [misdated 1581], *LCM*, 7:405.

89. Villeroy to Saint-Sulpice, 2 Oct. 1579, Cabié, *Guerres*, p. 515. Villeroy to Bellièvre, 3 Mar. 1581, FF 15906, vol. 1, fol. 219. Idem, 8 Feb. 1589, FF 15909, fol. 235.

90. Mariéjol, *Catherine*, pp. 418–20, 428–29.

91. Villeroy to Maisse, 14 Apr. 1584, FF 16092, fol. 219. Villeroy to Bellièvre, 13 June 1584, FF 15907, fol. 483. Bellièvre to Nevers, 1 Sept. 1586, FF 3372, fol. 186. Bellièvre to Henry III, 16 Jan. 1576, CCC 8, fol. 23.

92. Villeroy to the bishop of Paris, 9 Dec. 1585, FF 6627, fol. 72. Villeroy to Maisse, 16 Dec. 1587, FF 16093, fol. 219. Bellièvre to Henry III, 9 Mar. 1581, FF 15891, fol. 164.

93. Bellièvre to Henry of Navarre, 25 Nov. and 3 Dec. 1581, FF 15891, fols. 274–75, 276–77. Henry of Navarre to Bellièvre, 29 Nov. 1581, *LM*, 1:419.

94. Memoir in Bellièvre's hand [1593], FF 15893, fols. 143–45; Kierstead, *Bellièvre*, pp. 46–48. Bellièvre to Catherine, 27 May and 3 June 1585, FF 15891, fols. 403, 411. Bellièvre to Brulart, 20 Apr. 1588, FF 3402, fol. 8. Villeroy to Mauvissière, 5 May 1576, CCC 472, fols. 39–41; Sutherland, *Secretaries*, p. 199. Villeroy to Maisse, 5 July 1585, FF 16092, fol. 395. Idem, 4 Aug. 1585, FF 16092, fol. 402.

95. Villeroy to Bellièvre, 28 Sept. 1588, FF 15909, fols. 178–79; see also Villeroy to Mauvissière, 23 July 1579, CCC 472, fol. 9.

96. Poirson, *Histoire*, 4:213. Pagès, *Monarchie*, p. 59. Buisseret, "The *Intendants*." Major, "Henry IV." Mousnier, *Assassinat*, pp. 271, 237.

97. Villeroy to La Fontaine, 10 Oct. 1597, HMC, *Salisbury*, 7:407; Sully described a similar method of consultation, *ER*, 2:289. Villeroy to Béthune, 3 Dec. 1603, Henry IV, *Correspondance*, p. 426. Bellièvre

to Henry IV, 22 July 1594, "Lettres," p. 310. Bellièvre to Margaret of
Valois, [early 1584], FF 15891, fol. 343. Villeroy to Bellièvre, 16 Apr.
1584, FF 15907, fol. 418.

98. Villeroy to Du Vair, 1 Aug. 1594, Dupuy 3, fol. 7. Nouaillac,
Villeroy, p. 270. Villeroy to Montmorency, 29 May 1599, FF 3588, fol.
56; Sillery to Villeroy, 24 July 1607, FF 15579, fol. 61. Henry IV to
[?], 11 May 1594, *Lettres . . . 1581–1601*, p. 68. Henry IV to Bellièvre,
25 Nov. 1594, ibid., pp. 131–33.

99. Wiley, *Gentleman*, chaps. 3, 10. Henry IV to Sully, 8 Apr.
1607, *ER*, 2:201.

100. Henry IV to Elizabeth, 15 Nov. 1597, *LM*, 4:877–78. Henry
IV to the countess of Gramont, 15 July 1590, *LM*, 3:216. Henry IV
to the *échevins* of Lyons, 30 June 1595, *LM*, 4:380. "Ce que le roy a
dit à Messrs du Parlement," 13 Apr. 1597, *LM*, 4:743–44. Poirson,
Henri IV, vol. 1, p. 311. Henry IV to the constable [Montmorency],
8 June 1595, *LM*, 4:365. Henry to Catherine of Bourbon, 7 June 1595,
LM, 4:364. Villeroy to Bellièvre, 17 Feb. 1596, FF 15910, fol. 302.
Henry IV to Villeroy, 15 Apr. 1597, *LM*, 4:739; Villeroy complained
that "We are lodged here in the worst place in the world . . . We are
nearly dead of cold, for we are lodged in the open, or very nearly"
(Villeroy to Nevers, 22 Mar. 1597, FF 7784, fol. 295). Villeroy to
Montmorency, 8 Oct. 1600, FF 3591, fol. 151. Henry IV to the Assembly of Notables, Nov. 1596, *LM*, 4:657.

101. "The king has so much courage that he furnishes some to everyone . . ." (Villeroy in a postscript to a letter of Henry IV to the constable, 12 Mar. 1597, *LM*, 4:698–99). Villeroy to Montmorency, 3
Apr. 1597, FF 3548, fol. 53. Villeroy to Bellièvre, 27 Aug. 1597, FF
15911, fol. 111. Villeroy to La Fontaine, 10 Oct. 1597, HMC, *Salisbury*, 7:408. Bellièvre to Henry IV, 2 Jan. 1595, FF 15912, fol. 170.
Idem, 14 June 1595, FF 15912, fol. 226. Idem, 30 July 1595, FF 15912,
fol. 249. Villeroy to Montmorency, 2 Sept. 1600, FF 3591, fol. 130.

102. Henry IV to Elizabeth, 25 Oct. 1596, 2 June and 16 Aug.
1597, *LM*, 4:652–53, 770–71, 828. Henry was determined on peace by
early 1597: Cardinal de Medici to Clement VIII, 8 Mar. 1597, Leo XI,
Lettres, pp. 112–16; Henry IV to [the constable, Montmorency], 29
Apr. 1597, *LM*, 4:756. Henry IV to Piney-Luxembourg, 11 Aug.
1597, *LM*, 4:826. Poirson, *Henri IV*, 2:414–22. Henry IV to Bellièvre and Sillery, 14 Apr. 1598, Mornay, 8:320. Bellièvre and Sillery
to Villeroy, 3 Apr. 1598, Mornay, 8:265. Idem, 12 February 1598,
Mornay, 8:62.

103. Villeroy to Boissise, 12 Apr. 1599, FF 4128, fol. 50. *ER*, 2:314–

15. Villeroy to the duke of Luxembourg, 8 Mar. 1597, FF 16047, fol. 6. Quoted in Anquez, *Henri IV*, p. 86; Villeroy to Sully, 1 June 1599, *ER*, 2:327.

104. See the dispatches of Giovannini, Desjardins, vol. 5, passim. Henry admitted granting the promise: Henry IV to Beaumont, 22 June 1604, *LM*, 6:257. Villeroy to Sully, 3 and 12 July 1604, *ER*, 2:577–78. Henry IV to [Beaumont], 6 Mar. 1605, *LM*, 6:357.

105. Giovannini, 19 Sept. 1604, Desjardins, 5:547. Giovannini, 24 Nov. 1599, Desjardins, 5:376. Henry IV to Bellièvre, 11 Aug. 1599, *LM*, 5:155–56. Sillery to Bellièvre, 9 Dec. 1602, FF 15899, fol. 107; Bellièvre to Villeroy, 10 Dec. 1602, FF 15894, fol. 547. Villeroy to Sully, 28 June 1604, *ER*, 2:576. Villeroy to Béthune, 8 Feb. 1605, FF 4017, fol. 402. Idem, 23 Mar. 1605, FF 4017, fol. 415.

106. Mousnier, in *Assassinat*, pp. 231–36, demonstrates the glorification of Henry IV begun during his lifetime and hastened by his untimely demise. Villeroy to Mornay, 22 May 1610, Mornay, 11:41.

107. Bellièvre to Catherine, 3 Oct. 1586, FF 15892, fol. 5; memoir, [1590], FF 15892, fols. 402–10. Bellièvre to Catherine, 9 Sept. 1578, FF 15891, fol. 26. Bellièvre to Nevers, 12 June 1586, FF 3372, fol. 147. Bellièvre to Epernon, 5 Oct. 1587, FF 15892, fol. 129. Bellièvre to Villeroy, Oct. 1594, FF 15912, fol. 124. Bellièvre to [Villeroy], late 1588, FF 15892, fol. 235. Bellièvre to the bishop of Evreux, Sept. 1599, Dupuy 194, fol. 88.

108. Catherine to Villeroy, 7 Oct. 1578, *LCM*, 6:60. Cecil to [the master of Gray], 14 May 1601, HMC, *Salisbury*, 14:176. Cheverny, *Mémoires*, p. 531. Cardinal de Medici to Clement VIII, 15 July 1597, Leo XI, *Lettres*, p. 160. Stafford to Walsingham, 17 July 1584, *CSP, Foreign* [1583–84], p. 621. Dolfin, 25 Nov. 1585, F. It. 1734, fol. 323. *ER*, 2:543, 546–647. Sully to Villeroy, 26 Apr. 1604, Sully, "Dix lettres," p. 139. Catherine to Morvillier, 13 Dec. 1575, *LCM*, 5:310. Stafford to Walsingham, 17 July 1584, *CSP, Foreign* [1583–84], p. 621. Thou, *Histoire*, 9:316. Bufalo, 22 Sept. 1604, *Correspondance*, p. 786; *ER*, 3:211. Bellièvre to the cardinal of Joyeuse, 18 May 1607, FF 6633, fol. 255. See Henry IV's letters to him between March and August 1607, *LM*, 7:123ff.

109. Villeroy to Bellièvre, 21 June [1589], FF 15909, fol. 293.

110. This does not include his dismissal in 1616 during Concini's ascendancy; see Nouaillac, *Villeroy*, pp. 543–56. Sutherland, *Secretaries*, p. 238. Henry III to Villeroy, [Aug. 1582], NAF 1245, fols. 127–28. Villeroy to Bellièvre, 3 Aug. 1582, FF 15906, vol. 2, fol. 729.

111. Villeroy to Bellièvre, 1 and 12 Mar. 1589, FF 15909, fols. 239,

241. Villeroy to Nevers, 7 Apr. 1589, FF 3629, fol. 129. Idem, 26 Apr. 1589, FF 3422, fol. 37.

112. Villeroy, *Mémoires,* pp. 140–216. Villeroy to Du Vair, 1 Aug. 1594, Dupuy 3, fols. 5–23. Nouaillac, *Villeroy,* pp. 259–64. Mocenigo, 29 Sept. 1594, F. It. 1743, fol. 9.

113. Villeroy's memoir on the affair, 3 May 1604, CCC 1, fols. 289–92; Nouaillac, *Villeroy,* pp. 315–16. Sillery to Villeroy, 24 Apr. 1604, FF 15578, fol. 219. Villeroy to Bellièvre, [late Apr.] 1604, FF 15896, fol. 502. Idem, 30 Apr. 1604, FF 15896, fol. 449.

114. Aarssens to the States-General, 6 July 1599, Buzanval, *Lettres,* p. 228. Giovannini, 28 Apr. 1601, Desjardins, 5:463. Bellièvre to Margaret of Valois, [summer 1599], FF 15894, fol. 362. Bellièvre to Sillery, 7 June 1598, Mornay, 9:19. Bellièvre to Pinart, 16 May 1585, FF 15891, fol. 407. Bellièvre to [?], n.d., FF 15893, fols. 143–48. Bellièvre to Henry III, 25 Apr. 1588, FF 3402, fols. 14–15. Bellièvre to [?], June 1590, FF 15892, fol. 399. Bellièvre to [?], Oct. 1590, FF 15892, fol. 382; Bellièvre to Bouillon, 22 June 1592, FF 15893, fol. 40; Bellièvre to Henry IV, [late 1590]; memoir [late 1590], FF 15892, fols. 400, 402–10.

115. Bellièvre to Henry IV, 10 Dec. 1602, FF 15894, fol. 437. Ibid. See Henry IV, *Lettres . . . 1604.* Bellièvre to Du Perron, 1 Jan. 1605, FF 15894, fol. 606. Badoer, 23 Nov. 1604, F. It. 1753, fols. 130–31; Thou, *Histoire,* 9:716. Du Perron to Sillery, 23 Feb. 1605, *Ambassades,* p. 288. L'Estoile, *Mémoires-journaux,* 8:339.

116. Sutherland, *Secretaries,* pp. 185–87. Villeroy to Nevers, 10 Oct. 1574, cited in Sutherland, *Secretaries,* p. 187. Villeroy to Bellièvre, 29 Nov. 1602, FF 15896, fol. 375. Henry IV to [the landgrave of Hesse], 22 Nov. 1602, *LM,* 5:697–98.

117. Henry IV to Marshal Ornano, July 1594, *Lettres . . . 1581–1601,* pp. 80–82. Bellièvre to Henry IV, 17 Nov. 1601, FF 15894, fol. 435. See Kierstead, *Bellièvre,* pp. 124–34. Bellièvre to Villeroy, 10 Dec. 1602, FF 15894, fol. 547. Ibid. Bellièvre to Villeroy, 28 May 1603, FF 15894, fol. 562. Sully to Bellièvre, 13 Oct. 1599, FF 15897, fol. 519.

118. Bellièvre to the bishop of Evreux, Sept. 1599, Dupuy 194, fol. 88.

119. Villeroy wrote him: "If you were beside the king we would be relieved of the trouble we have of writing you so much . . . ," 29 May 1601, FF 15896, fol. 317.

120. Villeroy to Bellièvre, 6 Jan. 1589, FF 15909, fol. 226. Bellièvre to Brulart, 26 Sept. 1588, FF 3420, fol. 71. Bellièvre to [?], [early

1589], FF 15892, fol. 307. Villeroy to Bellièvre, 26 Feb. 1589, FF 15909, fol. 236. Bellièvre to [?], 1588, FF 15892, fol. 238. Villeroy to Nevers, 18 Apr. 1594, FF 3622, fol. 104.

121. Bellièvre to Du Perron, 1 Jan. 1605, FF 15894, fol. 607. L'Estoile, *Mémoires-journaux*, 8: 339. Villeroy to Bellièvre, 28 Sept. 1588, FF 15909, fol. 178. Bellièvre to Du Haillan, 17 Apr. 1593, FF 20480, fol. 163.

3. War and Foreign Policy

1. See Hale, "Armies," pp. 171–74.

2. Clark, *War*, p. 6.

3. Bellièvre to [?], 19 Oct. 1580, FF 15891, fol. 62. Bellièvre to Morvilliers, 25 June 1576, FF 15560, fol. 83. Villeroy to Saint-Sulpice, 30 Jan. 1577, Cabié, *Guerres*, p. 329. Villeroy, *Mémoires*, p. 161. Villeroy to Maisse, 1 Jan. 1588, FF 16093, fol. 223.

4. Bellièvre to Rambouillet, 29 Dec. 1591, FF 15892, fol. 487. Bellièvre to Sillery, 28 June 1600, FF 15894, fol. 403. Villeroy to La Boderie, 2 June 1606, CCC 475, fol. 23. Villeroy to Joyeuse, 28 Feb. 1607, FF 6633, fol. 120. Villeroy to La Boderie, 20 Mar. 1610, CCC 475, fols. 356–57.

5. Bellièvre to Henry III, 22 Nov. 1580, FF 15891, fol. 74.

6. Bellièvre to Du Perron, Sept. 1599, Dupuy 194, fol. 87.

7. Villeroy to Bellièvre, 9 Mar. 1581, FF 15906, vol. 1, fol. 245. Idem, 13 Feb. 1591, FF 15909, fol. 366. Idem, Apr. 1591, FF 15909, fol. 377. Bellièvre to Nevers, Mar. 1591, FF 15892, fol. 451.

8. Bellièvre to Morvilliers, 19 June 1576, FF 15890, fol. 417. Bellièvre to Nevers, 20 Sept. 1586, FF 3372, fol. 214. Villeroy to Saint-Sulpice, 25 Feb. 1578, Cabié, *Guerres*, p. 393. Bellièvre to Henry III, 18 Nov. 1581, FF 15891, fol. 270. Bellièvre to Catherine, 3 Apr. 1585, FF 15891, fol. 389. Villeroy to La Fontaine, 11 Oct. 1597, HMC, *Salisbury*, 7:408.

9. Bellièvre to Villeroy, 10 Aug. 1595, FF 15912, fol. 260. Idem, 30 June 1597, FF 15893, fol. 454. Villeroy to Bellièvre, 31 Aug. 1597, FF 15911, fol. 116.

10. FF 15894, fol. 582.

11. Villeroy to La Boderie, 20 Mar. 1610, CCC 475, fol. 355. Bel-

lièvre to Nevers, 18 Mar. 1587, FF 3398, fol. 66. Idem, 13 Feb. 1587, FF 3398, fol. 63. Bellièvre to Brulart, 20 Apr. 1588, FF 3402, fol. 8. Villeroy to Béthune, 22 Mar. 1603, FF 4017, fol. 169.

12. "Touchant les divisions de la Chrétienté," FF 15892, fol. 11. Henry IV to Sillery, 24 May 1600, *Lettres . . . 1600*, p. 86. Clark, *War*, p. 16.

13. Villeroy to Maisse, 28 Mar. 1587, FF 16093, fol. 150.

14. Villeroy to Béthune, 3 Dec. 1603, Henry IV, *Correspondance*, pp. 426–27.

15. In his study of Richelieu and the other councillors of Louis XIII, Orest Ranum sums up the problem of determining the influence of royal ministers on their masters: "In the complex problems of government, where goals and political policies were defined, Louis's role is more difficult to determine . . . The great affairs of state were usually discussed, and decisions were reached in the *Conseil d'en haut*. . . . No minutes were taken, and to our knowledge not even a detailed description of one of these sessions is extant." Later Ranum points out that in the royal letter, "the most important diplomatic medium of communication, the legal fiction that the king was responsible for all decisions again makes it impossible to think in terms of ministerial responsibility. In this greatest of sources for diplomatic history, the roles of the king, Richelieu, Chavigny, and all the other ministers become indistinguishable and unified" (*Richelieu*, pp. 16, 97).

16. Pagès, *Monarchie*, p. 51. Bellièvre to Henry IV, 10 June 1604, FF 15894, fol. 596. Baudrillart, "Politique," p. 413. Villeroy to Henry IV, 30 Oct. 1603, *Archives*, ser. 2, 2:231–32. Henry IV to Beaumont, 22 June 1604, *LM*, 7:249.

17. Henry IV to Montmorency, 4 June 1601, *LM*, 5:422. Henry IV to Rosny (Sully), 12 July 1604, *LM*, 6:268. Henry IV to Ornano, 2 Sept. 1601, *LM*, 5:462. Henry IV to Fresnes-Canaye, 4 Mar. 1603, *LM*, 6:42–43.

18. Henry IV to Fresnes-Canaye, 11 Nov. 1602, *LM*, 5:694. Henry IV to Clement VIII, 13 Dec. 1601, *LM*, 5:513.

19. There exists no general study of Franco-Spanish relations during this period. For Henry III's reign see Jensen, *Mendoza*. Drouot, *Mayenne*, treats the years 1587–96. Relations between Henry IV and Philip III have been studied in detail by Philippson, *Heinrich IV*.

20. Bellièvre to Catherine, 15 Apr. 1585, *LCM*, 8:434.

21. Idem, 9 Sept. 1578 and 20 Oct. 1580, FF 15891, fols. 25–26; *LCM*, 7:451. Villeroy to Bellièvre, 9 Oct. 1578, FF 15905, fol. 151; 15

Mar. 1581, FF 15906, vol. 1, fol. 264. Villeroy to Mauvissière, 18 Oct. 1579, CCC 472, fol. 201. Villeroy to Bellièvre, 29 Nov. 1580, FF 15905, fol. 638. Villeroy to Henry III, 2 June 1582, FF 6628, fol. 102.

22. Villeroy to Bellièvre, 2 Mar. 1582, FF 15906, vol. 1, fol. 214; Villeroy to Henry III, 6 and 11 Mar. 1582, FF 3385, fols. 114, 119. Idem, 12 Sept. 1582, FF 6631, fols. 68–69. Villeroy to Maisse, 23 July 1583, FF 16092, fol. 121.

23. See Jensen, *Mendoza*, pp. 43–92, 131–70. Mendoza to Philip II, May 1588, Croze, *Guises*, 2:342. Jensen, *Mendoza*, pp. 148–50.

24. Stafford to Burghley, 17 Nov. 1586, *CSP, Foreign* [1586–87], p. 147. Mendoza to Philip II, 20 May 1587, *CSP, Spanish*, 4 [1587–1603]:87. Villeroy to Maisse, 28 Feb. 1587, FF 16093, fol. 142. Villeroy to [Bellièvre], 20 Feb. 1584, FF 15567, fol. 1; Villeroy to Maisse, 4 Mar. 1584, FF 16092, fol. 203. Bellièvre to Navarre, [1586], FF 15892, fol. 2.

25. For Villeroy's role as a league diplomat, see Nouaillac, *Villeroy*, pp. 159–264. Villeroy to Mauvissière, 14 Oct. 1589, Dupuy 3, fol. 111. Villeroy to Nevers, 25 Oct. 1589, FF 3977, fol. 312. "Advis de M. de Villeroy à M. le duc de Mayenne, publié à Paris après la mort du roi, sur la fin de l'an 1589," CCC 483, fols. 17–27. Villeroy to Bellièvre, 27 Nov. 1591, FF 15909, fol. 427. Villeroy to Fleury, 18 Apr. 1592, Mornay, 5:300. "Harangue faicte par M. de Villeroy, pour estre prononcée en l'assemblée des prétendus estats de Paris," Villeroy, *Mémoires*, pp. 234–54. Villeroy to Nevers, 17 Jan. 1590, FF 3978, fol. 29.

26. Bellièvre to [Matignon], 16 June 1590, FF 15892, fol. 366. Bellièvre to Jacques Faye d'Espesses, 14 July 1590, FF 15892, fol. 289. Bellièvre to Cheverny, 25 Nov. 1590, Bellièvre to [?], 29 May 1591, FF 15892, fols. 389, 454–55. Villeroy to Bellièvre, 26 Dec. 1592, FF 15895, fols. 231–39; Bellièvre to Villeroy, 30 Dec. 1592, Dupuy 88, fols. 177–82. Bellièvre, "Lettre," pp. 20, 10. "Un escrit contre la convocation des pretendus estats de la Ligue," FF 15893, fols. 68–96.

27. The best account of Henry IV's pacification of France remains Poirson, *Histoire*, vols. 1–2.

28. The peace negotiations are described in detail in Kermaingant, *Boissise*, 1:146–219.

29. Bellièvre to Nevers, 10 Nov. 1594, FF 3622, fol. 138; Villeroy to Mornay, 26 Dec. 1594, Mornay, 6:127. "The origin is in Spain, where they say that they have sworn the death of His Majesty by such means" (Villeroy to Bongars, 27 Dec. 1594, FF 15591, fol. 355). Nouaillac, *Villeroy*, pp. 362–63. Villeroy to Joyeuse, 10 Mar. 1595, NAF 2750, fol. 12. Bellièvre to Henry IV, 17 Apr. 1595, FF 15912, fol. 200. Idem, 7 Apr. 1595, FF 15912, fols. 194–96. Idem, 9 Nov.

1594, FF 15912, fol. 132. Bellièvre to Epernon, 7 Oct. 1594, FF 15912, fol. 96. Bellièvre to Henry IV, 30 June 1597, FF 15893, fol. 451; Villeroy to Bellièvre, 20 and 24 Aug. 1597, FF 15891, fols. 100, 102. Bellièvre to Villeroy, June 1598, Mornay, 9:24.

30. Bellièvre to Villeroy, 15 Sept. 1597, FF 15893, fol. 462. Idem, 30 June 1597, FF 15893, fol. 454. Villeroy to Béthune, 2 June 1602, Henry IV, *Correspondance*, p. 229. Villeroy to Du Tour, 12 Dec. 1602, FF 20651, fol. 41. Villeroy to Jeannin, 2 Feb. 1609, *Négociations*, p. 594. Sully to Jeannin, 2 Dec. 1608, *Négociations*, p. 502.

31. See Bufalo, *Correspondance*, pp. 106–9. Villeroy to Bellièvre, 2 Sept. 1601, FF 15896, fol. 331. Henry IV to the constable (Montmorency), 2 Aug. 1601, *LM*, 5:446; Henry IV to Cardinal Ossat, 24 Dec. 1601, *LM*, 5:518–21. Villeroy to Brunault, 19 July 1602, Kermaingant, *Boissise*, 1:159. Henry IV to Du Tour, 17 Sept. 1602, *LM*, 5:669–74.

32. The king ranted against "the insatiable ambition and unbearable pride of this nation," and charged that "if [the Spanish] were not held back by fear of my arms and the Dutch war, they would tyrannize all the other princes..." (Henry IV to Beaumont, 14 May 1604, *LM*, 6:247, 249). Villeroy to Béthune, 26 Jan. 1604, FF 4017, fol. 279. Badoer, 26 May and 9 June 1604, F. It. 1753, fols. 33–41. Villeroy to Beaumont, 3 May 1604, Kermaingant, *Beaumont*, 1:210. Bellièvre to La Guische, 13 May 1604, FF 15894, fol. 593. Henry IV to Sully, 12 July 1604, *LM*, 6:267. Idem, 17 Oct. 1604, *LM*, 6:308. Idem, 12 July 1604, *LM*, 6:268. Kermaingant, *Beaumont*, 1:228–30.

33. Henry IV to Brèves, 31 Aug. 1609, *LM*, 7:760–65. Villeroy to Jeannin, 6 Apr. 1609, *Négociations*, pp. 648–49. Idem, to La Boderie, 6 Feb. 1610, CCC 475, fol. 324. See the dispatches of the archduke's ambassador, Pecquius, in Aumale, *Condé*, appendixes. Villeroy to La Boderie, 9 May 1610, CCC 475, fol. 373.

34. Villeroy to Béthune, 11 Feb. 1602, FF 4017, fol. 40. Idem, 24 Aug. 1603, Henry IV, *Correspondance*, p. 417. Henry IV to Brèves, 31 Aug. 1609, *LM*, 7:760. Bellièvre to Nevers, 24 Aug. 1593, FF 3985, fol. 104. Thuau, *Raison d'état*, pp. 242–48. Villeroy to Loménie, 7 Nov. 1608, Dupuy 3, fol. 109.

35. See Pagès, "Richelieu and Marillac."

36. See Read, *Walsingham*, vol. 1, chap. 5; vol. 2, chap. 8; vol. 3, chap. 14.

37. Villeroy to Mauvissière, 18 May 1579, CCC 472, fol. 11. Idem, 8 Mar. 1583, CCC 472, fol. 123. Villeroy to Maisse, 6 Dec. 1585, FF 16092, fol. 449. Bellièvre and Chateauneuf to Henry III, 18 Dec. 1586, FF 15892, fol. 46.

38. See Cheyney, *History*, vol. 1, passim.

39. Villeroy to Bellièvre, 29 Nov. 1595, FF 15910, fol. 274. Villeroy to Mornay, 26 Feb. 1596, Mornay, 6:461. Bellièvre to Henry IV, 29 Apr. 1596, FF 15893, fol. 343. Nouaillac, *Villeroy*, p. 369. Bellièvre and Montmorency to Henry IV, 26 June 1596, FF 15893, fol. 351. Villeroy to La Fontaine, 11 Oct. 1597, HMC, *Salisbury*, 7:409.

40. Bellièvre and Sillery to Villeroy, 12 Feb. 1598, Mornay, 8:62. Villeroy to Henry IV, 18 Aug. 1598, Dupuy 3, fol. 37. Bellièvre to Villeroy, [summer 1598], FF 15894, fol. 150.

41. Villeroy to Beaumont, 19 Feb. 1605, Bibliothèque Nationale, Mélanges Colbert 25, fol. 266. Bellièvre to Villeroy, 31 May 1603, FF 15894, fol. 563. Villeroy to Montmorency, 13 July 1603, FF 3599, fol. 58. Bellièvre to [Villeroy], [summer 1603], FF 15894, fol. 583. Willson, *James VI*, p. 273. Villeroy to Béthune, 4 June 1603, FF 4017, fol. 193. Villeroy to La Boderie, 28 June 1608, CCC 475, fol. 216. Villeroy to Jeannin, 22 Dec. 1607, *Négociations*, p. 247. Villeroy to La Boderie, 11 June 1606, CCC 475, fols. 15–16. Idem, 2 June 1606, CCC 475, fol. 22. Idem, 27 Feb. 1610, CCC 475, fol. 337.

42. Bellièvre to Henry III, 26 Aug. 1583, FF 15891, fol. 314.

43. Villeroy to Boissise, 12 Jan. 1599, FF 4128, fol. 24.

44. Villeroy to Béthune, 1 Aug. 1602, 6 May 1603, FF 4017, fols. 84, 183.

45. The most detailed account of Franco–Dutch relations remains Motley, *History*, passim. Buisseret, *Sully*, p. 82. Villeroy to Henry IV, 30 Oct. 1603, *Archives*, ser. 2, 2:231–32.

46. Villeroy to Mauvissière, 12 Feb. 1578, CCC 472, fol. 89. Villeroy to Bellièvre, 9 Oct. 1578, FF 15905, fol. 151. Bellièvre to Henry III, 29 Aug. 1578, FF 15891, fols. 19–20. Villeroy to Bellièvre, 29 Apr. 1584, FF 15907, fol. 428. Villeroy to Maisse, 6 July 1584, FF 16092, fol. 248. Stafford to Walsingham, 12 Feb. and 3 Mar. 1585, *CSP, Foreign* [1584–85], pp. 274, 320–21.

47. Villeroy to Henry IV, 7 Nov. 1598, 3 Mar. and 21 Oct. 1599, Dupuy 3, fol. 41; Dupuy 1, fols. 51, 56. Aarssens to Valcke, 21 Nov. 1600, *Lettres*, p. 90. Bellièvre to Villeroy, June 1598, Mornay, 9:24. Henry IV to Bellièvre, 3 Mar. 1599, *Lettres . . . 1581–1601*, pp. 241–42. Aarssens to the States-General, 6 July and 15 Aug. 1599, Buzanval, *Lettres*, pp. 227, 262. See Aarssens's correspondence in *Lettres;* Buzanval, *Lettres;* and Barneveldt, *Gedenkstukken*. For details, see Nouaillac, *Villeroy*, pp. 445–61. Pruili, 16 Jan. 1607, F. It. 1756, fols. 124–26.

48. Henry IV to La Boderie, 14 Apr. 1607, *LM*, 7:179–80. Villeroy to La Boderie, 23 Apr. 1607, quoted in Nouaillac, *Villeroy*, p. 462. See Henry's letters to Jeannin during the summer of 1607 in *Négocia-*

tions, pp. 57–140 passim. See Villeroy's letters for the same period, ibid. Villeroy to Jeannin, 4 Aug. 1607, *Négociations,* p. 115.

49. Villeroy shared Jeannin's admiration for the Dutch rebels' willingness to be "torn into little pieces rather than give [their liberties] up" (Jeannin to Villeroy, 6 Oct. 1607, *Négociations,* p. 166). Villeroy to Jeannin, 1 Jan. 1609, *Négociations,* p. 549.

50. See Anquez, *Henri IV;* Baudrillart, "Politique," pp. 408–82; Labouchère, "Guillaume Ancel."

51. Villeroy to Mauvissière, 23 Oct. 1575, CCC 472, fols. 21–22. Bellièvre to Casimir, 11 Aug. 1576, Dupuy 502, fols. 108–10. Bellièvre to Henry III, 27 July and 17 Aug. 1578, FF 15891, fols. 1–2, 6; Villeroy to Hautefort, 5 Sept. 1582, FF 15565, fol. 78. Bellièvre to Navarre, [1586], FF 15892, fols. 1–2. Villeroy to the bishop of Paris, 26 Nov. 1585, FF 6627, fol. 70. Villeroy to Maisse, 5 Dec. 1587, FF 16093, fol. 216.

52. Baudrillart, "Politique," pp. 444–47.

53. Villeroy to Bongars, 20 Apr. 1597, Anquez, *Henri IV,* pp. 47–48.

54. Idem, 23 July 1601, 7 Dec. 1605; ibid., pp. 57, 59. Villeroy to Beaumont, 2 Feb. 1604, Nouaillac, *Villeroy,* p. 327. Villeroy to Bunickhausen, 19 Dec. 1609, CCC 426, fol. 101. Villeroy to La Boderie, 16 Apr. 1610, CCC 475, fol. 362.

55. See Rott, *Henri IV,* passim.

56. See Raulich, *Carlo Emmanuele I;* Bergadini, *Carlo Emmanuele I.*

57. Villeroy to Henry III, 11 June 1582, FF 3385, fol. 108. Bellièvre to Nevers, 11 Oct. 1586, FF 3372, fol. 226. Villeroy to Bellièvre, 26 Oct. 1588, FF 15909, fol. 205. Bellièvre to Villeroy, 10 Aug. 1595, FF 15912, fols. 260–61. Raulich, *Carlo Emmanuele I,* pp. 383–447. Villeroy to Bellièvre and Sillery, 14 Mar. 1598, Mornay, 8:178.

58. Villeroy to Rochepot, 16 and 27 July 1600, FF 16137, fols. 36, 32. Ibid. Bellièvre to Sillery, 14 July 1600, FF 15894, fol. 405. Villeroy to Boissise, 14 Sept. 1600, FF 4128, fol. 205. Richard, "Légation Aldobrandini." [Bellièvre to Henry IV, 1600], FF 15894, fol. 375. Villeroy to Boissise, 5 Jan. 1601, Kermaingant, *Boissise,* 2:280; Villeroy's continued discontent with this treaty is testified to by Giovannini, 10 Jan. 1601, 4 Nov. 1602, 27 Jan. 1603, Desjardins, 5:453, 505, 508.

59. Villeroy to Henry IV, 24 Feb. 1601, Dupuy 3, fol. 59. Villeroy to Béthune, 14 Aug. 1602, Henry IV, *Correspondance,* p. 270. Villeroy to Servières, 15 Oct. 1602, FF 16912, fol. 99. Nouaillac, *Villeroy,* pp. 439–40. Ibid., p. 511.

60. Rott, *Henri IV,* p. 130.

61. Bellièvre to Nevers, 11 Oct. 1586, FF 3372, fol. 226. Giovannini, 8 July 1600, Desjardins, 5:430. Bellièvre to Montmorency, 21 Sept. 1594, FF 3547, fol. 35.

62. Vinta, 20 Jan. 1601, Desjardins, 5:455. Villeroy to Béthune, 24 Feb. 1603, FF 4017, fol. 161. Rott, *Henri IV*, bks. 2–3 passim. Nouaillac, *Villeroy*, pp. 404–9; Villeroy to Béthune, 5 July 1604, FF 4017, fol. 331. Villeroy to Béthune, 10 Apr. 1604, FF 4017, fol. 308. Villeroy to Bellièvre, 17 July 1604, FF 15896, fol. 465; Villeroy to Béthune, 21 Sept. 1604, FF 4017, fols. 359–61.

63. See Pastor, *History*, passim.

64. Villeroy to Cardinal Du Perron, 3 June 1605, Du Perron, *Ambassades*, p. 351.

65. Villeroy to Maisse, 11 Oct. 1585, FF 16092, fol. 426. Bellièvre to Nevers, 3 Aug. 1586, FF 3372, fol. 174. Bellièvre to Villeroy, 27 May 1587, FF 15892, fol. 121. Bellièvre to [?], 24 Feb. 1591, FF 15892, fol. 444. Kierstead, *Bellièvre*, p. 64. Bellièvre to Nevers, 24 Aug. 1593, FF 3985, fol. 101. Idem, 5 Nov. 1593, FF 3987, fol. 21. Villeroy to Bellièvre, 24 Aug. 1593, FF 15910, fol. 46. Bellièvre to Villeroy, 28 Oct. 1594, FF 15893, fol. 201. Bellièvre to Henry IV, 2 Jan. 1595, FF 15912, fols. 167, 168. Villeroy to Bellièvre, 18 Sept. 1596, FF 15910, fol. 352.

66. Bellièvre to Villeroy, [Aug.] 1598, FF 15894, fol. 149; Villeroy to Henry IV, 18 Aug. 1598, Dupuy 3, fol. 37. Feret, "Nullité." Villeroy to Cardinal Joyeuse, 20 Dec. 1599, NAF 2750, fol. 62. Villeroy to Béthune, 17 Nov. 1602, FF 4017, fols. 113–14. Idem, 24 Apr. and 7 May 1602, FF 4017, fols. 58–59, 63–64. Idem, 20 Oct. 1604, Nouaillac, *Villeroy*, p. 411; for the nuncio's role as mediator, see Bufalo, *Correspondance*, pp. 114–17. Villeroy to Bellièvre, 11 Apr. 1605, FF 15894, fol. 509; Bellièvre to Du Perron, 20 Apr. 1605, Du Perron, *Ambassades*, p. 304. Villeroy to Joyeuse, 6 May 1605, NAF 2750, fol. 128. Villeroy to Brèves, 6 July 1609, FF 3541, fol. 24.

67. Nouaillac, *Villeroy*, pp. 428–35.

4. Society and the Economy

1. Buisseret, *Sully*, p. 176.

2. Bellièvre to [?], 12 Apr. 1592, FF 15893, fol. 24. Sillery to Villeroy, 24 July 1607, FF 15579, fol. 61. Sutherland, *Secretaries*, p. 281. Nouaillac, *Villeroy*, pp. 536–37. Kierstead, *Bellièvre*, p. 134.

3. Villeroy to Hautefort, 7 Mar. 1583, FF 15566, fol. 80. Villeroy to Bellièvre, 9 Apr. 1594, FF 15910, fol. 84. Bellièvre to [?], 21 Mar. 1593, FF 15893, fol. 101. Bellièvre to the constable (Montmorency), [1593], FF 15893, fol. 114. See Sutherland, *Secretaries*, pp. 278–82. Bellièvre to Epernon, 5 Oct. 1587, FF 15892, fol. 129. Villeroy to Bellièvre, 27 Aug. 1588, FF 15909, fol. 132. Bellièvre to Villeroy, 28 Dec. 1590, FF 15892, fols. 397–98.

4. Villeroy to Saint-Sulpice, 5 July 1579, Cabié, *Guerres*, p. 489. Bellièvre to Nevers, 9 June 1587, FF 3398, fol. 107. Bellièvre to Henry III, 17 Oct. 1581, FF 15565, fol. 134. Bellièvre to Navarre, 3 Dec. 1581, FF 15891, fols. 276–77. Villeroy to Maisse, 19 Aug. 1595, FF 16093, fol. 464. Villeroy to Matignon, 30 Sept. 1595, FF 3356, fol. 99. Bellièvre to Henry IV, 12 Feb. 1596, FF 15893, fol. 301. Villeroy to Mornay, 23 Nov. 1595, Mornay, 6:371.

5. Memoir on the trial of Biron, 1 July 1602, FF 15894, fol. 173. Bellièvre to Henry IV, 11 July 1602, Dupuy 194, fol. 99; Villeroy to Bellièvre, 17 July 1602, FF 15896, fol. 324. Henry IV to Bellièvre, 28 July 1602, *LM*, 5:643; Villeroy to Bellièvre, 29 July 1602, FF 15896, fol. 359. Villeroy to Beaumont, 25 Aug. 1603, quoted in Nouaillac, *Villeroy*, pp. 327, 328. Villeroy to Bongars, 9 Sept. 1605, Anquez, *Henri IV*, p. 108. Bellièvre to Loménie, 15 Aug. 1603, FF 15894, fol. 574. Villeroy to Bellièvre, 8 Apr. 1606, FF 15896, fol. 530.

6. Bellièvre to Matignon, 23 Apr. 1582, FF 3351, fol. 19. Villeroy to Henry III, 11 Jan. 1581, FF 15564, fols. 7–9; idem, 20 Jan. 1583, FF 6629, fol. 3. Villeroy to Mauvissière, 7 Feb. 1576, CCC 472, fol. 47. Bellièvre to Catherine, 11 Dec. 1580, FF 15891, fol. 84.

7. Fontenay-Mareuil noted in his memoirs that those in the *conseil des affaires* were, "with the exception of Sully, of humble birth" (cited in Nouaillac, *Villeroy*, pp. 274–75). Bellièvre to Villeroy, 22 Mar. 1587, FF 15892, fol. 216. Villeroy to Béthune, 19 June 1602, Henry IV, *Correspondance*, pp. 237–38. Mornay to Henry of Navarre, 9 Mar. 1584, Mornay, 2:554. Memoir on reform of the king's council, [1601], FF 15894, fols. 438–39. Buisseret, *Sully*, p. 176.

8. "Avis au roy," [1575], FF 15890, fols. 387–89.

9. Bellièvre to Henry III, 19 Oct. 1580, FF 15891, fols. 62–63. Cheverny to Bellièvre, 27 Jan. 1581, FF 15906, vol. 1, fol. 85. Bellièvre to Henry III, 25 Jan. 1581, FF 15891, fol. 144. Henry III to Bellièvre, 16 Feb. 1581, FF 15906, vol. 1, fol. 131. Cheverny to Bellièvre, 9 Feb. 1581, FF 15906, vol. 1, fol. 118. Bellièvre to Catherine, 5, 7, and 15 Apr. 1585, FF 15891, fols. 391, 393, 395. Drouot, *Mayenne*, 2:323–28.

10. For a succinct definition of the chancellor's powers, see Mous-

nier, *Séguier*, 1:21–26. See below, pp. 142–43. Buisseret, *Sully*, pp. 91–92. Sully urged Bellièvre to punish a financier "with the rigorous punishment that he deserves to prevent others from doing the same thing in the future" (Sully to Bellièvre, 13 July [1605], FF 15897, fol. 529); the king forbade Bellièvre to act until Sully had returned from the assembly of Huguenots at Chatellerault (Henry IV to Bellièvre, 18 and 25 July 1605, *LM*, 6:480–81, 488). Buisseret, *Sully*, p. 91. Bellièvre to [Villeroy], 29 Nov. 1602, FF 15894, fol. 545.

11. Bellièvre to Henry IV, 12 July 1603, FF 15894, fol. 567. Idem, 14 July 1601, FF 23196, fol. 528. Idem, Sept. 1600, FF 15894, fol. 372. Address to the Parlement of Paris, n.d., FF 15894, fol. 390. See Kierstead, *Bellièvre*, p. 139.

12. Bellièvre to [?], 29 Nov. 1602, FF 15894, fol. 545. Buisseret, *Sully*, pp. 91–92.

13. Memoir, [1601], FF 15894, fols. 438–39. Villeroy to Bellièvre, 2 Sept. 1601, FF 15896, fol. 330. Henry IV to Bellièvre, 2 Sept. 1601, *Lettres ... 1581–1601*, p. 313. Villeroy to Bellièvre, 29 Sept. 1601, FF 15896, fol. 340. Henry IV to [Marie de Medici], 23 Oct. 1601, *LM*, 5:507. Groulart, *Mémoires*, p. 588; Bellièvre himself warned Sillery, who was negotiating an alliance with the Swiss, that "if you show yourself ready to make too many difficulties, you will not evade calumny"; he may have been thinking of himself (Bellièvre to Sillery, 2 Oct. 1601, FF 15894, fol. 435).

14. Major, "Henry IV," pp. 364–67.

15. "Advis au roy sur le reiglement des affaires de son royaume," 28 Jan. 1580, cited in Sutherland, *Secretaries*, pp. 211–12. Villeroy to Hautefort, 2 Nov. 1582, FF 15565, fol. 117. Villeroy to Henry III, 4 Apr. 1582, FF 3385, fol. 126. Mastellone, *Reggenza*, pp. 149–50.

16. Mastellone, *Reggenza*, pp. 169–226. Ibid., pp. 109–10.

17. There is no general treatment of the French clergy for this period; much useful information is contained in Martin, *Gallicanisme*, and in Serbat, *Assemblées*. See Neale, *Age of Catherine*, pp. 11–13, for a brief summary of the state of the clergy. See Martin, *Gallicanisme*, pp. 290–95. For continuing suspicion of the sincerity of Henry's conversion, see Mousnier, *Assassinat*, pp. 142–66.

18. Villeroy to Du Perron, 26 Jan. 1605, *Ambassades*, pp. 284–85. Du Perron to Villeroy, 19 June 1604; Du Perron to Bellièvre, 30 June 1604, *Ambassades*, pp. 189, 197. See Ossat, *Lettres*. Villeroy to Bellièvre, 14 Jan. 1591, FF 15909, fol. 354. Bellièvre to Nevers, 24 Aug. 1593, FF 3985, fols. 100, 102–3. Bellièvre to Villeroy, 15 Mar. 1596, FF 15893, fol. 327. Villeroy to Henry III, 3 June 1581, FF 15564, fol.

127. Bellièvre to Nevers, 24 Aug. 1593, FF 3985, fols. 103–4. Bellièvre to Villeroy, [Aug.] 1598, FF 15894, fol. 149. Bufalo, *Correspondance*, pp. 114–17.

19. Serbat, *Assemblées*, passim. Ibid., pp. 91–109; Martin, *Gallicanisme*, pp. 143–65. Bellièvre's address to the clergy, July 1579, FF 15891, fols. 43–47. Saulnier, *Bourbon*, pp. 157–59; Serbat, *Assemblées*, pp. 116–27; Martin, *Gallicanisme*, pp. 220–29. Villeroy to Maisse, 1 and 14 Mar. 1586, FF 16093, fols. 31, 35. Serbat, *Assemblées*, pp. 136–38. Address to the clergy, FF 15893, fols. 311–15. Bellièvre to Villeroy, 15 Mar. 1596, FF 15893, fol. 327.

20. Villeroy to Béthune, 6 May 1603, FF 4017, fol. 184. Villeroy to Sillery, 17 June 1599, FF 15777, fol. 234. Ibid., fols. 233–35.

21. See Martin, *Gallicanisme*, pp. 320–25.

22. See the nuncio's dispatches in *Ragazzoni*, pp. 471, 482. Villeroy to the bishop of Paris (Gondy), 6 Jan. 1586, FF 6627, fol. 92. Villeroy to Bellièvre, 18 Sept. 1596, FF 15910, fol. 352; Cardinal de Medici, 10 Mar. 1597, 4 Sept. 1598, Leo XI, *Lettres*, pp. 119, 249. Martin, *Gallicanisme*, pp. 312–27. Ibid., p. 314; Bellièvre to Sillery, 20 Apr. 1600, FF 15894, fol. 400. Thou, *Histoire*, 9:329. Villeroy to [Du Perron], 10 Sept. 1605, Dupuy 3, fol. 94.

23. See Fouqueray, *Histoire*, pp. 505–690. Bonciani, 28 Dec. 1594, Desjardins, 5:296; Henry IV to Bellièvre, 16 Mar. 1595, *Lettres... 1581–1601*, p. 159. Henry IV to Villeroy, Oct. 1598, *LM*, 5:54. Villeroy to Béthune, 17 Jan. 1602, FF 4017, fol. 32. Idem, 9 Apr. 1602, FF 4017, fol. 54. Idem, 18 Nov. 1603, FF 4017, fols. 247–49. Idem, 3 Nov. 1603, FF 4017, fol. 243. Idem, 11 Jan. 1604, FF 4017, fol. 274. Cardinal de Medici, 10 Mar. 1597, Leo XI, *Lettres*, p. 119.

24. Villeroy to Béthune, 6 May 1603, FF 4017, fol. 184. Ibid., fols. 184–85. Villeroy to Béthune, 7 Oct. 1603, Henry IV, *Correspondance*, p. 422. Villeroy to Bellièvre, 4 Aug. 1604, FF 15896, fol. 477. Idem, 27 Nov. [1591], FF 15909, fol. 427.

25. Bellièvre to Henry III, 6 and 11 Sept. 1583, FF 6629, fols. 74, 78. See Kierstead, *Bellièvre*, pp. 140, 145.

26. For a good survey of the economic and social effects of the wars, see Livet, *Guerres*, pp. 73–106.

27. Bellièvre to Henry III, 17 and 19 Oct. 1580, FF 15891, fols. 60, 62–63. Villeroy to Bellièvre, 25 Aug. 1593, FF 15910, fol. 47. Idem, 11 Sept. 1593, FF 15910, fol. 62. See above, pp. 85–86.

28. Bellièvre to Mayenne, 21 Jan. 1590, FF 15892, fol. 361; Bellièvre to Biron, 13 May 1592; Bellièvre to Belin, 24 May 1592, FF 15893, fols. 30, 31. Bellièvre to Alincourt, 14 Mar. 1592, FF 15893,

fol. 13. Villeroy to Bellièvre, 29 Apr. 1589, FF 15909, fol. 252. Idem, 13 Feb. 1591, FF 15909, fol. 366. Bellièvre to Montmorency, 1593, FF 15893, fol. 114. Bellièvre and Sillery to Villeroy, 5 Aug. 1598, FF 15894, fol. 147.

29. Henry IV to Bellièvre, 5 Sept. 1604, *Lettres . . . 1604,* pp. 68–69. Bellièvre to Henry IV, 2 Nov. 1605, FF 15894, fol. 609.

30. Bellièvre to Henry IV, 13 Oct. 1594, FF 15912, fol. 98. Idem, 8 May 1595, FF 15912, fol. 209. FF 15893, fols. 387–88. Bellièvre to Henry IV, [1602], FF 15894, fols. 455–56.

31. Bellièvre to [?], [1590], FF 15892, fol. 438; Villeroy to Bellièvre, Apr. 1591, FF 15909, fol. 377.

32. Léonard, *Histoire,* 2:82–149.

33. Bellièvre to Catherine, 16 Apr. 1585, FF 15891, fol. 405.

34. Idem, 30 Oct. 1580, *LCM,* 7:452.

35. Avis au roy, Jan. 1577, Dupuy 24, fols. 65–68; Saracini, 8 and 13 Feb. 1577, Desjardins, 4:108, 110; Thou, *Histoire,* 5:359. Villeroy to Saint-Sulpice, 30 Jan. 1577, Cabié, *Guerres,* p. 329. Villeroy to Henry III, 8 Sept. 1577, Sutherland, *Secretaries,* p. 199. Villeroy to Bellièvre, 27 Mar. 1579, FF 15895, fol. 57; Catherine to Villeroy, 27 Apr. 1580, *LCM,* 7:280. Bellièvre to Henry III, 25 Jan. 1581, FF 15891, fol. 144. Bellièvre to Nevers, 11 Sept. 1586, FF 3372, fol. 208. Villeroy to Maisse, 11 May 1585, FF 16092, fol. 371. Idem, 5 July 1585, FF 16092, fol. 395. Bellièvre to Nevers, 13 Feb. 1587, FF 3398, fol. 63; Villeroy to Nevers, 26 Jan. 1587, FF 3398, fol. 54. Bellièvre to Brulart, 20 Apr. 1588, FF 3402, fol. 8. Memoir in Bellièvre's hand: "Touchant les divisions de la Chrétienté," FF 15892, fol. 12.

36. "You judge better than I that war cannot put an end to this war" (Bellièvre to La Noue, 25 Sept. 1590, FF 15892, fol. 381). Bellièvre to Sancy, [1591], FF 15892, fol. 434. Bellièvre to Villeroy, 30 Dec. 1592, Dupuy 88, fol. 177. Bellièvre to Henry IV, 3 Mar. 1596, FF 23195, fol. 271. Bellièvre to Schomberg and Thou, 27 Dec. 1597, CCC 32, fol. 257; Bellièvre and Sillery to Villeroy, 7 Apr. 1598, Mornay, 8:288. Villeroy to Schomberg, 1 Apr. 1597, FF 4047, fol. 284. Villeroy to La Fontaine, 10 Oct. 1597, HMC, *Salisbury,* 7:407. Villeroy to Thou, 21 Feb. 1598, CCC 32, fol. 121. Villeroy to Henry IV, 7 Nov. 1598, Dupuy 3, fol. 41; Villeroy to Boissise, 27 Nov. and 29 Dec. 1598, 12 Jan. 1599, FF 4128, fols. 8, 21, 24.

37. Villeroy to Béthune, 25 Feb. 1602, FF 4017, fol. 43. Idem, 3 Dec. 1602, Henry IV, *Correspondance,* p. 323. Pruili, 14 Feb. 1606, F. It. 1754, fol. 148. Villeroy to Joyeuse, 15 Feb. 1606, NAF 2750, fol. 141. See Patry, *Mornay,* pp. 383–97. Bellièvre to Du Perron, 3

July 1600, *Ambassades*, pp. 243–45. Villeroy to Boissise, 6 May 1600, FF 4128, fol. 172. Villeroy to Mornay, 12 Aug. 1605, Mornay, 10:117–19.

38. Bellièvre's address to the assembly of Montauban, Aug. 1584, FF 15891, fol. 372. "Touchant les divisions de la Chrétienté," FF 15892, fol. 12.

39. Bellièvre to [?], 12 Aug. 1593, FF 15893, fol. 131. Villeroy to Maisse, 14 July 1596, FF 16093, fol. 498. "Touchant les divisions de la Chrétienté," FF 15892, fols. 12, 15.

40. Mornay to Villeroy, 29 Mar. 1585, Mornay, 3:9. Mornay to Buzanval, 28 Sept. 1594, Mornay, 6:92. Mornay to Henry of Navarre, 9 Mar. 1584, Mornay, 2:552; Mornay to Bellièvre, 28 Mar. 1585, Mornay, 3:7–8. Mornay to Henry IV, 2 June 1596, Mornay, 6:489. Bellièvre to Du Perron, 3 July 1600, *Ambassades*, pp. 243–45. See Nouaillac, *Villeroy*, pp. 181–84, 213–25. Fleury to Mornay, March 1592, Mornay, 5:219–20.

41. For a survey of the economic history of the sixteenth century, see Sée, *Histoire*, pp. 79–143.

42. Bellièvre to Nevers, 27 Oct. 1574, FF 3315, fol. 107. See Mariéjol, "Réforme," pp. 223–37. Henry IV to the Parlement of Paris, 1 Oct. 1595, *LM*, 4:416. Buisseret, *Sully*, chap. 4. Mastellone, *Reggenza*, pp. 166–67; Tapié, *France*, pp. 90–94.

43. Bellièvre to Catherine, 3 Oct. 1586, FF 15892, fol. 5. Idem, 27 May 1585, FF 15891, fol. 403. Bellièvre to [Henry III], 19 Oct. 1580, FF 15891, fols. 62–63. Henry III to Bellièvre, 22 Oct. 1578, FF 15905, fol. 172. Bellièvre to Henry III, 18 Sept. 1587, FF 6631, fol. 74. FF 15890, fols. 463–65, 467–69, 471–72. Bellièvre to Henry III, 18 Sept. 1587, FF 6631, fol. 74. Idem, 13 Nov. 1586, FF 3373, fol. 5. Idem, 15 Nov. 1587, FF 15892, fols. 138–41.

44. Henry IV to Bellièvre, 28 Nov. 1594, *LM*, 4:266–67. Bellièvre to Nevers, 18 Nov. 1594, FF 3622, fol. 142. See Kierstead, *Bellièvre*, pp. 76–89. Bellièvre to Henry IV, 8 May 1595, FF 15912, fol. 210. Idem, 7 Apr. 1595, FF 15912, fol. 195. Henry IV to Bellièvre, 17 Jan. 1595, *Lettres . . . 1581–1601*, p. 145. Villeroy to Montmorency, 14 Nov. 1595, FF 3556, fol. 28. Memoir, [late 1596], FF 15893, fol. 386. Bellièvre, Cheverny, and Sancy to Montmorency, 31 Nov. 1595, FF 3578, fol. 19. Bellièvre to Henry IV, 29 Apr. 1596, FF 15893, fols. 340–41. Mariéjol, "Réforme," pp. 407–8.

45. Buisseret, *Sully*, pp. 72–73. Ibid., p. 77. Mousnier, "Sully," pp. 68–86.

46. Bellièvre to Villeroy, 10 Dec. 1602, FF 15894, fol. 547.

47. Sully to Bellièvre, 13 July [1605], FF 15897, fol. 529. Henry IV to Bellièvre, 18 and 25 July 1605, *LM*, 6:480–81, 488.

48. Bellièvre to Henry IV, [1602], FF 15894, fols. 455–56.

49. Mousnier, "Sully," p. 82.

50. Villeroy to Bellièvre, Oct. 1587, Nouaillac, *Villeroy*, p. 307. Villeroy to Mauvissière, 21 June 1582, CCC 472, fol. 107. Villeroy to Bellièvre, 29 Nov. 1602, FF 15894, fol. 375. Idem, 13 Dec. 1602, FF 15896, fol. 377. Bellièvre to Villeroy, 29 Nov. 1602, FF 15894, fol. 543. Villeroy to Bellièvre, 13 Dec. 1602, FF 15896, fol. 377. Idem, 10 Mar. 1603, FF 15896, fol. 387.

51. Buisseret, *Sully*, pp. 170–75. Bellièvre to Henry IV, 3 Apr. 1601, FF 15894, fols. 413–14; Villeroy to Bellièvre, 21 May 1601, FF 15896, fol. 312. Memoir on the finances, [late 1596], FF 15893, fol. 387.

52. Sully to Jeannin, 26 Feb. 1608, *Négociations*, p. 280; Buisseret, *Sully*, p. 178. The only reference either minister made to the New World was Bellièvre's facetious suggestion that perhaps some troublesome Irish refugees might be settled in Canada (Bellièvre to Villeroy, 2 Nov. 1605, FF 15578, fol. 246). Villeroy to Henry III, 8 Aug. 1582, FF 6631, fol. 36. Bellièvre to Henry IV, 27 May 1595, FF 15912, fol. 222. Buisseret, *Sully*, p. 170.

53. "Mémoire sur les parties casuelles," [Dec. 1602], FF 15894, fol. 454. Buisseret says that "there is no means of accurately calculating the proportion of income devoted to the payment of holders of various offices" (*Sully*, p. 103). "Mémoire sur les parties casuelles," [Dec. 1602], FF 15894, fol. 454. Hobsbaum, "Crisis"; he says that "government enterprise in the new absolute monarchies fostered industries, colonies and export drives which would not otherwise have flourished, as in Colbertian France" (p. 43). Villeroy to Béthune, 18 Nov. 1603, FF 4017, fol. 250.

Conclusion

1. Bellièvre to [?], Dec. 1592, FF 15893, fols. 44–45.

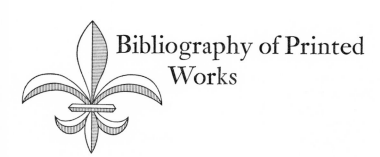

Bibliography of Printed Works

Primary

AARSSENS, FRANÇOIS D'. *Lettres inédites de François d'Aerssen à Jacques Valcke, 1599–1603.* Edited by J. Nouaillac. Paris, 1908.

Archives ou la correspondance inédite de la maison d'Orange-Nassau. Edited by G[uillaume] Groen van Prinsterer. Series 1 and 2. 14 vols. Leiden, 1835–62.

BARNEVELDT, JAN VAN OLDEN. *Gedenkstukken van Johan van Olden-barnevelt.* Edited by M. van Deventer. Vols. 2–3. The Hague, 1862.

BELLIÈVRE, POMPONNE DE. "La lettre d'état de Pomponne de Bellièvre au président Jeannin, 13 décembre 1592." Edited by J. Nouaillac. *Documents d'histoire* 4 (1913) : 1–20.

———. "Lettres inédites de M. de Bellièvre au roi Henri IV au sujet de l'emprisonnement du duc de Nemours." *Revue du Lyonnais* 17 (1858) : 306–16.

BUFALO, INNOCENZO DEL. *Correspondance du nonce en France, Innocenzo del Bufalo, évêque de Camerino (1601–1604).* Edited by Bernard Barbiche. Rome and Paris, 1964.

BUZANVAL, P. CHOART, SIEUR DE. *Lettres et négociations de P. Choart, sieur de Buzanval, ambassadeur ordinaire de Henri IV en Hollande.* Edited by G. Vreede. Leiden, 1846.

CABIÉ, EDMOND. *Guerres de religion dans le sud-ouest de la France, 1561–1590.* Paris, 1906.

CATHERINE DE MEDICI. *Lettres de Catherine de Médicis.* Edited by Hector de La Ferrière and [Gustave] Baguenault de Puchesse. 9 vols. Paris, 1880–1905.

CHEVERNY, PHILIPPE HURAULT, COUNT OF. *Mémoires.* In *Nouvelle collection des mémoires pour servir à l'histoire de France,* edited by Michaud and Poujoulat. Series 2, vol. 11. Paris, 1837.

DESJARDINS, ABEL. *Négociations diplomatiques de la France avec la Toscane.* Vols. 4–5. Paris, 1872–75.

DU PERRON, JACQUES DAVY. *Les ambassades et négociations du cardinal Du Perron.* Paris, 1623.

GREAT BRITAIN. *Calendar of State Papers, Foreign Series.* 17 vols. (1572–89). London, 1876–1950.

———. *Calendar of State Papers, Spanish Series.* Vols. 2–4. London, 1894–99.

———. *Calendar of State Papers, Venetian Series.* Vols. 7–11. London, 1890–1904.

GROULART, CLAUDE. *Mémoires.* In *Nouvelle collection des mémoires . . .* , edited by Michaud and Poujoulat. Series 1, vol. 11. Paris, 1838.

HENRY IV. *Correspondance entre Henri IV et Béthune, ambassadeur de France à Rome, 1602–1604.* Edited by J. E. M. Lajeunie. Geneva, 1952.

———. *Lettres inédites de Henri IV.* Edited by A. Galitzin. Paris, 1860.

———. *Lettres inédites du roi Henry IV à monsieur Bellièvre, 1602.* Edited by E. Halphen. Paris, 1881.

———. *Lettres inédites du roi Henri IV à monsieur de Sillery, 1 avril–27 juin 1600.* Edited by E. Halphen. Paris, 1866.

———. *Lettres inédites du roi Henri IV au chancelier Bellièvre, 1581–1601.* Edited by E. Halphen. Paris, 1872.

———. *Lettres inédites du roi Henri IV au chancelier Bellièvre, 16 mars–28 octobre 1604.* Edited by E. Halphen. Paris, 1883.

———. *Recueil des lettres missives de Henri IV.* Edited by [Jules] Berger de Xivrey. 9 vols. Paris, 1843–76.

HISTORICAL MANUSCRIPTS COMMISSION. *Calendar of the Manuscripts of the Marquis of Salisbury.* Vols. 2–12 (1580–1603). London, 1887–1910.

JEANNIN, [PIERRE]. *Négociations diplomatiques et politiques du président Jeannin, 1598–1620.* Edited by J.-A.-C. Buchon. Paris, 1875.

[LEO XI]. *Lettres du cardinal de Florence sur Henry IV et sur la France (1596–1598).* Edited by R. Ritter. Paris, 1955.

L'ESTOILE, PIERRE DE. *Mémoires-journaux de Pierre de L'Estoile.* Edited by Brunet, Champollion, et al. 12 vols. Paris, 1875–96.

MORNAY, PHILIPPE DE. *Mémoires et correspondance de Duplessis-Mornay.* 12 vols. Paris, 1824–25.

OSSAT, ARNAUD D'. *Lettres du cardinal d'Ossat.* Edited by Amelot de La Houssaye. 5 vols. Amsterdam, 1714.

RAGAZZONI, GIROLAMO. *Girolamo Ragazzoni, évêque de Bergame;*

nonce en France, 1583–1586. Edited by Pierre Blet. Rome and Paris, 1962.

STATES-GENERAL. *Procès verbaux des états de 1593.* Edited by Auguste Bernard. Paris, 1842.

SULLY, MAXIMILIEN DE BÉTHUNE, DUKE OF. "Dix lettres inédites de Sully." Edited by J. Nouaillac. *Revue des questions historiques* 95 (1914) : 136–45.

———. *Mémoires des sages et royales œconomies d'estat de Henry le Grand.* In *Nouvelle collection des mémoires . . .*, edited by Michaud and Poujoulat. Series 2, vols. 2–3. Paris, 1837.

THOU, JACQUES AUGUSTE DE. *Histoire universelle.* Vols. 5–12. London, 1734.

VILLEROY, NICHOLAS DE NEUFVILLE, SIEUR DE. *Mémoires d'estat.* In *Nouvelle collection des mémoires . . .*, edited by Michaud and Poujoulat. Series 1, vol. 11. Paris, 1838.

Secondary

ALLEN, J[OHN] W[ILLIAM]. *A History of Political Thought in the Sixteenth Century.* London and New York, 1960.

ANQUEZ, LÉONCE. *Henri IV et l'Allemagne.* Paris, 1887.

AUMALE, HENRY D'ORLÉANS, DUKE OF. *History of the Princes de Condé in the Sixteenth and Seventeenth Centuries.* Translated by Robert Brown Borthwick. Vol. 2. London, 1872.

BAGUENAULT DE PUCHESSE, GUSTAVE. "La politique de Philippe II dans les affaires de France, 1559–1598." *Revue des questions historiques* 25 (1879) : 5–66.

BAUDRILLART, A. "La politique d'Henri IV en Allemagne." *Revue des questions historiques* 37 (1885) : 408–82.

BERGADINI, ROBERTO. *Carlo Emmanuele I (1562–1630).* Turin, 1932.

BRAUDEL, FERNAND. *La Méditerranée et le monde méditerranéen à l'époque de Philippe II.* Paris, 1949.

BUISSERET, DAVID. "A Stage in the Development of the *Intendants:* The Reign of Henri IV." *Historical Journal* 9 (1966) : 27–38.

———. *Sully and the Growth of Centralized Government in France, 1598–1610.* London, 1968.

CHEYNEY, EDWARD P. *A History of England, 1558–1604.* 2 vols. London, 1914–26.

CHURCH, WILLIAM FARR. *Constitutional Thought in Sixteenth-Century*

France: A Study in the Evolution of Ideas. Cambridge, Mass., and London, 1941.

CLARK, SIR GEORGE NORMAN. *War and Society in the Seventeenth Century*. Cambridge, 1958.

CROZE, JOSEPH DE. *Les Guises, les Valois, et Philippe II*. 2 vols. Paris, 1866.

DODU, G. "Henri III." *Revue historique* 164 (1930) : 1–42.

DROUOT, HENRI. *Mayenne et la Bourgogne: Etude sur la Ligue (1587–1596)*. 2 vols. Paris, 1937.

FERET, PIERRE ."Nullité du mariage de Henri IV avec Marguerite de Valois." *Revue des questions historiques* 20 (1876) : 77–114.

FOUQUERAY, HENRI. *Histoire de la Compagnie de Jésus en France des origines à la suppression (1528–1762) .... 5 vols.* Paris, 1910–25. Vol. 2 (1913).

GARNIER, ARMAND. "Un scandale princier au XVIe siècle." *Revue du seizième siècle* 1 (1913) : 153–89, 355–91, 561–612.

HALE, J. H. "Armies, Navies, and the Art of War." In *The New Cambridge Modern History*, vol. 3, *The Counter Reformation and the Price Revolution*. Cambridge, 1968.

HANOTAUX, G. *Histoire du cardinal de Richelieu*. Vol. 1. Paris, 1893.

HAUSER, HENRI. *La modernité du XVIe siècle*. Paris, 1963.

HEXTER, J. H. "The Education of the Aristocracy in the Renaissance," *Reappraisals in History*. New York, 1963.

HOBSBAUM, E. J. "The Crisis of the Seventeenth Century." In *Crisis in Europe, 1560–1660*, edited by Trevor Aston. New York, 1967.

JENSEN, DE LAMAR. *Diplomacy and Dogmatism: Bernardino de Mendoza and the French Catholic League*. Cambridge, Mass., 1964.

KERMAINGANT, P. LAFFLEUR DE. *L'ambassade de France en Angleterre: Mission de Jean de Thuméry, sieur de Boissise, 1597–1602*. 2 vols. Paris, 1886.

———. *L'ambassade de France en Angleterre sous Henri IV: Mission de Christophe de Harlay, comte de Beaumont, 1602–1605*. 2 vols. Paris, 1895.

KIERSTEAD, RAYMOND. *Pomponne de Bellièvre*. Evanston, 1968.

KOSSMAN, ERNST. *La Fronde*. Leiden, 1954.

LABOUCHÈRE, G. "Guillaume Ancel, envoyé résident en Allemagne, 1576–1613." *Revue d'histoire diplomatique* 37 (1923) : 160–88, 348–67.

LAFUE, PIERRE. *Henri III et son secret*. Paris, 1949.

LÉONARD, EMIL. *Histoire générale du Protestantisme*. Vol. 2. Paris, 1961.

L'EPINOIS, H. DE. "La réconciliation de Henri III et du duc de Guise, mai–juillet 1588." *Revue des questions historiques* 39 (1886) : 52–94.

LIVET, GEORGES. *Les guerres de religion.* Paris, 1966.

MAJOR, J. RUSSELL. "The French Renaissance Monarchy As Seen through the Estates General." *Studies in the Renaissance* 9 (1962) : 113–25.

———. "Henry IV and Guyenne: A Study concerning the Origins of Royal Absolutism." *French Historical Studies* 4 (1965–66) : 363–83.

———. "The Renaissance Monarchy: A Contribution to the Periodization of History." *Emory University Quarterly* 13 (1957) : 112–24.

MARIÉJOL, JEAN H. *Catherine de Médicis.* Paris, 1920.

———. *A Daughter of the Medici.* Translated by J. Peile. New York and London, 1929.

———. *Henri IV et Louis XIII, 1598–1643.* Vol. 6, pt. 2, *Histoire de France illustré depuis les origines jusqu' à la révolution,* edited by Ernest Lavisse. Paris, 1911.

———. "La réforme et la Ligue—l'édit de Nantes, 1559–1598." In *Histoire de France . . . ,* edited by Ernest Lavisse. Vol. 6. Paris, 1911.

MARTIN, V. *Le Gallicanisme et la réforme catholique.* Paris, 1919.

MASTELLONE, SALVO. *La reggenza di Marie de Medici.* Florence, 1962.

MATTINGLY, GARRETT. *The Armada.* Boston, 1959.

———. *Renaissance Diplomacy.* Boston, 1955.

MESNARD, PIERRE. *L'essor de la philosophie politique au XVIe siècle en France.* Paris, 1936.

MOTLEY, JOHN L. *History of the United Netherlands, 1584–1609.* 4 vols. London, 1860–67.

MOUSNIER, ROLAND. *L'assassinat d'Henri IV.* Paris, 1964.

———. "Le conseil du roi de la mort de Henri IV au gouvernement personnel de Louis XIV." *Etudes d'histoire moderne et contemporaine* 1 (1947) : 1–40.

———. *Lettres et mémoires adressés au chancelier Séguier (1633–1649).* 2 vols. Paris, 1964.

———. "Recherches sur les soulèvements populaires en France avant la Fronde." *Revue d'histoire moderne* 4 (1958) : 81–113.

———. "Sully et le conseil d'état et des finances." *Revue historique* 192 (1941): 68–86.

NEALE, JOHN E. *The Age of Catherine de Medici.* New York, 1962.

NOUAILLAC, J. "La retraite de Pomponne de Bellièvre, septembre 1588–mai 1593." *Revue historique* 81 (1914) : 129–67.

———. *Villeroy, secrétaire d'état et ministre de Charles IX, Henri III, et Henri IV, 1543–1610.* Paris, 1909.

PAGÈS, GEORGES. "Autour du 'Grand Orage': Richelieu et Marillac; deux politiques." *Revue historique* 179 (1937) : 63–97.

———. "Le conseil du roy sous Louis XIII." *Revue d'histoire moderne* 12 (1937) : 293–324.

———. *La monarchie d'ancien régime en France (de Henri IV à Louis XIV).* Paris, 1929.

PASTOR, LUDWIG VON. *The History of the Popes.* Edited by R. F. Kerr. Vols. 19–25. London and St. Louis, 1930–37.

PATRY, R. *Philippe du Plessis-Mornay, un huguenot homme d'état, 1549–1623.* Paris, 1933.

PHILIPPSON, MARTIN. *Heinrich IV und Philippe III.* 3 vols. Berlin, 1870–76.

POIRSON, M. *Histoire du règne de Henri IV.* 4 vols. Paris, 1856.

PORSHNEV, BORIS. *Les soulèvements populaires en France de 1623 à 1648.* Paris, 1963.

RANUM, OREST A. *Richelieu and the Councillors of Louis XIII: A Study of the Secretaries of State and Superintendents of Finance in the Ministry of Richelieu, 1635–1642.* Oxford, 1963.

RAULICH, ITALO. *Storia de Carlo Emmanuele I, 1588–1598.* Vol. 2. Milan, 1902.

RICHARD, P. "La légation Aldobrandini et le traité de Lyon, septembre 1600–mars 1601." *Revue d'histoire et de littérature religieuse* 7 (1902) : 481–509; 8 (1903) : 25–48.

READ, CONYERS. *Lord Burghley and Queen Elizabeth.* New York, 1960.

———. *Mr. Secretary Walsingham and the Policy of Queen Elizabeth.* 3 vols. Oxford, 1925.

ROTT, EDOUARD. *Henri IV, les Suisses, et la haute Italie: La lutte pour les Alpes (1598–1610).* Paris, 1882.

SAULNIER, EUGÈNE. *Le rôle politique du cardinal de Bourbon (1523–1590).* Paris, 1912.

SÉE, HENRI. *Histoire économique de la France.* Vol. 1. Paris, 1948.

SERBAT, L. *Les assemblées du clergé de France, 1561–1615.* Paris, 1906.

STONE, LAWRENCE. *The Crisis of the Aristocracy, 1558–1641.* Oxford, 1967.

SUTHERLAND, N. M. *The French Secretaries of State in the Age of Catherine de Medici.* London, 1962.

TAPIÉ, VICTOR. *La France de Louis XIII et de Richelieu.* Paris, 1952.

THUAU, ETIENNE. *Raison d'état et pensée politique à l'époque de Richelieu.* Paris, 1966.

VAISSIÈRE, PIERRE DE. *Henri IV.* Paris, 1928.

WILEY, W. L. *The Gentlemen of Renaissance France.* Cambridge, Mass., 1954.

WILLSON, D. H. *King James VI and I.* Oxford, 1967.

WOLF, JOHN. *Louis XIV.* New York, 1968.

Index

Aarssens, Francis van, 108
Absolutism, royal: and bureaucracy, 126; and divine sanction, 43–45; and Henry IV, 71; and law, 49–50, 148; and popular authority, 47; theory of, 42; and tradition, 45–46; and utility, 42–43
Alincourt, Charles de Neufville, sieur de, 14
Anjou, François, duke of, 14, 15, 40, 45, 95–96, 104, 107–8
Assemblies of notables, 32–33, 48–49
Aumale, Charles de Lorraine, duke of, 61, 62, 63
Aumont, Jean d' (marshal of France), 63
Auvergne, Charles de Valois, count of, 14

Barricades, Day of the, 45, 55, 64
Bavaria, John Casimir, prince of, 11
Bellièvre, Albert de, 14, 131
Bellièvre, Claude, 3
Bellièvre, Nicholas de, 14–15, 120
Bellièvre, Pomponne de: ancestry, 3; career, 4–5, 6–7; Catherine de Medici, relation with, 4, 66–67, 70; contemporary estimates of, 78; dismissal by Henry III, 55–59; education and intellectual interests, 23–26; Henry III, relation with, 52; Henry IV, relation with, 60, 71–73, 76; honor of, 79–81; personality, 8–10; physical health, 15–16; retirement, 20; values, 10–15; Villeroy, relation with, 17–23, 77
Bergerac, Peace of, 70
Biron, Charles de Gontaut, duke of, 13–14, 29, 36, 44, 121
Biron plot, 94, 101, 111, 113

Bodin, Jean, 42
Bologna, Concordat of, 126
Bon Français, 17, 35, 103
Bouillon, Henry de la Tour d'Auvergne, duke of, 29, 110–11, 121, 137
Brulart de Sillery. See Sillery, Nicholas Brulart de
Bufalo, Innocenzo del (cardinal), 127
Bureaucracy: Bellièvre's reform efforts, 122–25; and the paulette, 125; and royal absolutism, 126; Villeroy's views, 125–26

Casimir, John, 11
Catholic League: and Henry III, 5, 59–66; and Philip II, 96–98; right to rebel, 41–42
Cavriana, Filippo, 56
Cecil, Robert (earl of Salisbury), 77
Chambéry, 39
Chambres mi-parties, 134–35
Charles Emmanuel I. See Savoy, duke of
Chastel, Jean, 43, 99, 115
Cheverny, Philip Hurault, count of (chancellor), 7, 13, 77
Clément, Jacques, 13
Clement VIII, 114, 115–16
Clergy: Bellièvre family benefices, 131; dons gratuits, 127–28; Jesuits, 129–30; and the crown, 127; Trentine decrees, 128–29; Villeroy's views on reform, 128, 130–31; and the Wars of Religion, 126–27
Colonization, 144
Conflans, 25
Conseil d'en haut, 31, 32
Conseil d'état et des finances, 32, 82
Councils, royal, 31–34
Customary law, 49–50

Dévots, 17, 35, 103
Diplomacy, government by, 28–29, 68–70
Divine right of kings, 43–45
Dons gratuits, 127–28
Droit annuel, 142
Du Haillan, Bernard, 25
Du Perron, Jacques Davy (cardinal), 25, 81, 127, 137
Dutch Republic, 107–9

Economic views, of Bellièvre and Villeroy, 144–45; 149–50
Elizabeth I, 11, 39, 104–5
England, relations with France: under Elizabeth I, 104–5; under James I, 105–6
Entragues, Catherine Henriette de Balzac d', 14, 76
Epernon, Jean-Louis de Nogaret, duke of, 12, 18, 19, 62, 63, 65, 120
Estrées, Gabrielle d', 75–76

Faye d'Espesses, Jacques, 15
Fiscal policies: Bellièvre, 140–41; Sully, 141–43; Villeroy, 143
Fiscal problem, France, 139
Folembray, Edict of, 120
Foreign policy: Bellièvre's and Villeroy's approach to, 90–91, 117, 148–49; Bellièvre's and Villeroy's influence on, 91–95
France: as Catholic kingdom, 38, 40–41; and dynastic patriotism, 35–37; as historic entity, 38; as linguistic unit, 38, 40; as territorial unit, 38, 39–40
Fronde, 36–37

Gens de robe (robins), 122. *See also* Bureaucracy
German Protestant principalities, 109–11
Gloire, and Henry IV, 72–75
Gondy, Pierre de (bishop), 126–27
Government, Bellièvre's and Villeroy's philosophy of, 30–31, 68–70
Greenwich, Treaty of, 104
Grignon, 25

Guise, Henry, duke of, 55, 59–65, 110

Halle, Treaty of, 110, 111
Henry III: Bellièvre, relation with, 52; and the Catholic League, 55, 59–66; dismissal of Bellièvre and Villeroy, 55–59; foreign policy of, 92, 93; and government by diplomacy, 28; and Henry of Navarre, 45, 60, 61–63, 66, 69; shortcomings as king, 51, 54–55; Villeroy, relation with, 5, 51–53, 62
Henry IV (Henry of Navarre): Bellièvre and Villeroy, relations with, 5–6, 37, 71–73, 76; and Elizabeth I, 104–5; foreign policy approach, 92–94; and *gloire,* pursuit of, 73–75; and government by diplomacy, 28–29; and Henry III, 45, 60, 61–63, 66, 69; historians' views of, 70–71; and *honneur,* 73, 75; mistresses, 75–76; war against Spain, 98–99
Huguenots: and Catholic League, 59–63; and right to rebel, 41–42; rise and fall of, 133; and secular view of the state, 138–39; toleration of ministers toward, 133–38

James I, 105–6
Jesuits (Society of Jesus), 116, 129–30
Juliers-Cleves affair, 101–2

La Fin, Jacques de, 44,
Laubespine, Magdalene de, 5
Law, customary. *See* Customary law
League estates, 47–48, 97, 98
Leo XI (Alexander de Medici), 77, 116, 127
Lerma, Francisco Gómez de Sandoval y Rojas, duke of, 100
L'Estoile, Pierre de, 81
Lorraine, Charles de (cardinal), 25
Louis XIII, 34–35
Louis XIV, 35
Lyons, Treaty of, 112

Mantes, Edict of, 135
Mayenne, Charles of Lorraine, duke of, 5, 6, 15, 20, 36, 97

Mazarin, Jules (cardinal), 35, 37
Medici, Alexander de. *See* Leo XI
Medici, Catherine de: Bellièvre, relation with, 4, 66–67, 70; and the Catholic League, 60–62, 64; governing, philosophy of, 68; ministers of, 34, 40; Villeroy, relation with, 5, 67–68, 70, 77
Medici, Marie de, 6, 34, 40, 76, 102
Mendoza, Bernadino de, 13, 17, 57, 96
Mercantilism, 139–40, 144
Mercoeur, Philip Emmanuel of Lorraine, duke of, 29
Ministerial power, 81–83, 149
Ministers, relations between, 16–17, 160
Ministries, royal, 34–35
Mocenigo, Giovanni, 56
Monarchy, Renaissance, 27–28. *See also* Absolutism, royal
Monsieur, Peace of, 70
Montaigne, Michel Eyquem de, 25
Montmorency, Henry, duke of (constable), 81–82, 120
Mornay, Philippe de, 25, 137, 138
Morvilliers, Jean de (bishop), 4, 122

Nantes, Edict of, 133
Nemours, Jacques de Savoie, duke of, 15
Nemours, Treaty of, 60–61, 70, 135
Neufville, Nicholas I de, 4
Neufville, Nicholas II de, 4
Neufville, Nicholas III de (Villeroy). *See* Villeroy
Nevers, Louis de Gonzague, duke of, 68
Nobility, 119–22
Noblesse de robe. See Bureaucracy
Normandy, estates of, 48
Nouaillac, J., 57

Orléans, Louis d', 14
Ornano, Alphonse d' (marshal of France), 81
Ossat, Arnaud d' (cardinal), 25, 126–27

Pancarte, 141
Papacy: and Franco-Spanish relations, 116; French support of, 116–17; and

Henry of Navarre, 114–16
Paris, Treaty of, 112
Parlements, 49–51
Parma, Alessandro Farnese, duke of, 40, 97, 107
Patriotism, dynastic, 35–37, 148
Paulette, 7, 12, 124, 125, 142
Paul V, 114, 116
Peasantry: Bellièvre's and Villeroy's attitude toward, 132–33; and Wars of Religion, 131–32
Pensions, for nobility, 120–21
Philip II, 39, 48, 89, 96–99, 100
Philip III, 93–94, 99–100, 101, 102
Politiques, 69
Prices, rise of, 144
Provincial estates, 48
Puysieux, Pierre Brulart, marquis of, 6

Rebellion, as divine right, 41
Religion: of France, 38, 40–41; and religious toleration, 133–38, 149; and royal sovereignty, 43–45
Richelieu, Armand Jean du Plessis, duke of (cardinal), 35, 103
Rochepot incident, 94, 101

Salcède, Nicholas, 18
Salic Law, 45–46
Saluzzo, marquisate of, 111, 112, 113
Satyre Ménippée, 79
Savoy, 111–13
Savoy, Charles Emmanuel I, duke of, 39, 111, 113
Secretary of state, office of, 6
Sillery, Nicholas Brulart de, 7, 16, 22, 79
Sixtus V, 114, 115
Social order, 149
Spain, relations with France: and Anjou's ambitions, 95–96; Biron plot, 101; and Catholicism, 102–3; and Dutch revolt, 93, 107; Juliers-Cleves crisis, 101–2; Philip II and Catholic League, 96–98; Philip III's policy, 100; Rochepot incident, 94, 101; tariff war, 94, 101; war of 1595–98, 93, 98–99
Stafford, Sir Edward, 17, 37, 56

States-General, 47–48
Succession, royal. *See* Salic Law
Sully, Maximilien de Béthune, duke of
  (baron of Rosny): and Bellièvre, 22,
  32, 82; and the *paulette,* 7; as
  minister of finance, 34, 124, 141–43;
  and Spain, 100; and Villeroy, 77–78,
  81
Sutherland, Nicola M., 57

Taille, 131–33
Tariff war, 94, 101
Trentine decrees, 128–29
Tuscany, 113–14

Union, Edict of, 64

Valois, Margaret of, 14, 41, 55, 75, 116
Valtellina pass, 23, 114
Venice, 113–14

Vervins, Peace of, 99, 105
Villeroy, Nicholas de Neufville, sieur
  de: ancestry, 3–4; Bellièvre, relation
  with, 17–23, 77; career, 5–6; Catherine
  de Medici, relation with, 5, 67–68,
  70; and Catholic League, 5, 12, 18;
  contemporary estimates of, 77–78;
  dismissal by Henry III, 18, 55–59;
  education and intellectual interests,
  23–26; Henry III, relation with, 5,
  51–53, 62; Henry IV, relation with,
  5–6, 71–73, 76; honor of, 78–79; personality, 7–8; physical health, 15–16;
  values, 10–11, 12–15
Vindiciae contra Tyrannos, 41

War: Bellièvre's and Villeroy's views
  on, 12–13, 85–89, 148; contemporary
  views on, 85
Wars of Religion, 27, 126, 131–32